ADVANCES IN HETERODOX ECONOMICS

Fred S. Lee, University of Missouri–Kansas City, Series Editor
Rob Garnett, Texas Christian University, Series Editor

Over the past two decades, the intellectual agendas of heterodox economists have taken a decidedly pluralist turn. Leading thinkers have begun to move beyond the established paradigms of Austrian, feminist, institutional-evolutionary, Marxian, post-Keynesian, radical, social, and Sraffian economics—opening up new lines of analysis, criticism, and dialogue among dissenting schools of thought. This cross-fertiliezation of ideas is creating a new generation of scholarship in which novel combinations of heterodox ideas are being brought to bear on important contemporary and historical problems.

Advances in Heterodox Economics aims to promote this new scholarship by publishing innovative books in heterodox economic theory, policy, philosophy, intellectual history, institutional history, and
pedagogy. Syntheses or critical engagements of two or more heterodox traditions are especially encouraged.

The editor and associate editors work closely with individual authors to ensure the quality of all published works.

Economics in Real Time: A Theoretical Reconstruction
   John McDermott

Socialism after Hayek
   Theodore A. Burczak

Future Directions for Heterodox Economics
   John T. Harvey and Robert F. Garnett, Jr., editors

Are Worker Rights Human Rights?
   Richard P. McIntyre

Are Worker Rights Human Rights?

RICHARD P. MCINTYRE

The University of Michigan Press

Ann Arbor

Published in the United States of America by
The University of Michigan Press
Manufactured in the United States of America
☉ Printed on acid-free paper

2011   2010   2009   2008   4   3   2   1

A CIP catalog record for this book is available from the British Library.

Library of Congress Cataloging-in-Publication Data

McIntyre, Richard P., 1955–
     Are worker rights human rights? / Richard P. McIntyre.
        p.   cm. — (Advances in heterodox economics)
     Includes bibliographical references and index.
     ISBN-13: 978-0-472-07042-8 (cloth : alk. paper)
     ISBN-10: 0-472-07042-8 (cloth : alk. paper)
     ISBN-13: 978-0-472-05042-0 (pbk. : alk. paper)
     ISBN-10: 0-472-05042-7 (pbk. : alk. paper)
     1. Employee rights.   2. Labor—Standards.   3. Labor laws and
legislation.   4. Human rights.   I. Title.
     HD6971.8.M38   2008
     331.01'1—dc22   2008011490

CONTENTS

PREFACE AND ACKNOWLEDGMENTS

The controversy over labor standards is one of the central debates in the contemporary period of economic globalization. Economists have generally entered this debate through cost-benefit analysis, but there are important questions of morality and class that do not fit easily within the orthodox approach. In this book I draw on the Institutional and Marxist traditions in economics to present an analysis of worker rights and labor standards that takes both moral questions and class relations and interests seriously.

I argue that a prime and imminent tendency in the contemporary world economy is the lengthening of commodity chains through which the ultimate employer is able to wash his hands of moral responsibility for the conditions of work. This is true in globalized production networks, such as those operated by Nike and other global manufacturers, as well as in temporary and subcontracted work situations in the United States and elsewhere.

Asserting the rights of workers against such practices may be a promising strategy, but in failing to distinguish between the individual and collective meaning of rights the supporters of such slogans as "worker rights are human rights" may end up with something quite different from what they expected. The antislavery movement indirectly created support for capitalist forms of exploitation, the push for *individual* employment equality in the 1960s and 1970s contributed to the undermining of workers' *collective* rights, and contemporary corporate codes of conduct emphasize the rights of the individual but say little about collective rights. The definition of rights is influenced by class interest in ways that the supporters of such rights ignore at their own peril.

Recognizing that what constitutes a right is influenced by class relations and interests, and that the assertion of rights will necessarily have contradictory rather than simple effects, I examine the practices of the International Labor Organization (ILO), the interaction between labor law and U.S. foreign policy, and the activities of labor-based nongovernmental organizations in creating worker rights and enforcing labor standards. I argue for the strengthening of the ILO as an authoritative institution. Opponents of including labor standards in trade agreements point to the ILO as the appropriate forum for dealing with labor problems, though the organization has little enforcement power. Critics of the ILO contend that its weakness is by design, and there is something to this. But of all the existing multilateral organizations the ILO comes closest to the kind of global regulatory commission that could produce reasonable values by bringing all interested parties to the table, and its (rather arbitrary) definition of core labor standards is gaining widespread acceptance.

In the United States, workers have few legally guaranteed rights, and what rights they do have eroded over the last generation. The United States has an abysmal record in ratifying ILO conventions. Yet as the dominant economic power, and with a self-image as a promoter of democracy and freedom, the U.S. government sometimes puts itself in the vanguard of the international worker rights movement. I argue that while the reasons generally given in the United States for not adopting ILO conventions are specious, particularly those concerning freedom of association and collective bargaining, the United States' occasional support for international labor standards could be leveraged to improve worker rights domestically.

There is a long history of popular movements challenging the idea that "human rights" are discarded once one enters the factory or office door. Over the past decade a vigorous student movement demanding that university-logoed apparel be made sweat free has developed across the United States. While its goals are modest, I argue that this movement could have a large impact, to the extent that it builds organizing capacity in the newly industrializing countries while potentially creating a desire for class justice at home.

The classical socialist dream of the common experience of proletarianization and exploitation leading to working-class unity and revolutionary socialism was not realized. A desire for class justice must be cultivated; it does not flow inevitably from capitalist relations of production. In thinking openly and deeply about the constructed meaning of "worker rights as human rights" I hope to contribute to a positive, pragmatic discussion of how to improve material conditions and democratic participation for working people, not *just* to critique economic orthodoxy or deconstruct one of the sacred cows of the political Left. A popular politics that is more theoretically sophisticated and conscious of class than what is generally on offer in the United States has a real chance to make a concrete difference in twenty-first-century globalized labor markets, and also in the homely setting of the college classroom, as I argue at the end of this book.

My thanks go especially to Yngve Ramstad and Matthew Bodah with whom I developed some of these ideas. I thank Michael Hillard and Patrick McHugh for their thorough reading of the penultimate version of this manuscript, and to Mary Hashman for her careful copyediting. I acknowledge the University of Rhode Island's Center for the Humanities for its support of my research in Geneva, and the research laboratory IDHE at the Ecole Normale Supérieure-Cachan France for hosting me during my sabbatical. I appreciate the time given to me by the many people who were interviewed in the course of this research and my students in the Honors Program and the Schmidt Labor Research Center at the University of Rhode Island who graciously listened and questioned as I worked out the arguments in class.

I received helpful comments on earlier versions of some of these chapters at the annual meetings of the Association for Evolutionary Economics (2006) and the Canadian Industrial Research Association (2001), as well as at *Rethinking Marxism*'s Fifth International Conference in Amherst (2003), the Fourth International Marx Conference in Paris (2004), the 2006 Left Forum in New York, and the Conference on the Future of Heterodox Economics in Kansas City in 2003, as well as at seminars at ENS-Cachan, Université de Lyon II, and the University of Rhode Island. I thank Fred Lee and Rob Garnett for their editorial assistance, and my wife Deborah for her love and support.

CHAPTER 1

Class, Convention, and Worker Rights

In the summer of 1997, Nguyen Thi Thu Phuong died making Nike sneakers in a factory in Bien Jhoa, northeast of Ho Chi Minh City. She was struck in the heart by a piece of shrapnel that flew out of a machine that a co-worker was fixing. She died instantly. Nike's response to this (and other similar incidents) was "We don't make shoes" (Larimer 1998, 30). This was technically correct as Nike's core business strategy involves outsourcing *all* manufacturing to sub-contractors in poor Asian countries.

In November 2001, Rosa Ruiz died when the van she was riding in flipped over on Route 1 in southern Rhode Island. The van was carrying Ruiz and her co-workers from their job at a fish-processing plant back to their homes in the Providence area. Rosa was working at a company called Town Dock but had been hired through a temporary employment agency, Action Manufacturing Employment. The van was owned and operated by the agency. When the surviving workers publicly voiced complaints about conditions at the plant, they were all fired. Town Dock management's response to the incident was "Rosa Ruiz was not working for Town Dock on the day that she passed" (Ziner and Davis 2001).

The business strategy employed by Nike and Town Dock is not unusual. Specifically, each of these businesses has adopted the "sweating system" method of organizing work. In this system, the real employer takes no responsibility for the wages and working conditions of the employees. The sweating system is now being used not only by producers like Nike, who outsource production to low-wage countries but also by companies like Town Dock, operating in the United States.

Against this strategy, a variety of labor and community organizations have asserted "worker rights." Whereas business strategists (largely supported by orthodox economics) present their tactics as necessary responses to irresistible "globalization," labor activists put forward worker rights as an obvious and natural alternative. Rather than a conversation about what appropriate workplace standards might be, we are often left with a battle of competing truisms.

This book examines how worker rights are conceived and how these conceptions affect the activities of international organizations, governments, enterprises, and social movements. Focusing on the social processes by which rights are defined and the networks through which these definitions are distributed, I go beyond the recent controversies over sweatshops and globalization to show how worker rights have been contested from the antislavery movement to the present day. I analyze how class interest and conventional morality interact to define particular rights at particular times.

By defining slavery as *the* evil that must be destroyed, antislavery activists and reformers, many of them rising industrial capitalists and their allies, helped to create a concept of freedom as the right to sell one's labor time in a "free market." Responding to the social dislocations of industrialization and the perceived threat posed by the Bolshevik revolution, social democrats articulated a right to collective bargaining that was embodied in the New Deal and the constitution of the International Labor Organization (ILO). During the Cold War, American conservatives such as George Schultz argued for the adoption of ILO conventions to demonstrate the superiority of the American way of life. Bill Clinton sought to boost the presidential chances of Al Gore and contribute to "globalization with a human face" by linking labor standards to trade negotiations, contributing to the collapse of the WTO meetings in Seattle in 1999. The administration of George W. Bush shifted focus away from sweatshops per se to child labor and worker rights in the Middle East. In each case, class interest and moral convention both influenced how worker rights were conceived.

Economic Heterodoxy

I adopt the standpoint of heterodox economics to tell this story. In doing so, I follow Marx to some extent, in highlighting the material conditions that influence the formation of knowledge, but also certain postmodern and Institutional economists who see ideas, and especially moral conventions, as having a life of their own, a relative autonomy from economics. In emphasizing but not essentializing class relations and interests, I try to avoid both the economic determinism of classical Marxism and the hyperindividualism of neoliberalism.

Contemporary heterodox economics draws on elements from the Keyne-

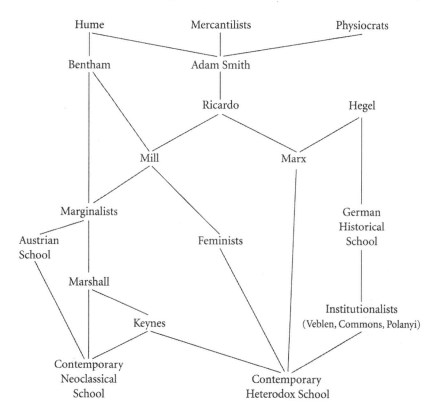

Fig. 1. Political economy: a simplified family tree

sian, Feminist, Marxian, and Institutional traditions (see fig. 1). In Marx and in some of his followers we find the most fully developed analysis of class relations and class interest and their influence on knowledge. The American Institutional school has been especially concerned with the roles of convention, custom, and tradition on how economic arrangements are evaluated.[1]

Human beings live in communities. These communities (states, towns, families, workplaces) create larger structures of meaning and understanding, and it is in terms of such structures that individuals understand the world and their place in it. Particular forms of class interest and desire limit both the behavioral choices and meanings available. Class and community create the context within which laws and social practices develop, and law and social practice affect the structuring power of class and community.

Conventional neoclassical economics enters this discussion with little to offer. It essentializes human preferences and technology as the uncaused causes of economic change, and it deploys a highly abstract notion of the market as its primary trope. It continues to spotlight relations between rational, autonomous individuals, "Robinson Crusoes on islands," and is concerned mainly with the conditions under which these interactions might produce a stable social order.

This neoclassical vision no longer fully defines orthodox economics because over the last generation vigorous research programs in institutional and behavioral economics have developed. Even at the level of the introductory textbook, economics as it is now conventionally taught often includes attention to various complexities such as information and transaction costs, as well as a more serious consideration of the psychological motivation of economic agents. This shift over the last several decades has been useful in making economists more sophisticated about human behavior and able to enter into exciting conversations across the social sciences.

But in public policy discussions a rather crude version of market economics still prevails, and all that noneconomists often know is the neoclassical version of orthodoxy. The study of worker rights is by necessity interdisciplinary, including law, moral philosophy, history, and sociology, as well as economics, and here the revival of Institutional thought is particularly helpful as Institutional economists have always ranged across these fields. However, I argue in the next chapter that the new Institutional and behavioral research programs are likely to help us understand the formation of worker rights only to the extent that class relations, class interest, and the social formation of knowledge are seriously thought about. We will find far more resources for considering these issues in heterodox than in orthodox economics.

If my theoretical approach lies at the intersection of Institutional thought and the Marxian critique of political economy, my political concerns flow from the array of social dislocations that have struck the industrialized world over the last generation, first as "deindustrialization" and more recently as "globalization."

Since the 1970s there has been a massive extension of the market both geographically and into new areas of social life. More and more things take the form of commodities, and more and more people have become wage laborers. How has this affected dominant moral convention? How have these changes in moral convention been influenced by class interest?

How, given our answers to these questions, should we interpret the relationship between globalization and the reinvigoration of international justice movements? Is the latter simply called forth by the former, as its dialectical opposite, or can (and should) this relationship be understood in a more complex way? How do conventional definitions of rights and class interest combine to overdetermine the agendas that these movements pursue? Does the antisweatshop movement, for instance, rooted as it is in a moral and often religious critique, allow itself to be used by "enlightened" capitalists to shift attention from the existence of exploitation in general to specific forms of exploitation that contemporary cultural conventions define as particularly egregious, such as forced labor and child labor?[2] Alternatively, can this movement create a desire for certain kinds of rights that does not exist now? Can it contribute to organizing and giving voice to subaltern groups?

Back to Work

In choosing class and convention as analytical entry points I want to be clear about what in Marx and what in Institutional thought I really want to use. The genius of classical Marxism was to produce in thought the class that would resolve the contradictions of capitalism. But the two-class model of the *Communist Manifesto* and the determinism of the famous preface to the *Contribution to the Critique of Political Economy* are now almost embarrassing in their optimism and scientism, however successful they once were polemically. On the other hand Marxist theory has long since left behind the base-superstructure model, and there is now a rich and extensive body of work that develops Marx's concept of class as exploitation without making class the determinant of everything else in society.[3]

As long as the drives to minimize labor costs and to privately appropriate public resources are promoted as normal and socially efficient there will probably always be some kind of Marxism that is denaturalizing and critiquing those drives and their effects. I assume with Marx that exploitation in production is linked to a host of social problems, without assuming that those links are simple or obvious. In addressing the role of social convention in combating exploitation I am drawn to those parts of the Marxian and Institutional traditions that find a relatively autonomous role for ideology in social life.

In the United States the Institutional tradition has left a bigger footprint on social theory and politics than has Marxism.[4] Although Thorstein Veblen is now more commonly read in sociology and cultural studies than in economics, there is a healthy industry in recycling his contrasts between the world of money making and the world of making goods, if not very often with his satirical wit. There has recently been a resurgence of interest in Karl Polanyi's work, particularly his analysis of the ways in which society protects itself from the outward thrust of the market, and the social turbulence that this double movement engenders.

Among the major Institutional theorists in the United States it was John R. Commons and his followers who had the biggest impact on labor relations and law. Paralleling Fabian socialism in England and the reformist wing of German social democracy, Commons argued that unionization and regulation could incorporate the working class within capitalism while tempering some of the social instability inherent in the capitalist process. And it was Commons's students (and his students' students) who prevailed in labor law and policy in the United States from the 1930s to the 1970s. In a sense, for Commons-brand institutionalism, the labor movement and the New Deal *were* the revolution that Marxists sought through other means.

This brand of policy and thought is now almost as dead as deterministic Marxism. Yet Commons's ideas are also regularly recycled in the New Institutional economics and in vague desires, usually at the end of books or conference addresses, for "some kind of global New Deal." I develop Commons's ideas directly and put them into conversation not with the neoclassical theory of the firm, as in so-called new Institutionalism, but with the Marx who recognized that the institutions, norms, and traditions of each country must be taken into consideration when analyzing the possibility of eliminating exploitation.[5]

Institutions and Class

How do economic rights emerge and evolve? I argue that the emergence and definition of worker rights are best understood as the interactive result of convention and class.

Why *worker rights?*[6] Because they are increasingly important—and understudied. The globalization of the late twentieth and early twenty-first centuries, that is, the extension of market relations to new parts of the globe and the deepening hold of markets and market-worshiping ideologies within the already (mostly) capitalist countries, was accompanied by an unexpected resurgence of the "labor problem." Antisweatshop activists and living wage campaigns put the problem of the labor market and the employment relationship squarely at the center of the public policy agenda at a time when many apostles of the "new economy" had assumed that these were solved problems of the industrial age (French 2002).

Economists have studied property rights at length, often believing that securing such rights is the critical condition necessary for a market-coordinated economy to work. Various kinds of property rights have figured prominently in global trade negotiations. While worker rights have snuck onto that agenda from time to time, they have hardly received anywhere near the analytical attention that property rights have.

Even many heterodox—radical, feminist, institutional, Marxian, Austrian, post-Keynesian, ecological, and so on—economists do not take worker rights seriously, seeing such rights as fine (and perhaps even supportable) as a political slogan but not worth serious academic consideration. I show here that clear understanding of the emergence and evolution of worker rights can make a strong contribution to the ongoing project of building a viable alternative to neoclassical theory and neoliberal policies.

Any approach to the labor market that takes institutional and sociological factors seriously must acknowledge that how hiring and production take place, how wages and unemployment are determined, and how income is distributed are all affected by what kinds of rights can be asserted and defended. It is hard to see how heterodox (or orthodox for that matter) students of labor and employment relations can make any headway without clear and sophisticated concepts of the formation and evolution of worker rights.

Most activists and human rights scholars pay little attention to economics, or indeed to the status of their own claims to workers having "rights." One of the purposes of this book is to demonstrate that a viable economics exists that can lend support to some human rights claims, while also critically engaging such claims. An encounter between worker rights activism, human rights theory, and economic heterodoxy can lead to the effective critique and strengthening of each.

Class and Conventional Knowledge

Rights emerge and evolve in the context of class processes, class interest, and conventional knowledge. Both *class* and *convention* have multiple meanings in general, and I will use both words to signify several things.

Its *class* approach to understanding social change is arguably the greatest contribution of Marxian theory to the social sciences. Marx posited that all but the most primitive societies are divided by class in that some people receive the surplus labor of others. This surplus is the labor over and above what is necessary for the replacement of the means of production and reproduction of the direct producers at a given standard of living. The appropriators of the surplus—slaveholders, feudal lords, capitalists, chiefs, in various types of societies—have a privileged position as the first receivers of the surplus, but they in turn must distribute at least part of the surplus to various individuals providing conditions of their continued existence as surplus appropriators—overseers, feudal retainers, merchants, bankers, churches, the state, etc. Tensions and contradictions both between the producers and appropriators of surplus and between the appropriators and the various groups that make claims on the surplus are understood to be the main forces driving social change. Examining those forces and the various possible alliances between people differently positioned with respect to the performance, appropriation, and distribution of surplus is the main object of Marxian scholarly and political work.

This is a different notion of class than is used in academic sociology, cultural studies, or the popular media. It is a thin definition in that it focuses on only a few processes, which it calls *class processes,* and does not presume a one-to-one correspondence between these class processes and the sociological or cultural meanings of *class.*

There is another, thicker meaning of *class* that I also deploy in this book: class interest. Those who are performers of surplus labor may have a class interest in ending that performance and appropriating the surplus for themselves. Those who are surplus appropriators may have a class interest in just the opposite outcome. Those who receive surplus from the appropriators may themselves come to perceive class interest either in their own groups or through some kind of alliance with surplus performers or appropriators.

It would be foolish to reduce people's behavior to their class positioning. Consideration of class interest is important though in understanding the formation and evolution of rights concepts. Rights cannot be understood as emerging from nowhere; they are always and everywhere affected by the class relations within which they circulate. Particular rights concepts will be more or less consistent with existing patterns of surplus production, appropriation, and distribution. I argue in chapter 4, for instance, that the critique of slavery was informed and limited by capitalists' desire to contrast slavery with an ideology of free labor. In other words, the (sometimes intended and sometimes unintended) effect of the attack on the slave class process was to create ideological conditions of existence for capitalist exploitation.

A more recent example is the emergence of rights-based governance of the employment relationship in the United States over the last twenty-five years. Developing out of the civil rights and feminist movements, employers are now legally constrained in their dealings with a whole array of people based on their gender, age, racial, and physical characteristics. But at the same time, capitalists were successful in channeling the complaints about work relations in the ways that were easiest for them to handle, that is, by granting *individual* rights rather than collective rights such as freedom of association and the right to bargain collectively. In chapter 7 I investigate how the definition of worker rights in the current moment of globalization is influenced by both convention and class, in that some corporations do in fact respond to consumer and investor complaints about sweatshops, but in ways that support individual rather than collective rights.

Class interest has its effects mostly indirectly through the formation of conventional knowledge. Here the Institutional economics tradition and the tendency in Western Marxism associated especially with the Italian theorist and labor leader Antonio Gramsci are not so far apart. Gramsci developed a subtle and acute analysis of how capitalists maintain their position not just through violence and economic coercion but also through various institutions—schools, churches, media, and so forth—in which the values of the capitalist class in general are promoted as the common sense of society. This creation of a hegemonic culture, Gramsci thought, was critical to capitalists' ability to get workers to consent to (and sometimes even to celebrate) their own exploitation, without resorting to direct or violent repression. In the case of Italy Gramsci thought the Catholic Church played an especially important role as a universal institution promoting a perceived unity of interests among those occupying different class positions. The precise workings of cultural hegemony differ from one society to another, but the key point is that a dominant capitalist economic class position is reproduced partly by creating conventional knowledge in which bourgeois values emerge as natural and normal (Gramsci 1971).

Not only did Gramsci raise the importance of cultural processes for socialists, but he pointed to the fact that the formation of a "historical bloc" capable of reproducing the hegemony of the dominant class required compromise and alliance with a variety of different groups. In the analysis of worker rights then, recognizing class interest points us toward the limits that the conventional wisdom will place on the formation of rights concepts as well as the real advances that might be made because of capitalists' desire and need to maintain hegemony in the cultural sphere.

Convention is at least as variously defined as *class,* and I will use the term in several senses. The notion that economic behavior is the complex product of the cultural and political setting in which it occurs is familiar in the older institutional economics of Thorstein Veblen, John R. Commons, Karl Polanyi, and John Kenneth Galbraith. Galbraith's notion of the "conventional wisdom"—widely and rarely questioned beliefs that ground behavior—is particularly well known, and given the emphasis Galbraith placed on advertising, his version of the consensus construction of reality is perhaps not so far from Gramsci's as it might first appear.

Various strands within Institutional thought are useful for offsetting a tendency to functionalism and structuralism within Marxism. There are, of course, Marxists who reject functionalist and structural explanations but oftentimes what Marxists and critical theorists seem especially good at is explaining how capitalist structures of power and exploitation are reproduced because that is somehow what capitalism requires. Institutional thought allows us to more easily incorporate conventional thinking, which is (of course) influenced by but not reducible to class interest.

The concept of convention is prominent in the new Institutional economics. Conventions, such as driving on one side of the road or another, allow people to coordinate their behavior without communicating with one another, drawing on ideas they share based on common experience. Conventions become widespread when the small numbers of people who deviate from them do less well than those who follow them. Conventions then are self-perpetuating patterns of behavior.

Class, Convention, and Worker Rights

How are worker rights established? Here is where Institutionalists might learn something from Marxism. In the next chapter I argue that it is necessary to bring Marx's ideas fully into the discussion of worker rights, rather than treating Marx—and the idea of class as exploitation—as a ghostly absence, which is currently the case for both orthodox and many heterodox economists.

In chapter 3 I use class and convention to argue that recent changes in the contemporary world economy have created something quite similar to sweatshop conditions on a global basis through an increase in social distance. By this I mean a situation in which the employer takes no moral responsibility for the condition of his employee. This is most obviously true in situations of lengthened commodity chains, such as Nike and other shoe and apparel manufacturers, in which the ultimate employer has never been to the country in which the ultimate producer is working. But it is also true in cases where employer and employee share the same physical space but are grouped into separate legal entities, as in the cases of outsourcing, subcontracting, and the use of temporary workers in the United States. In the concluding chapter I speculate that this imminent tendency has spread to define workplace morality even in traditional factory enterprises.

Can a politics of rights combat this tendency? "Rights talk" makes economists nervous, and there are good reasons for this. While not all discussions of rights are "hot air on stilts," I show in chapter 4 that the assertion of rights claims as a primary strategy used by those who want to challenge (or defend) the political-economic status quo is more an accident of history than a testament to the strength of rights theory. What is and is not constituted as a right is influenced not just by the desires of social movements and intellectuals but by material interest. I argue that the right to freedom from forced labor, one of the four "core" rights established by the International Labor Organization, fits well with the contemporary human rights regime, whereas the right to freedom of association and collective bargaining does not. And if the latter is the more potent tool in developing a countermovement to corporate globalization, then neglecting the discursive constitution of rights comes at a high price.

In the later chapters I show that a class-conscious deployment of Institutional economics is the most useful way to think about the contemporary international organization of worker rights through case studies of the International Labor Organization, the international labor policy of the U.S. government, and the student antisweatshop movement. If the growth of social distance through lengthening commodity chains explains much about contemporary labor markets, I argue that the creation of a language of international labor rights and an international law of labor standards through an authoritative institution is a pressing priority.

Chapter 5 is concerned with the nascent version of such an institution, the International Labor Organization (ILO). The most completely articulated argument for labor rights is the ILO's Declaration on Fundamental Principles and Rights at Work. The ILO, both in the programs and policies it promotes, and in its own governance, is very close to that part of the Institutional tradition associated with Commons. For this reason it deploys a way of thinking about rights that is alien to the other multilateral organizations such as the International Monetary Fund (IMF) and the World Bank. The ILO's discursive construction of rights creates space to address the moral dimensions of the contemporary employment relationship, while creating awkward translation problems within economics.

The United States has not ratified the core ILO conventions on labor rights, in particular the rights to freedom of association and to bargain collectively. Defenders of the U.S. record argue variously that the U.S. federal system prevents such ratification, that our current system of employment law reflects a fragile balance of interests that should not be disturbed by international considerations, and that in practice U.S. workers have their rights protected more effectively than workers in those countries that have ratified these conventions. I show each of these claims to be specious. The resistance to ratification flows more from class interest than from legal constraint or the virtues of our current arrangements. Perhaps nothing would be more educational on these issues than a Senate debate on ratification of the conventions on freedom of association and collective bargaining, and because of contradictions between U.S. foreign policy and the class desires of U.S. capitalists, such a debate may be possible.

Resistance to dictatorship inside the workplace is as old as or older than capitalism itself, and today a variety of labor-based nongovernmental organizations are engaged in cultivating a desire for class justice at work, by breaking down the mysteries of the commodity and encouraging people to link the commodities they consume to the social relations under which they were produced. Prominent among these in the United States are United Students Against Sweatshops and the Worker Rights Consortium. I argue that while the stated goals of the student antisweatshop movement are modest, its unintended effects may be quite large, especially when judged against the record of earlier worker rights movements.

In the concluding chapter I will draw the various strands of the argument together and consider some effects of the spread of the sweating model and mentality beyond the global factory networks, as well as the resistance to that model and mentality. To reverse the old 1960s slogan, this resistance takes the form of thinking locally while acting globally, of repositioning faceless others as our neighbors, while building global networks of solidarity.

Neither class nor morality is part of the standard conversation in economics today although both once were. Before becoming famous as the author of the *Wealth of Nations,* Adam Smith, professor of moral philosophy at Edinburgh, wrote *The Theory of Moral Sentiments,* a book recently rediscovered by new Institutional economists. Karl Marx was not only the last of the classical political economists; he also developed the most sophisticated approach to class in social theory. The next chapter provides a new economic approach to worker rights that incorporates both morality and class.

CHAPTER 2

Class, Convention, and Economics

In economics, but also in political science and sociology, a new Institutionalism has arisen since the 1980s to compete with if not displace the older neoclassical orthodoxy. As institutional ideas have always had a prominent place in labor economics, it is not surprising that new Institutional concepts play a prominent role in that subdiscipline.

This chapter begins with one of the central ideas of the new Institutionalism: convention. I find this concept both useful for understanding how ideas about worker rights are developed and disseminated, but also inadequate unless issues of class are explicitly discussed. In my view, Marxian notions of class are critically important in understanding the most important material interests affecting power and meaning. Some Marxists have recently explored subjectivity in ways that are consistent with Institutional accounts. Who has rights and what those rights are depends on the way we conceive economic subjects and what we think they are capable of doing.

As with any research program that is contending for hegemony, there is a tendency to categorize potential rivals as subsumable to the new orthodoxy. This is more or less what the new Institutionalism does with Marx. I say more or less because the new Institutionalism actually makes two contradictory moves: (1) what is interesting in Marx can be subsumed under the Institutional banner; (2) there is nothing interesting in Marx. I illustrate this with examples drawn from the three subfields most relevant to a consideration of the problem of worker rights: labor economics, development, and economic history.

The policy-oriented reader, impatient with intramural debates among social scientists, may want to skip ahead to the next chapter. These debates are important though in order to establish the diversity of voices within economics on the question of rights and the necessity for considering both class and convention in the formation of rights.

Conventions Are Ever Present and Subject to Class Interest

In a widely cited paper, Robert Sugden argues that conventions are the product of an evolutionary process and spread from one sphere of life to another by analogy. For example, if "first come first served" is a convention in one area of social life, people may begin to apply it to others. Precisely because conventions spread by analogy there is no presumption that they are efficient. "First come first served" may be perfectly reasonable when it comes to pumping gasoline but it may make no sense when distributing health care, for instance.

Sugden contends that conventions that establish themselves are those that take root most quickly in a convention-free world. This is both vague and idealist. In any contemporary social situation in which we are likely to have interest, conventions are always already present, and the goal of social analysis might more properly be seen as trying to understand why certain conventions are overthrown and replaced by others. Slavery was considered to be fine and normal; then it wasn't. Doctors considered cigarette smoking relatively harmless; now they do not.[1]

One need not believe that new conventions are more consistent with reality or more efficient than older ones, and it is just as likely that conventions develop through leaps of imagination or class interest as through reason or public interest. I will consider how this might occur in a situation in which conventions help maintain the dominance of the few over the many. Before doing so I want to emphasize the peculiarity of thinking of conventions emerging in a convention-free world, because it is here that I think the new Institutionalism especially falls into an idealist trap that Marxists usually avoid.

The first example Sugden develops is about who gets to gather wood on a beach. He imagines a convention in which the first person on the beach gets it all, and is able to leave some there for a time if he also leaves a mark, such as two stones on top of the pile. For Sugden, somehow such a convention must have emerged in a convention-free world. It is more than a little ironic that Marx wrote a series of newspaper articles in 1842 about peasants being prosecuted for taking wood from forests owned by the Kaiser. In fact, the debates on the law on thefts of wood in the Rhine Provincial assembly is what first turned Marx's attention to economic issues (1970, 1).

In these articles Marx demanded that the customary rights of the poor to the common land be recognized against the abstract legal arguments of the government (1842). Marx was later to revise some of his thinking on how pre-capitalist rights should be treated, but the point here is that a convention was overthrown through legal arguments, behind which lurked organized class interest:

> His description of the villainies committed by the landowners and of the way in
> which they trampled underfoot logic and reason, law and justice, and in the last
> resort the interests of the State, in order to satisfy their own private interests at
> the expense of the poor and the dispossessed reveals the fierce anger against injustice which moved him. "In order to destroy the poacher and the pilferer the
> Diet has not only broken the limbs of the law, but it has pierced it to the very
> heart." On the basis of this one example Marx wished to show what might be expected of a class assembly of private interests when once it seriously set about
> the task of legislating. (Mehring 1966)

Sugden's wood-gathering parable demonstrates a lacuna in the new Institutionalism, one that I believe calls for explicit class analysis of the formation of conventions. I agree that economic behavior is largely conventional, and that such conventions are not the product of reason or collective choice *or* class interest alone. Conventions are not necessarily efficient and cannot generally be justified on moral or social welfare grounds. Of course some conventions do come to be defined in moral terms.

Following Hume, Sugden argues that conventions become norms when virtue is annexed to justice, because of a human desire for approval from others. (One might easily argue that it is equally "human" to desire disapproval from others, but let us go along with Sugden here.) Conventions, as they become norms, are internalized as the right thing to do, not just as the thing that we do.

Conventions that favor some over others can become norms. Sugden uses the wood gathering example again, arguing that if the second person on the beach breaks the convention he must presume that the third person on the beach will still support it. His argument is based on reason—the third person will support the convention because he in fact hopes that at another time he will be first. But isn't it more likely that the wood-gathering convention will become a norm because (1) the first person is the Kaiser's agent; (2) newspapers, schools, and churches proclaim that the convention is virtuous; and (3) freedom of assembly is prohibited so that the second and third persons are not allowed to talk to each other?

Wood-gathering peasants may hate the regime in which they live but prefer that small groups not revolt if such revolts are easily defeated with nasty repercussions for *all* peasants. If a small group legitimately expects that all other peasants will follow a revolt, then communication between peasants must be prevented. Without such communication, nonrevolt is in the interest of each peasant who also hates the Kaiser's regime, so that continued obedience may become a *norm* that acquires moral force among the peasants. Not gathering wood in "the Kaiser's forest" is not done, and it is not right to do it.

Of course, it is possible that new conventions will be introduced that challenge and do not reinforce the rule of property. The attempt to create conventions around the decent treatment of wage laborers is one such example. Beginning in the late eighteenth century and continuing in fits and starts up to the present, liberal reformers, socialist agitators, and Christian moralists have attempted to overturn conventions under which once one stepped across the factory or office gates only the owner's rules applied. Unilateral rule by owners was certainly the predominant thinking in industrializing England, yet in the first half of the nineteenth century a series of laws was passed that constricted capitalists' ability to rule in the workplace, particularly regarding the length of the working day.

Yet this battle between the claims of democracy and the claims of property has a certain *Groundhog Day* quality to it, in that the same struggle seems to have to happen over and over. Describing the labor struggles of the 1930s, the son of Thomas Gertler, head of Republic Steel and leader of the viscerally antiunion "little steel" coalition, uses the following analogy: workers engaged in sit-down strikes were like people who stood in front of your house and would not let you in. In the film *Roger and Me,* when Michael Moore tries to interview autoworkers about to be laid off by General Motors, he is thrown off the property because he "doesn't represent anyone" and the layoff is a "private family time." There is more than a little class interest at work here.

Using Conventions to Establish Norms

If the evolution of conventions and norms cannot be explained by the social benefits they engender, and if inefficient conventions and norms are just as likely as efficient ones, and if conventions that favor the exploiter over the exploited can actually become norms, then some active intervention is necessary to shift both conventional thinking and normative evaluation. One can think of the *conventions* promoted by the International Labor Organization as being precisely such an intervention. As I will discuss in more detail in chapter 5, through moral suasion and technical training the ILO and allied organizations seek to create a convention, in the sense that those who respect core labor rights will be rewarded and those who don't will be punished. But in a sense the causality flows backward here. These "conventions" in the legal sense are actually norms, which the ILO hopes that through moral suasion and technical assistance will become conventions in the sense that new Institutional and Evolutionary economists use the term. The ILO and labor-based nongovernmental organizations need to be analyzed as teachers of norms (Finnemore 1993), and that is precisely what I do in chapters 5 and 7.

Conventional rules for behavior and normative evaluations are learned, and political economists since David Hume have emphasized the role of the market in promoting and undermining moral behavior. For Hume and his followers, people are naturally induced to follow the governing rules once they come to understand that unrestrained selfishness undermines society. As rules are developed to regulate social behavior they become customary and are handed down from one generation to another so that eventually the rules themselves become both the common sense of society, and normative. Markets teach that rule-generating institutions are necessary and that there is self-interest in submitting to the norms thus established.

Adam Smith basically followed Hume, seeing the spread of industry as promoting conventions of industriousness, punctuality, and so forth. Believing that humans, in their nature, have the capacity for sympathetic identification with others, self-interest would be held within socially acceptable bounds. So markets would produce not just the wealth of the nation but also better people. But Smith also consciously worried about the effects of the division of labor on the human spirit, arguing that it tended to produce people who were as stupid as it is possible for human beings to become, so that the social order had to be "fabricated" not just through conventional knowledge and its accompanying normative evaluation but by the constitution and preservation of moral order by virtuous people, especially, in Smith's view, by the church.

Today, while the spread of the market across the globe and into new areas of social life arguably increases the shared experiences from which tolerance and mutual understanding might grow, the deepening division of labor and the geographic fragmentation of production reduce those shared experiences, splintering the social space and making sympathetic behavior the less likely. This is happening as primary socialization through the family has been in rapid eclipse, and market signals appear to be creating a narcissistic society in which all are encouraged to grab what they can without regard to others. Unable to see their mutual interdependence, unaware of relevant moral norms, and unwilling to take responsibility for their own actions, the pessimist case today is that the deepening division of labor and pressures of competition are eroding the moral norms upon which the functioning of a market economy rests. I will investigate this case in more detail in the concluding chapter. But I now turn to how it is that both the old (neoclassical) and new (institutional) orthodoxies in economics can be so blind to class issues.

Neoclassical, Institutional, and Marxian Labor Economics

Neoclassical economics is descended from Adam Smith's liberal and optimistic view of coordination through markets, but with important differences. Smith utilized a labor theory of value whereas neoclassicals posited that value was established subjectively through marginal utility's intersection with marginal cost. And whereas Smith was explicit in establishing his concept of the "impartial spectator" as the agent for connecting the market process with morality, neoclassicals have generally disdained such notions.

Neoclassical economics came to prominence in the 1870s when the utilitarian approach was proclaimed more or less simultaneously in England, France, and Austria. It was the most prominent tendency in economics from that time through the Great Depression. The inability of neoclassicals to come up with persuasive explanations for or responses to the Depression, and the greater success enjoyed by Institutional and Keynesian explanations and responses, led to neoclassicism being displaced as a hegemonic discourse.[2]

Beginning in the 1960s and gathering strength in the 1970s through early 1990s, neoclassical theory made a comeback. With it came a set of policy recommendations often labeled "neoliberal," and it was against the latter that the antiglobalization and global justice movements of the late 1990s and early 2000s took aim. For Institutional economists, though, the formal apparatus of neoclassical theory is as much of a problem as its policy recommendations.

Neoclassical economists focus on rational individuals interacting through markets, and they do not consider the labor market to be qualitatively different from other markets. Thus "labor economics" is merely an applied field of price theory rather than an interdisciplinary research program as is true (in different ways) for Institutionalists and Marxists. Reading published neoclassical research one finds a dull monotony of cursory and mostly unidisciplinary literature review, deductive formal reasoning, and formal statistical modeling generally leading to unsurprising results: markets work, or where they don't any interference with market outcomes will lead to even worse results. Surely the dullness of dry-bones neoclassicism is partly responsible for the energetic research programs in behavioral economics and the reinvigoration of the Institutional approach at the beginning of the twenty-first century.

The original Institutional school, prominent especially in the United States in the first half of the twentieth century, focused on law, history, and the creation of mediating institutions to handle the conflicts that were seen as the inevitable result of the capitalist organization of society. There was a merger of sorts in the 1930s with Keynesian economics. Although the simple story of the Depression is often told as Keynesian theory gaining ground at the expense of neoclassicism, it was actually Institutional economists that were most influential in the United States in the 1930s. Some of these were the students of John R. Commons who came to Washington from Wisconsin and elsewhere to write the laws and staff the agencies created by the New Deal. John Kenneth Galbraith was also part of this merger, an avowed young Keynesian in macroeconomics who also rejected the apparatus of neoclassical price theory.

The young labor economists of the World War II period, while more intimately familiar with and inclined to utilize price theory than was Commons, carried their research out in an inductive case study method. This neoinstitutional group included figures that would influence labor policy through the 1990s and beyond including John Dunlop and Clark Kerr.[3]

The new Institutionalism has developed from the perceived failings of neoclassicism, while often adopting the individualistic assumptions of that approach. It has emphasized bounded rationality, incomplete information, and particularly the incompleteness of the labor contract. In other words, economic agents are assumed to have limited ability to process information and limited information to process, leading them to rely on rules and conventions. Because the labor contract does not specify how much work will be done for a particular wage, the link between wages and productivity breaks down, and there is a role for psychology and even biology in determining wages and output.

The public persona of economics as a science always creates a desire for unity when ruptures open, and economists reviewing these new literatures have been quick to find it, with the new approaches either subsumable to neoclassicism or forming something new ("modern economics") with it.[4] The new behavioral and new Institutional work has made conversation in economics more interesting but still often willfully blind to class issues.

The treatment of Marxian labor economics in these attempted syntheses is one of simultaneous absorption and dismissal. For Marx, the wage is set just like any other value, at the cost of the reproduction of the thing being sold. Thus in chapter 6 of *Capital*, volume 1, Marx presumes that the labor market is fair in the precise sense that the wage is equal to what it costs to clothe, feed, house, and transport the worker as well as the next generation at a socially and customarily determined standard of living. It is *inside* the employment relationship that one must go to understand processes of conflict and cooperation and in this sense the new Institutionalism has just gotten to where Marx was almost a century and a half ago.

What the capitalist wants to buy is labor (i.e., work), but what he can buy is labor time. This distinction causes two kinds of conflict. One key locus of conflict is the length of the working day. If capitalists can lengthen the working day without increasing the (daily) wage, more of the output returns to them—surplus labor time and the surplus product (labor time and production above what is necessary to socially reproduce the worker and the means of production) increases—and under the capitalist rules of the game this accrues to the capitalist. And indeed the beginning of the modern labor rights discourse can be found in the struggle to limit the working day, first for women and children and then for all workers.

A second area of conflict is reduction in necessary labor time, or what Marx called relative surplus value. Technical changes that increase the pace of production or allow skilled or high-status workers to be replaced by unskilled or low-status workers, speedup that gets the worker to work harder, or moving production to regions with a lower standard of living all increase the relative part of the product that accrues to the capitalist.

While workers may struggle (sometimes successfully) against these two forms of exploitation, their success is limited by a number of factors, including the coordination problems emphasized by the new Institutionalism but also the existence of the reserve armies of the unemployed who are ready to take employment under lower standards than incumbent workers.

In his mature political economy, especially the three volumes of *Capital* and some of the preparatory studies for that monumental work, Marx articulated a number of arguments that have only recently received much attention from labor economists. For Marx, people were social even before they were human, so that the methodological individualism of orthodoxy makes no sense.[5] Marx understood markets to be artificial, not natural, and the extraction of labor from labor power is really very close to the new Institutional emphasis on the incompleteness of the labor contract.

But there are differences with institutionalism, and these generally revolve around the handling of conflict and the understanding of change. Conflict is common and oftentimes not solvable through negotiation, as Institutionalists assume. Only one man can be king. Marx saw the dynamism of the capitalist mode of production as lying in the competition that develops technology and business cycles. Politics and culture (including conventional wisdom) tend to be structured so that those who prefer not to adjust to these dynamic factors are overridden. For Marx and his followers, violence is understood to be a foundational aspect of the capitalist mode, in the formative phase to clear out the peasantry and to dominate the noncapitalist colonies, today in the form of interelite conflicts due to uneven development between and within regions, and in rationalizing declining advanced areas and incorporating new ones into the international division of labor.

Some of these new areas are geographically defined. For instance, the incorporation of China into the world market has been accompanied by mass protest and state violence, however little reported this is in the Western press. But some of these areas are social, such as the movement of women in the United States and northern Europe out of the household mode of production and into the capitalist mode, which has itself been accompanied by much turmoil.

Capitalism, as it is described by economic orthodoxy, is a remarkably flat and peaceful thing, always tending toward some kind of equilibrium. In *Capital* Marx goes to some length to demonstrate that the economic surplus does not arise from market exchange but through the appropriation of other people's labor time. This is less obvious in capitalism than in feudal or slave modes, because in capitalism the rule of law and seemingly impartial market forces appear to be the primary mechanisms coordinating society. Yet it remains the case that capitalism channels the fruits of economic development to those who appropriate rather than perform surplus labor. Marxists and critical theorists have examined the normalization of this process through the ideological apparatuses—the schools, the churches, the media, and so on—in some depth over the last thirty years.[6] Nonetheless, the state and its ability to deploy violence remain critical for enforcing the capitalist rules of the game.

The state plays a key role in both Institutional and Marxist thought, but whereas for Commons emphasis is on the law and the courts, until recently Marxists have focused on the repressive power of the state. This is not to deny an independent or relatively autonomous role for law. For instance, Tigar and Levy demonstrate the importance of legal theory in the rise of the European bourgeoisie, showing a complex and rich relationship between class struggle and legal ideology. Commons read the history of English common law and found an emphasis on reasonableness and fairness; Marx and his followers read a similar history and found the law as a tool of class struggle. One may argue for either Commons's or Marx's interpretation, but clearly one cannot introduce law and the state as "exogenous variables" that influence already existing market equilibria, as is the case in economic orthodoxy; the state as a cultural, political, *and* economic actor was present at capitalism's creation and is integral to its evolution, including the very definition of the categories within which we understand "economy" and "freedom."

It was a particular kind of freedom that wage laborers enjoyed during the emergence of capitalism in nineteenth-century America. In fact, work in early America existed along a spectrum of arrangements including various forms of freedom and unfreedom (Tomlins 1993; Steinfeld 1991). The free/unfree labor binary was constructed in the antebellum period in the context of the growing tensions between North and South. While the classical economists viewed the "work or starve" choice presented to wage laborers as the natural product of market forces, it is in fact better understood as "historically contingent, located in the actions of the state to narrow the range of alternative possibilities" (Rockman 2006, 352).

A "free" labor market meant a different kind of coercion and sometimes a different set of workers than an "unfree" market. Economic pressure was perhaps not as important as legal pressure in the nineteenth-century Northern states. Workers were legally restricted in their ability to shift employers at will and stood to lose up to three months pay and possible imprisonment if they did not complete the term of their contract. They were legally prohibited from withholding their labor collectively through the prosecution of conspiracy cases, of which there were none in the colonial period but many in New England, New York, Philadelphia, and Baltimore between 1806 and 1847. They were often unable to withhold labor individually, because of the enforcement of vagrancy and trespass laws (Rockman 2005, 2006).[7]

In his more polemical and journalistic writings Marx argued that the common experience of proletarianization would lead to revolutionary socialism. Labor historians influenced by Marxism have often argued that the common experience of degradation faced by skilled workers would lead them to a common, revolutionary, and socialist political project.

It is out of common experience that conventions and norms flow. But it is now clear that neither proletarianization nor degradation produced a unified, revolutionary, and socialist working class. Slavery and household labor provided crucial and negative comparisons through which wage labor, a degraded form in the ideology of the producer's republic of the revolutionary period, became "free labor" with the victory of the North in the Civil War.

We need then to investigate how a desire for class justice—a convention that would say that those who perform surplus labor should also have some say in how it is performed, appropriated, and distributed—might be *produced,* and what kind of system of normative evaluation would be consistent with class justice. It is here that some of the new Institutional work might help, although new Institutionalists seem to be so busy denying they have anything to learn from Marx or Marxists that such a conversation has not taken off.

Was Marx a Minor Pre-Institutional Labor Economist?

Economics contains a variety of discourses or stories, and this is often unsatisfying both to the consumers of economic knowledge and to professional economists. Students want straight answers, politicians want one-handed economists, and economists want to be scientists, not humanities professors.

Given the public and professional demands for a unified and scientific approach to economic questions, and the vigilance with which dissenting theories are often hunted down and killed (Lee 2004), the continued existence of a plurality of economic discourses might be seen as a testament to the diversity of economic life and the human condition. In any case, it is out of this diversity that anything resembling scientific progress is likely to come.

In economics generally and in labor economics particularly a "new Institutional school" has emerged in the last two decades. Like the old Institutionalism, this school sees individual behavior as guided primarily by social norms rather than utility maximization, while giving broader scope to the influence of markets than previous Institutional labor economists had, and using formal and deductive reasoning in the manner of neoclassicism. Neoclassical economists have reacted to this by arguing that their own tradition has become sufficiently flexible to absorb institutional and neoinstitutional critiques (Boyer and Smith 2001). Some Marxists have characterized the new Institutionalism as being merely a reentrenchment of the hegemony of bourgeois power within the discipline of economics, after the disruption of the hegemonic status of neoclassicism (Madra 2004). In any case something different from either the older Institutional or neoclassical traditions seems to have emerged from their interactions and social changes external to the discipline.

Yet in any new synthesis there are exclusions, and that is the case here. In particular, Marxian analysis of labor problems, and especially the role of class, is not explicitly a part of this new orthodoxy, although it continues to live a subterranean existence.

For a decade and a half I have been teaching a course in labor economics primarily oriented to master's degree students in labor relations and human resources. Except for two years I have used a textbook by Bruce Kaufman (with Julie Hotchkiss as co-author on later editions), and this has worked reasonably well. These students tend not to have a strong background in economics, and *Economics of Labor Markets* is, for the most part, clear and only as difficult as necessary. For my part I favor this book because it presents paradigmatic difference as important, telling the story of labor economics at least partly as a struggle between neoclassical and Institutional ideas and providing at least a rough sense, in the first chapter, that this struggle and these schools have changed over time.

When one teaches with a book for some time it becomes possible to see the conscious and perhaps unconscious rhetorical strategies of the authors. A typical chapter in *Economics of Labor Markets* begins with a presentation of relevant data, presents the neoclassical theory of the issue in question (hours of work, labor force participation, marginal productivity theory, etc.), sometimes presents dissenting, mostly institutional theories more or less briefly, and then has several boxed policy applications and treatments of issues "in the news." This gives the student the feeling that labor economics is empirically based, which is certainly true since at least the mid-1970s, perhaps to the point that the field has become measurement without theory (Freeman 1997/98, 2002). Differences between labor economists are presented as mostly about different weights given to market, institutional, and sociological forces.

"Market forces" at first are just supply and demand, but later in the book they are linked to the rational actor model and various forms of economizing behavior. By "institutional forces" Kaufman and Hotchkiss mean unions, corporations, and the state, and by "sociological forces" they mean family, class, culture, and custom. "Empirical testing" is presented as critically important in the opening chapter as a way of deciding between various explanations of labor market phenomena. The ease with which the chapters move from data to theoretical discussion to application and policy creates the image of the policy-engaged scientist that economists love so much.

Given their sensitivity to paradigmatic difference and the historical evolution of ideas, Kaufman and Hotchkiss's treatment of Marx is peculiar. They deal with Marx in a footnote in their introductory chapter, and how this footnote has changed across editions is instructive. In the late 1980s and early 1990s editions, Marx was identified as the founder of a third school of thought that, while minor in the United States, had influence in Japan and Europe. While a bit insular (and cavalier about the United States), this at least had the virtue of providing an excuse for jokes comparing Marx and Marxism to various over-the-hill baseball players and defunct rock 'n' roll bands who were "big in Japan."

In later editions both Marxism and Feminism were identified as "minor schools." In the most recent edition, the authors claim, in reference to Marxism and Feminism, that "both schools of thought share a number of features with the institutional school." And although Marx does not appear in the name index at the end of the book, he pops up again in the chapter on unions and collective bargaining as grounding a perspective in which management-labor conflict is inevitable, but unions are not the ultimate solution to the conflict. Marx's reserve army of the unemployed is mentioned as logically consistent with efficiency wage theory, but this connection is not developed. Neo-Marxist contributions to wage theory and the economics of discrimination appeared more explicitly in earlier editions, although there is still a reasonable citing of radical and neo-Marxist work in the end-of-chapter bibliographies.

Perhaps Marx simply *was* a pre-Institutional labor economist? Or perhaps, Marx's and Marxist work in labor economics is more distinctive, and a process of psychological (and perhaps political) repression and evasion is going on. Some evidence for the latter interpretation is in a separate essay Kaufman wrote entitled "The Evolution of Thought on the Competitive Nature of Labor Markets (1994), in a book co-edited by Clark Kerr.[8] Kaufman frames this history as a disagreement over how competitive labor markets really are. He surveys the work of Adam Smith, Alfred Marshall, the Institutionalists, institutionally informed neoclassicals like Paul Douglas, the post–World War II Institutionalists like Kerr and Richard Lester, the Chicago school, and what he calls the Cambridge group, Solow, Thurow, Freeman, Piore, Osterman, and so on, all contemporary Institutionalists in one way or another.

The essay is a tour de force even if one disagrees with the basic organizing concept (presence or lack of competition as the defining factor in differentiating between theorists and schools). But after the passage on Smith, and at the beginning of the section on Marshall there is the following: "Marshall had the greatest influence on the development and shape of economic science of anyone who wrote on the subject in the one hundred years that followed Adam Smith. (Karl Marx would be the closest challenger.)"

Yet there is no section of the essay on Marx. There is a section on Marx in an earlier chapter by another author (George Hildebrand), which is a more general survey of labor in classical and neoclassical economics, but while there are full chapters devoted to the Commons school, the postwar "Social Economics Revisionists" (Kerr et al.), and human capital theory, no such attention is given to Marxian work.

Recently Kaufman has become more aggressive in criticizing neoclassical theory, seeing it as a special case, that case being the never-existing one of labor exchange without transaction cost. He distinguishes two ways neoclassicism has responded to the new Institutionalism: "price theory," the conventional utilitarian, supply-and-demand stories still taught to hordes of college fresh-men and sophomores, and "choice theory," exemplified by the work of Gary Becker and more popularly by that of Steven Leavitt, which applies the rational actor model to all forms of human behavior. Rational actor theory often pro-vides explanations for institutions and outcomes not envisioned in pure price theory. Such seeming puzzles as the persistence of discrimination, unemploy-ment, and wages below marginal product are now explicable as resulting from rational choice. This does not provide a compelling defense of Smith's invisible hand, but "modern" economists seem to flip between choice theory when they want to explain something specific and price theory (and government failure) when they want to defend laissez-faire.

Kaufman continues to discuss, absorb, and dismiss Marx in his most recent work. In his global history of the field of industrial relations (2004b), he pro-vides a history of the rise of capitalism that is quasi-Marxist but does not effec-tively reference Marx. When discussing the problem of extracting labor from labor power he writes "as Commons and Marx before him emphasize," a strange way of discussing this key Marxian insight (108).[9] More than in his ear-lier texts, Kaufman here acknowledges a distinct Marxian tradition, but it is the Marx of the *Communist Manifesto,* all class struggle and private property, with-out much attention to Marx's specific analysis of the capitalist form of the em-ployment relation in *Capital.* It is Marx the economic determinist that is on of-fer, who dismissed reform as impossible and unnecessary given the inexorable laws of capitalism. Marxist thought on unions is presented essentially as a car-icature of Leninism, with vanguards of college professors leading the prole-tariat. No attention is given to the alternative tradition of Rosa Luxemburg, the New Left, and its contemporary offspring.

One does not have to investigate obscure texts to dispense with the eco-nomic determinist reading of Marx. In chapter 10 of volume 1 of *Capital* Marx gives an analysis of the length of the working day that is thoroughly institu-tionalist, reformist, *and* revolutionary. Kaufman is giving an interpretation of Marx- and Marxist-influenced work that since 1970 has been rejected by a vari-ety of antiessentialist readings of *Capital* and the Marxian tradition more broadly.[10]

This rejection of Marx on the "inevitable march of history" has involved reading Marx's many caveats and qualifications in *Capital* itself—his more complete theoretical analysis of class in the second and third volumes of *Capital*, his subtle analysis of class politics in his journalism and letters, analyses showing contingency, accidents of history, relative autonomy of the state, and so on—and subjecting the Marxian tradition to the same kind of analysis that Marx makes of the capitalist mode of production: critical, not hagiographic. It is not enough to dismiss Marx as having constructed a theory irrelevant to political pragmatism within capitalism, which is what Kaufman does here, as do both traditional institutional labor economics (Kerr 1994) and the new Institutional economics. A contemporary, nonessentialist reading of Marx leads one past Marx's grand *Manifesto* pronouncements and prefatory statements into a set of concepts and analyses that are consistent with the methods of the German historical school and its American Institutionalist offspring, that is, careful analysis of historical contingency, specificity, incremental change, and so forth, but with a careful attention to class exploitation and class interest that Institutionalism generally lacks.

One can get to the issue of the indeterminacy of labor effort through the language of the labor versus labor power distinction or through the incompleteness of the labor contract, so that a certain kind of radical economics has now merged with a certain kind of neoclassicism to form the new Institutional approach. But most of Marx's other insights continue to be evaded.

This subsumption of Marx and the ambiguity surrounding his importance is characteristic of the most thoughtful people in the field. Take, for instance, Michael Piore's characterization of research programs in a recent conference paper on the economics of the French Conventions school of economics and its attempt to deal with how order is (or is not) achieved by individuals acting spontaneously with each other through markets: "There are three distinct research approaches to this problem: the *standard* (I borrow this term from the background paper), the *psychological* (or behavioral), and the *sociological,* a fourth if one includes Marxism (where, however, the analytical apparatus leads one to expect both the stability and the chaos which these other approaches are trying to explain)" (2003).

Piore clearly believes, with the new Institutionalists, that the existence of such an order is unlikely, and it will be unstable where it does exist. He wants to take neoclassical economics (the standard approach) seriously only because it is what most economists are trained to do, not because it is a serious scientific enterprise. But the emergence of order and disorder can only really be understood by studying institutions, thereby moving economics into the realms of politics, sociology, and cognitive psychology. Whether there is a fourth research program or not is left vague, consistent with Piore's long-standing but ambiguous engagement with Marxist work (1983).

This tendency to subsume Marx and Marxist work under the Institutional banner, while also bringing it up independently and dismissing it, goes beyond the subdiscipline of labor economics. In perhaps his most important book, the wide-ranging survey *Institutions, Institutional Change, and Economic Performance,* Nobel Prize–winning new Institutional economist Douglass North argues that neither orthodox economic theory nor economic historians have sufficiently appreciated the role of institutions as "humanly derived constraints" that structure incentives in human political, economic, and cultural exchange. North is unfriendly to the neoclassical story, believing that by presuming innate rather than institutionally created incentives, that story is worthless.[11]

North credits Marx as an exception to the tendency to treat technological change exogenously and with an early "pioneering" attempt to integrate the constraints of technology and human organization. But because the Marxian tale ends with the bourgeoisie producing the proletariat, the class that can create the better society, he sees it as overly optimistic, "whereas the institutional analysis in this study provides no guarantee of a happy ending" (North 1990, 132).

Above and beyond the utopianism of the class struggle story, North finds Marxian political economy deficient relative to Institutional theory in that it needs a fundamental change in human behavior—from greed to altruism—to "achieve its results" (1990, 132). In particular he sees changes in ideology as able to overcome free rider problems in the short run but as ineffective in the long run if not consistent with "the behavioral sources of individual wealth maximizing."

On the other hand, he finds certain "Marxist models that do crucially depend on institutional considerations" as consistent with his framework. Marxist work on imperialism and dependency theory are mentioned as examples of "models" in which "institutional constructs" result in exploitation and uneven growth patterns. "To the extent that these models convincingly relate institutions to incentives to choices to outcomes they are consistent with the argument of this study."

This subsumption or evasion of Marx occurs in institutionally oriented work in development economics also. Prahnab Bardhan is an important, eclectic development economist whose work touches on several labor problems. He has given one of the ILO's prestigious social policy lectures, and he codirects the

MacArthur program on income inequality. In an essay devoted largely to showing the impact of the waning of neoclassical theory and the rise of the new institutionalism in development, he writes, "The political stumbling blocks to beneficial institutional change in many poor countries may have more to do with distributive conflicts and asymmetries in bargaining power. The 'old' institutional economists (including Marxists) used to point out how a given institutional arrangement serving the interests of some powerful group or class acts as a long-lasting barrier (or 'fetter', to quote a favorite word of Marx) to economic progress . . . the new institutional economists sometimes understate the tenacity of vested interests, the enormity of the collective action problem in bringing about institutional change, and the differential capacity of different social groups in mobilization and coordination" (Bardhan 2001, 283).

He mentions North as an exception to what he sees as the new Institutionalists' own unwarranted optimism and then favorably compares Robert Brenner's comparative Marxist analysis of the transition to capitalism to the standard new institutional story. Rather than demographics or market behavior Brenner emphasizes the cohesiveness of class-based groupings, their ability to make alliances, and their relative bargaining power.

So in labor economics, economic history, and economic development, important economists believe that a superior new Institutional approach has displaced or can at least contend with neoclassical theory, and this approach subsumes Marxism for the most part, although there are emergences of Marx that seemingly cannot be contained. But can Marx really be tamed in this way? Was Marx a minor preinstitutional economist, or is he a specter still haunting economic science?

It was Paul Samuelson who first labeled Marx as a "minor post-Ricardian," and we may learn something from his attempt to exclude and absorb Marx. While this is a pretty dismissive characterization, Samuelson in fact often struggled with Marx, lurking in the back of the Marxist seminars as an undergraduate at Harvard, writing several major essays on Marx in the 1960s and 1970s, and acknowledging Marx's unique contribution, his emphasis on class struggle.[12]

The new Institutional theory restores to orthodox economics an ability to deal with issues of politics and culture that were excluded in the period of neoclassical dominance. New Institutionalism has been helpful to me in explaining the emergence, distribution, and enforcement of concepts of labor standards, as will be seen in the chapters that follow. Yet the boundary setting of the new Institutional school is itself open to question because, as in all such cases, such boundary setting is hardly purely scientific. I argue that Marx did provide a distinct and important approach to labor problems that cannot be fully subsumed under the institutional research program.

Both class *and* convention are important for understanding worker rights and labor standards. Marxism provides a rich set of concepts for this study, even if we reject the economic determinism that characterizes much Marxist work. We are much more likely to take from Marx what is most useful if we confront his work directly.

Rather than trying to synthesize these approaches I draw eclectically from them as needed in the chapters that follow. While I emphasize that there is plenty of room for dialogue and overlapping views, there are also some important indices of difference between Marxists and Institutionalists and some surprising commonalities, which I summarize in table 1.

First, Commons's model and subsequent Institutional thinking starts from the extension of the market, not from the commodity and exploitation, and this makes a difference. In his crucial article on the shoemakers, Commons poses the extension of the market as undermining the position of the independent producer, with union membership coming from the desire to protect the skilled artisan's position vis-à-vis the market and "green hands." But subsequent research has shown that the Knights of St. Crispin blamed the factory system and the power of the bosses, not the market and the new unskilled labor force entrants, for their trouble (Dawley 1976, 147–48). If the Marxian tradition, especially the "new" labor history of the E. P. Thompson school, has sometimes overplayed the importance of proletarianization, it still explains a lot and is not a concept in the institutional arsenal.[13]

By *reasonable value* Institutionalists mean the price that could be negotiated if all market participants were involved in bargaining on equal terms. This is a useful concept that I will develop further in the next chapter. Marxian theories focus on the performance, appropriation, and distribution of surplus, and Institutionalists are loath to discuss this. The particular Marxian focus on ex-

TABLE 1.   Institutional and Marxian Economics: Difference and Unspeakable Commonality

	Marxism	Institutional Thought
Entry point	Class/proletarianization	Extension of the market
Labor process	Exploitation	Reasonable value
Political economy	Complex class analysis	Stabilization/exceptionalism
Reform	Can be good	Is good and is *the* goal

ploitation is a useful contrast to the Institutional tendency to underemphasize the specificity of the capitalist employment relationship. The price bargain between the merchant and manufacturer, and the loan arrangement between the industrial capitalist and the banker are important and part of Marx's value theory as he laid it out in the third volume of *Capital*. But they are not analogous to the capitalist employment relationship as Institutionalism at least implies. Industrial capitalists certainly struggle with merchants and financiers, but they rarely shoot up the board meeting or get federal troops called out against them. As Dawley argues, "Merchants, manufacturers, and bankers have been callous and ruthless with one another's fortunes and reputations, but the denial of food and shelter and bullet bargaining have been reserved for disputes between those who sell their labor and those who buy it" (1976, 181).

Third, there is an unspoken commitment to American exceptionalism and middle-class liberalism that permeates contemporary Institutional thought. Liberal critics of deindustrialization and globalization generally rely on a supposed outbreak of social disorder that will inevitably follow the "hollowing out" of the economy to try to sell their preferred reforms.[14] Marxists' greater awareness and analysis of fascist forms of capitalism stands as a critical, "realist" corrective to this. Labor economics textbook writers still rely on a supposed and largely unexamined American preference for individualism and lack of class identity or consciousness (Kaufman and Hotchkiss 2005, 576). But the political sympathies of both organized and disorganized labor in the United States might be better explained by the particular social conditions of American industry than by this cultural essentialism (Lichtenstein 2002; Resnick and Wolff 2006, 341–53).

Finally, I close with a commonality between Institutional and Marxist thought that both camps are loath to admit, Institutionalists perhaps because of fear of radicalism and Marxists because of pride in their credentials as revolutionaries: certain kinds of reform within capitalism are perfectly consistent with Marx's political economy.

The Institutionalist and Marxist traditions share the common assumption that conflict in and about the workplace is to be expected. Where they part ways is on what is the appropriate *resolution* of this conflict. For Institutionalists, class conflict is a threat to social order, a "primitive democracy" to be channeled and ultimately repressed.[15]

Marxists are famed for predictions of a proletarian-led revolution that, in the outlines Marx proposed, never came to fruition. Less famously, Marx proposed that the working class could, through struggle, improve its position within an existing economic system *without* overthrowing it. His prime example in *Capital* was the British working class's victorious struggle to shorten the working day and reduce child labor in the fifty years up to and including the 1860s. It has been the political quest of working-class parties in advanced capitalist countries to improve the quality of life for workers and for society, seeking to change capitalism by minimizing economic insecurity, reducing or eliminating poverty, promoting safety and health and labor standards (e.g., limiting hours worked, eliminating child labor), and the provision of public goods (e.g., education, child care, public space). The labor movements of various countries have also sought regulatory and union agreements that grant expanded worker rights and decreased property rights, such as legal guarantees over the right to a job, workplace decision-making power, and a significant stake in corporate governance.

The quality of economic and social life in a particular nation is a path-dependent outcome of the strength and degree of past and current success of its labor movement. There is of course no reason to believe that these improvements will lead to revolutionary change, but such improvements are good in themselves and explain many of the differences between the varieties of capitalism now on offer.

Marx and Engels were careful to stress that within capitalism, the state *could* be pressed by circumstance into opposition to the interests of capitalists. A politically empowered working class labor movement can shape, and has shaped, capitalist societies to be different from each other. The moments when the state leans against the interests—espoused and practical—of the capitalist class are restricted to those conjunctures when a combination of pressure from below and a host of other circumstances—political, economic, and ideological—combine to produce a change in the state that reacts back on the economy.[16]

The representation of the labor market laid out in the next chapter is primarily Institutionalist in its inspiration but it is good to keep Marxist objections at hand. The new Institutional tendency to both ignore and claim to subsume Marx and Marxian thought is part of a long tradition in social science of arguing with Marx's ghost (Williams 1964). We would be better off if we acknowledged now real commonalities and real differences rather than their ghostly representations.

CHAPTER 3

Not Only Nike Is Doing It

The chain of subcontracting typical of globalized production is best understood as a *sweating system*. This system is not peculiar to global production networks but is commonly used in domestic manufacturing and nonmanufacturing businesses.

The prevalence of the sweating system is illustrated by the examples of Nike and Town Dock with which I began chapter 1 and that are developed in more detail here. Orthodox neoclassical economics pays little attention to these issues and provides little in the way of help in trying to reverse the negative effects on workers. In contrast, one of the founders of the Institutional school, John R. Commons, *did* develop an interpretation of the labor market that provides a fruitful point of entry into contemporary sweating. In a report he made to the U.S. Industrial Commission over a century ago, Commons laid out an analysis of the sweating system that comes close to the core of how many firms organize the production and sale of commodities today (1977 [1901]). In addition, Commons illuminated the economic basis of sweating in the extension of the market in his article on the evolution of the wage bargain for American shoemakers (1964).

In application to the labor market, the terms *sweat* and *sweating* are generally employed to signify the practice of paying workers inappropriately low wages for long hours of work under conditions that may be unsafe or unsanitary. Consistent with this interpretation, the U.S. government defines a *sweatshop* as "a business that violates more than one federal or state law governing wages and hours, child labor, health and safety, workers' compensation, or industry registration" (U.S. General Accounting Office 1994).

In a report submitted in 1901 to the U.S. Industrial Commission, Commons provided an alternative definition—one presumably governing the meaning he associated with the term in the shoemakers article published eight years later—focused on labor market processes rather than on the actual terms of a wage bargain. "The term 'sweating' or 'sweating system,'" Commons observed, "originally denoted a system of subcontract, wherein the work is let out to contractors to be done in small shops or homes. . . . The system to be contrasted with the sweating system is the 'factory system' wherein the manufacturer employs his own workman" (1977, 45).

Commons emphasized that contractor control of information is a crucial element of the sweating system. It is worth quoting him at length on this point:

> [The labor contractor] deals with people who have no knowledge of regular hours. He keeps them in the dark with regard to the prevailing number of hours people work.
>
> The contractor is an irresponsible go-between for the manufacturer, who is the original employer. He has no connection with the business interests of the manufacturer nor is his interest that of his help. His sphere is merely that of a middleman. He holds his own mainly because of his ability to get cheap labor, and is in reality merely the agent of the manufacturer for that purpose.
>
> Usually when the work comes to the contractor from the manufacturer and is offered to his employees for a smaller price than has previously been paid, the help will remonstrate and ask to be paid the full price. Then the contractor tells them, "I have nothing to do with the price. The price is made for me by the manufacturer. I have very little to say about the price." That is, he cuts himself completely loose from any responsibility to his employees as to how much they are to get for their labor.
>
> The help do not know the manufacturer. They cannot register their complaint with the man who made the price for their labor. The contractor, who did not make the price for their labor, claims that it is no use to complain to him. So however much the price for labor goes down there is no one responsible for it.
>
> In case the help form an organization and send a committee to the manufacturer, the manufacturer will invariably say, "I do not employ you and I have nothing to do with you." (1977, 46)

By means of three cases to be presented here, I will demonstrate the relevance to the current setting of Commons's characterization of the sweating system and also of his understanding of its economic causes. I see the three cases as visible moments in an ongoing process of labor market transformation centered on the creation of social distance, whatever the physical location, between employer and employee so as to subject the latter ever more effectively to destructive competition, that is, to a race to the bottom. By the phrase *creation of social distance*, I am referring to the severing of a direct bargaining transaction relationship between the worker—the actual producer—

and the entity for which the productive activity is ultimately performed. I understand this severing to be the crucial step in implementing a sweating system of production.

Commons believed that regulation, in other words, the establishment and enforcement of labor market standards, is the appropriate remedy for destructive competition. This contrasts with the classical Marxist approach of building organizations capable of taking state power.

As a third alternative, it is of course possible that moral and empathic appeals to consumers and employers might provide a method of remedying the problem. Neoclassical economic theory, premised on the ubiquity of self-interested action, provides little insight into the process(es) by which such appeals might alter the behavior of market participants. Indeed, price theory has no place for the concept of destructive competition itself and tends to locate the remedy for low wages, contingent employment, and so forth in an elevation of the human capital possessed by workers rather than in an alteration of employer practices.

In contrast, the founder of conventional market economics, Adam Smith, understood economic actors to exercise restraint in granting dominion to their self-interested impulses. Specifically, Smith submitted that "natural liberty" (or, in modern language, the exercise of "free choice") incorporates an appropriate degree of restraint occasioned by, first, "sympathy," and, second, the moral principles embraced by an "impartial spectator" internal to each individual. If Smith was essentially on target about human nature (however dated his terminology), moral and empathic appeals have the potential to influence how employers will proceed in their unregulated negotiations with workers.

I will first describe three quite dissimilar contemporary cases in which the sweating system has been, or is being, implemented. I will next review Commons's conception of the sweating system, summarize how he understood industrial development to bring about sweating, and call attention to the close correspondence between the three cases and Commons's characterization. Because moral and empathic appeals have been utilized in some highly publicized recent situations involving sweating, and because Smith's ideas are not without some merit, I will also briefly summarize Smith's conception of self-regulated transactional behavior. I will then attempt to make clear why I am skeptical that Smithian self-regulation will prove to be an effective means of reversing the dynamic engendering a growing reliance on sweating. This skepticism informs the next chapter on the moral philosophy of worker rights and the chapters that follow that favorably compare regulation and worker organizing as alternatives to the "name and shame" approach.

Nike Does It

CEO Phil Knight formulated Nike's strategy of total outsourcing while he was at Stanford Business School in the early 1960s. The money saved through outsourcing would then be poured into marketing, primarily using high-profile celebrity endorsements. Significantly, "the manufacture of these sneakers was based on an arm's-length and often uneasy relationship with low paid, non-American workers" (Spar and Burns 2000, 2–3). Initially Knight subcontracted with firms in South Korea and Taiwan, but by the early 1990s most production had shifted to lower-cost East Asian countries, especially Indonesia.

The production of Nike shoes in Indonesia coincided with a period of rising labor unrest in that country. But Nike officials insisted that labor conditions in contractor factories were not their concern. Even if legal violations existed, the company's Jakarta general manager said, "I don't know that I need to know" (Spar and Burns 2000, 5). Nike did draft a corporate code of conduct for its suppliers in 1992 that addressed working conditions, safety, environmental practices, and workers' insurance. Contractors were required to certify that they were following relevant laws and regulations.

Media attention to conditions in developing country factories increased between 1992 and 1996, exploding in the latter year with revelations that the clothing line endorsed by Kathy Lee Gifford was made by child workers in Honduras. When Gifford called on other celebrity endorsers to investigate conditions in the factories where the products they endorsed were made, Michael Jordan denied any personal responsibility for the sneakers bearing his name (Nike Air Jordans), saying the company was responsible. Nike continued to maintain that this was not their problem.

Following congressional hearings in May 1996, President Clinton convened the Apparel Industry Partnership, which was meant to be a meeting ground for the companies and their critics. Nike quickly joined. Later that year they formed a new "labor practices department." They also hired former U.S. ambassador to the UN Andrew Young to evaluate the effectiveness of Nike's supplier code of conduct. The denial strategy had been replaced by one of engagement. According to Knight, "In labor practices as in sport, we at Nike believe 'there is no finish line'" (Spar and Burns 2000, 7).

Things got worse for Nike in May 1997 when the popular comic strip *Doonesbury* ran a week's worth of biting criticism of Nike plants in Vietnam. Young's largely positive reports were heavily criticized for failing to address the issue of wages and as methodologically flawed, a celebrity endorsement rather than real research.

In the spring of 1997 Nike aided a team of graduate students at Dartmouth's Tuck School of Business who wanted to conduct a study of "the suitability of wages and benefits" paid by Nike's Vietnamese and Indonesian subcontractors (Calzini et al. 1997, 5). The faculty member coordinating the student group claimed that "workers made enough to eat a good diet, house themselves simply but comfortably, dress nicely, buy basic consumer goods, and, primarily in the Indonesian case, save for the future" (Mihaly 1998). He argued that Nike and other multinationals were supporting social progress in these very poor countries, and that labor critics actually understood this but were pandering to the self-interests of U.S. trade unionists.

This argument is consistent with what orthodox economics teaches about international trade. In their best-selling international economics textbook, Paul Krugman and Maurice Obstfeld summarize the orthodox lesson: "The proposition that trade is beneficial is unqualified. That is, there is no requirement that a country be 'competitive' or that trade be 'fair'" (2000, 23). They use a version of David Ricardo's classical model of comparative advantage, believing that it demonstrates that competitiveness based on low wages does not hurt importing countries (so long as the opportunity cost of producing the imported good in terms of the home country's *own* labor is high). Further, in their model, trade does not exploit poor countries because wages are correlated with productivity.

I am skeptical about both the empirical results of the Dartmouth study and the orthodox model more generally. The Dartmouth team had no language skills, so local interpreters had to be used. Factory managers selected the workers to be interviewed. The students did not look at pay stubs or various deductions from wages, which are often greater than managers' or hand-picked workers' memories make them out to be. While the Dartmouth study implied a "living wage" was being paid to Nike workers, this does not appear to be the case.[1]

But the more serious problem is a theoretical one. This and other similar studies focus on labor market *outcomes* rather than the social aspects of the employment relation.[2] Nike's subcontracting network may or may not be a string of sweatshops in the traditional sense of low wages, long hours, and unsafe conditions. Yet, Nike's network clearly exhibits the separation of the worker from the price bargain and from a contractual relationship with the manufacturer that was, for Commons, the definition of the sweating system. "We don't make shoes" and "I don't know that I need to know" may make for bad public relations strategy, but they reflect the core of a business model in which the ultimate manufacturer tells the worker, "I do not employ you and I have nothing to do with you."

Fish Processors Do It

Fish processing may seem to have nothing to do with sneaker production. Sneakers are branded items, sold at remarkable prices because of the image that their consumers wish to convey. Fish are, well, just fish. The strategies that organizers have used to name and shame footwear and apparel companies may be less successful in fish processing. But the strategy of creating social distance in labor relations occurs in both branded and unbranded products, and not only by creating far-flung manufacturing networks.

Rosa Ruiz was a worker employed by a temporary employment agency working in a fish-processing plant in Galilee, Rhode Island, who was killed when her agency-owned van tipped over on Route 1 as she was returning home from work. After Rosa Ruiz was killed, the Rhode Island Worker Rights Board held hearings. Worker rights boards are nongovernmental organizations that attempt to use moral suasion and public pressure to expose and resolve labor problems. The use of moral suasion and public pressure reflects a popular response to the absence of governmental attention to the labor market problems since the 1980s. The members of this particular board included two Latino labor activists, an AFL-CIO field representative who is also a state legislator, clergy, and a member of the Rhode Island Human Rights Commission. The board met on December 19, 2001, at St. Teresa's Church in the heart of one of Providence's Latino neighborhoods. The fish-processing company and the temporary help agency were invited to attend but declined. The phone number that was listed for the temp agency was a fax machine.

Many of the workers at Town Dock could neither read nor speak English. For instance, Nasario Barrera, Rosa Ruiz's husband, could not identify the specific company he worked for in the days prior to the hearing because he can neither read nor write English. He and other workers testified that they earned less than the minimum wage and were not paid overtime. Workers were often paid in cash, with neither overtime nor holiday pay recognized, and with no documentation of hours worked. Rosa Ruiz's sister-in-law, Tomasa Barrera, claimed that female employees were subjected to sexual abuse by male supervisors. According to Barrera, women were verbally abused and had their pictures taken while working and in the bathroom. The Barreras and other workers testified that health and safety standards were routinely violated.

The owner of New England Employment Service, Rosa Noriega, did testify. Her company supplies workers to the fish-processing industry, though she was not involved in the Town Dock case. She said she received $7 per hour payment from the companies and paid the workers $5.75 per hour. (The Rhode Island minimum wage at this time was $6.15.) The companies faxed the number of hours each worker worked to her.

The board sent a recommendation to the state Department of Business Regulation, the Department of Labor and Training, and the regional OSHA office, calling for a "complete investigation" of the industry in the state, with special attention to Town Dock and one other firm. Angela Lovegrove, a member of both the Workers' Rights Board and the Rhode Island Commission on Human Rights, specifically requested that there be no retaliation against those workers who had testified. Two days after the hearings, nineteen workers at Town Dock were fired, including Nasario Barrera, Rosa Ruiz's husband. Through a translator, Barrera told a reporter that the company sought out him and his brother because their names had appeared in the newspaper. He claimed he was present when a Town Dock supervisor spoke to the van driver hired by the temp agency for which he was then working. According to Barrera, the supervisor asked the driver to inform the workers that they had been fired. This action dramatically illustrates the critical importance of social distance in understanding contemporary labor market trends.

The company's vice president maintained he had no knowledge of any workers being fired. According to a report in a local newspaper, the *Narragansett Times*, "Clark [the vice president] also said the workers are supplied to the company by the temporary agency and they are 'ordered' based on the number of workers Town Dock needs." To quote this manager directly, "It's important that everyone knows these people are not Town Dock employees" (Novak 2002a). Clark went on, "We have been in business for twenty years, and we are a highly regulated business. We're federally inspected annually. I disagree with the allegations. They are completely false as far as Town Dock is concerned, but my condolences go out to the family" (Novak 2002a). This was the family in which one adult was now dead and two had lost employment.

Eventually, thirty-five workers were fired. The temporary agency that had employed them told the workers Town Dock had asked for "all new people" after the initial Workers' Rights Board hearing. In a subsequent hearing, one of the immigrant workers, who had been making $5.90 per hour (25 cents less than the minimum wage) for very difficult work, expressed a strong desire to get his job back. He refused to give his name, fearing that he would be unable to find employment of any kind. Both workers and board members noted that the status of many workers as undocumented immigrants puts them in a particularly weak position.

The attorney for Town Dock claimed that "the company had simply decided to stop using New England Employment Services, an eight month old agency that supplied the workers" (Levitz 2002). It is common for temporary help agencies to go in and out of business quickly, changing names and sometimes phone numbers, without a change in the principals.

As a result of the second hearing, the legal counsel to the state's Department of Employment and Training said that the department would investigate both temp agencies and fish processors for violations of the minimum wage, workers' compensation, and safety standards. Paul Moura, a state representative, called for the revival of a state commission that had begun investigating labor problems in the industry in 1999 but was disbanded before issuing a report.

Two weeks after the second hearing, in late January 2002, the regional OSHA office held an informational meeting for fish-processing firms. OSHA's area director claimed that this meeting was unrelated to the problems at Town Dock and had been in planning for a year. At the meeting, OSHA announced that it would begin launching "surprise" inspections of seafood processors in Rhode Island. The justification was not the Town Dock incident but the relatively poor safety record of the industry nationally and recent inspections in Massachusetts that had turned up many violations. The main problems cited were inadequate machine guards, unsafe use of electrical equipment, work done in confined spaces, and accidental startup of machinery during maintenance or repair operation (the same problem that had killed Nguyen Thi Thu Phuong in Vietnam).

The director of the Rhode Island Seafood Council welcomed the free seminar but found the inspections unnecessary, arguing that most principals in seafood-processing companies work on the shop floor. Since they would be unlikely to expose themselves to hazardous conditions, inspections were unnecessary. One of the attendees, who refused to be identified by name, was happy that OSHA held an educational session prior to the inspections. "They're giving us a chance to do the right thing. Just because regulations are stated in black and white on a piece of paper doesn't always mean they are clear to us" (Novak 2002b). Apparently ignorance of the law *is* an excuse.

The Town Dock workers and their allies failed to get even the usual study commission and industry self-regulation that the Nike organizers achieved. Interviews with officials at the State Department of Employment and Training and the regional OSHA office indicate little follow-up. The state commission to study the industry was not revived.

Colleges and Universities Do It Differently

I turn briefly to another local case that strikes close to home. There is a strong trend for colleges and universities to outsource custodial and food services. I discuss one example of this to demonstrate the ubiquity of the strategy of creating social distance in employment relations.

In the spring of 2002, about fifty students from area colleges and universities rallied outside the gates of Providence College in support of janitors there who were working without a contract. They had originally wanted to hold the rally in front of Harkins Hall, the administration building, but the administration had told them to "take the demonstration off campus" (Milkovits 2002a). In fact, a university vice president, a priest, sent a letter to one of the students which read, in part: "While I respect our students' right to articulate their opinions, the college is not under any obligation to allow people it does not know to use Providence College's private campus as a public forum to air their grievances and concerns" (quoted in McIntyre 2002).

The unionized workers, members of SEIU Local 134, were seeking wages comparable to those at similar institutions in the area and the reinstatement of nine laid-off janitors. They came from a similar background as the Town Dock workers, predominantly immigrants with little English-speaking ability. These jobs were clearly a step up from Town Dock, however, and tended to be held by documented immigrants or those who had been in the country for some time. Still, many held second jobs and hoped, given their comparatively low wages, to reach parity with Brown, Bryant, and other area educational institutions.

The problem was that the janitors didn't actually work for Providence College, or as it is known locally, PC. The college had contracted janitorial services out to an independent company, UNICCO. The union representative expressed frustration at not being able to communicate directly with the college, and workers complained that they were "treated like they didn't work there." Although the workers were paid roughly $3 less than those doing similar work at area colleges and universities, and although the layoffs had left forty-one janitors to clean forty buildings, PC administrators attempted to wash their hands of the situation.

Students claimed that the college had a "moral responsibility" to guarantee adequate pay. The administration did not agree. Students called attention both to the recent student occupation of buildings in support of janitors at Harvard and the tenets of Catholic social doctrine. But according to Ed Caron, Vice

President for College Relations and Planning, the college could not dictate the level of compensation to a contractor:

> Unlike Harvard University, which directly employs its janitorial staff, Providence College is a UNICCO customer. As a UNICCO customer, Providence College does not and cannot have any role in the contract negotiations between UNICCO management and its employees. It is simply incorrect to suggest that the college can or should influence the outcome of the confidential labor-negotiation process that is underway. If Providence College did so, we would be interfering in an ongoing collective-bargaining situation between two other parties. (McIntyre 2002)

As in the Town Dock and Nike cases, management spokespersons convey the importance of social distance in contemporary labor relations most eloquently.

According to interviews I conducted with union staff, the discussion of Catholic social thought was a nonstarter. Although students and faculty were able to provide quantitative estimates of the inadequacy of the wage offer, given living costs in the area, and referred to specific papal encyclicals concerning salaries, social justice, and workplace dignity, they got no farther than the union did.

The union held a one-day strike in May and threatened to initiate a work slowdown that would have disrupted graduation ceremonies. This seemed to have more effect. Over the summer the UNICCO-provided Providence College janitors received a new contract, retroactive to January, which raised their base rate from $8.06 to $10.31 per hour, bringing them close to the area standard. The contract improved pension benefits and provided additional time off.

These cases are interesting but not unique. The safety problems in fish processing parallel those that Eric Schlosser documented in the meat-packing and chicken-processing industries (2001). More important for our purposes, the strategy of hiding behind shadowy temporary employment agencies or subcontractors is the domestic equivalent of Nike's outsourcing strategy. And just as export-oriented industrialization in East Asia has made a vast new labor supply available to Nike, the blowback from neocolonialism has presented American employers with an exploitable labor supply of both documented and undocumented immigrants (Gonzales 2001).

In the Nike, Town Dock, and Providence College cases, destructive competition in the labor market is promoted by an employer strategy that seeks to lengthen the chain between ultimate consumer and ultimate producer. In each case, currently available regulatory mechanisms are inadequate to deal with the problem. Internationally, the International Labor Organization (ILO) is not yet an adequate enforcer of international labor standards, and, as I will argue in chapter 7, company codes of conduct are not up to the job either. I argue in chapter 6 that the domestic legal and regulatory framework for maintaining worker rights has broken down in the United States. To date, popularly organized worker rights boards such as the one organized by Jobs with Justice in the Town Dock case have neither legal legitimacy nor the virtue of bringing all interested parties to the table (which the ILO does have).

The Sweating System

By "doing it," I mean implementing the sweating system. I now demonstrate that Commons's conception of the sweating system is useful in understanding these three cases.

For Commons all transactions have conflicts of interest at their core. He discerned that the fundamental conflict in all transactions is the interest of the consumer in higher quality and a lower price versus that of the producer in higher wages and better working conditions. The reality that the well being of a household is affected by a large number of price bargains but only by a single or small number of wage bargains requires that the social goal of a "good" price bargain be appropriately balanced with the need of the producers in individual households to negotiate a "good" wage bargain. Commons contended that private negotiations yield a "reasonable" balancing of this conflict when the parties to a bargain possess equal power to influence the other in their favor. That is, prices and wages are at their "correct" levels when consumers and producers are each exerting equal power to withhold what the other wants but does not own, namely, money and labor power.

Commons most effectively outlined the economic structure of sweating in his article on the American shoemakers (1964). The evolution of the shoemakers' market is summarized in table 2. Initially, under a system of itinerant production, the price bargain between the purchaser and the producer was in reality simultaneously a price bargain *and* an implicit wage bargain—significantly, one that was "reasonable" as Commons employed that term. As shown in table 2, extension of the market for shoes generated a series of adjustments in the system of production, which in turn created a chain of price bargains separating the purchasers of shoes from their producers—first, between the customer and the retail merchant; second, between the retailer and the capitalist merchant organizing the distribution of a specific shoe; and third, between the capitalist merchant and capitalist manufacturing firms.

The term *social distance* represents the social gap caused by the severing of a direct relationship between the producer and the eventual beneficiary of her effort. Commons (1964, 249) underscored that the timing and terms of the price bargains that now separated the eventual users of shoes from their producers, coupled with the producers' conversion into wage workers, shifted market power dramatically in favor of purchasers. Hence, the capitalist businesses at the end of the transactional chain, those within whose ambit shoes are actually produced, find they can earn a profit only by means of *sweating* their workers, that is, by worsening the wage bargain (from the worker's point of view). Commons made it clear that he considered sweating to be a *necessary* consequence of the increase in what I call social distance between the consumer and producer characterizing the evolution of the shoemakers' market (cf. Commons 1964, 246).

Commons's approach to the issue of sweating seems particularly relevant today. In particular, it is apparent that Commons's characterization of how the sweating system works corresponds fairly closely to the actual events that unfolded in all three of the case histories reviewed here, although contractor control of information did not characterize the PC case. All three enterprises said, in effect, "I do not employ you and I have nothing to do with your wages." Significantly, the common element in our three cases, which is why I am comfortable using the term *sweating system* in reference to all three, is the actual or attempted organization of production within a structure allowing the manufacturer *not* to "employ his own workman." What is evident from these cases is that outsourcing and labor contracting are simply alternative methods of ef-

TABLE 2. Evolution of the Wage Bargain

Stage	Bargains			
Custom order (personal market)	P/W Customer—Producer			
Retail shop (local market)	P Customer—Retailer	W Wholesaler—Producer		
Wholesale order (regional market)	P Customer—Retailer	P Retailer—Wholesaler	W Wholesaler—Worker (bargain prior to work)	
Wholesale speculative (regional, national, world market)	P Customer—Retailer	P Retailer—Capitalist	P Capitalist—Employer (bargain after work completed)	W Employer—Worker

Note: At all stages, workers seek "protective device" from "competitive menace": (1) protective organization (e.g., unions); (2) protective legislation (e.g., labor "standards").

Two bargains: P = Price bargain (Exchange of ownership of a produced good); W = Wage bargain (Exchange of ownership of labor power)

fecting this end, that is, to institute the sweating system. And as Commons's account makes clear, the crucial step in implementing a sweating system is the creation of a transactional gap between the worker and the entity capturing the results of her labor power being put into motion—as clearly occurred in all three cases. This severing of a direct transactional relationship between the worker and her substantive "original employer," recalling Commons's phrase, is the increase of social distance to which I am calling attention here.

In Commons's day, the principal organizers of the sweating system were people who were socially positioned to recruit immigrant workers. While not a necessary element of sweating, our three cases indicate this remains true today so long as we extend the meaning of "immigrant worker" to include migrants from the countryside to the city in the developing world. Moreover, as is evident from the three cases, sweated production is becoming far more general than the limited case of outsourced Kathy Lee clothing items made in Chinatown or Nike shoes made in Indonesia might suggest.

Commons's sweating model can be usefully supplemented by Marx's treatment of the labor process. Even in the case upon which Commons built his shoemakers model, workers blamed the factory system and the power of the bosses, not the market and the new unskilled labor force entrants for their trouble (Dawley 1976, 147–48). The tendencies to lengthen the working day, to reduce the necessary part of the working day, to re-create the reserve armies of labor, and to proletarianize new populations are all part of the tension over what "rights," if any, workers should have. The Commons approach provides a neat way of thinking about some of the effects of the extension of the market on social relations inside the workplace, but it is only part of the story.

Their limited focus leads Institutional writers to be overly confident about the establishment of a balance of power in the workplace. Without collective organization, political influence, and some command over the ideological apparatuses it is most difficult to overcome the class interest of organized capital. This will be demonstrated in subsequent chapters. Here I turn my attention to a different kind of overconfidence, belief in the effectiveness of moral suasion.

Adam Smith and the Likely Role of Moral and Empathic Appeals in Curtailing Sweating

I alluded earlier to the possibility that moral and empathic appeals represent a strategy for moderating the harmful consequences for labor of the sweating system. I further noted that Adam Smith furnished economists with a (long neglected) conception of human nature providing a possible rationale for this approach. I now review relevant facets of the argument Smith presented in *The Theory of Moral Sentiments* (1976 [1759, revised 1790]). The theory of "self-regulated" action Smith outlined in this work has been analyzed by countless scholars over the many years since its publication, and the main thrust of the analysis is now well understood.[3] However, the issue at stake here was never directly addressed by Smith in *Moral Sentiments*. That issue is forbearance in market relations, by which I mean the "act" of refraining from fully exercising one's market power over another despite one's legal right to do so, that is, the "choice" of negotiating a transaction on terms less favorable to oneself than one is capable of obtaining legally in order to improve the terms from the perspective of the other transactor. In order to deal with this issue, therefore, interpretation and extension of Smith's often subtle reasoning is required.[4]

Contrary to standard textbook representations, Smith never claimed that people's economic actions are intended only to further their own selfish interest. Smith began *Moral Sentiments* by calling attention to the pervasiveness of benevolence in human action. However, Smith acknowledged that human action reveals an even stronger propensity for self-love (more on this later). Perceiving that an appeal to another person's self-interest is the most reliable method of eliciting a desired response, Smith inferred that self-interest is the behavioral impetus upon which a system of "natural liberty" must be based.[5] But Smith also made clear in *Moral Sentiments* his concomitant belief that unfettered self-interested action is moderated "naturally" by other inborn traits and that virtue and morality hence will generally typify "free" behavior.

According to Smith, we all possess an empathetic capacity he dubbed "sympathy," which occasions us to experience inside ourselves, via our imagination, emotions that are displayed by others or that, based on our own past experiences, can be situationally imputed to them. Our sympathy with displayed or imputed feelings, however, depends upon our approval of their appropriateness, that is, upon our reading of the propriety of their causes. Smith observed that the force of an empathic experience—of sympathy—wanes with the weakening of the link between oneself and another. For example, given the power of self-love, one empathizes most completely with oneself, somewhat less with family members, less yet with close acquaintances, and very weakly if at all with those "with whom we have no particular connection" (Smith 1976, 135). What this means is that one's empathetic identification with one's own emotions will clearly tend to overshadow the empathetic experience occasioned by the emotions displayed by or imputed to another with whom one does not have a strong personal connection. But if so, how can the potential impact of an act on another's interests (imagined feelings) become a factor regulating one's pursuit of one's own attainments? Or, to put it slightly differently, how can that imagined potential impact induce an economic principal to forbear?

Smith perceived that in addition to an empathetic capacity, upon achieving maturity individuals also bring within themselves an "impartial spectator" to whom they transfer the power to render judgments concerning the morality of their own actions. This internalized "spectator," he insisted, remains outside the pull of individual self-interest and therefore stands ready to approve or disapprove of a specific economic actor's affections as she would those of any another person—on the basis of the acceptability of their causes within the moral code and general rules of conduct of the broader society (Smith 1976, 109–10). And, Smith decreed, actors desire to deserve the approval of this internalized "spectator" (Smith 1976, 116–17) and hence they have a strong internal inducement—albeit one that "self-love" sometimes subverts—to limit their actions to ones generating only effects that are justifiable under conventional moral standards or general rules of behavior.

The foregoing suggests that when operative, sympathy can orient us toward restraining our selfish and indulging our benevolent affections (Smith 1976, 25), that is, can cause us to forbear somewhat from fully exercising our economic power in negotiations when the attainable outcome can be inferred to entail negative, painful, consequences for others or when conventional morality or general rules of behavior decree that such an exercise of power is morally wrong or improper.[6]

What, then, do the three cases suggest regarding the role that forbearance occasioned by the two "Smithian" restraining forces is likely to play in limiting sweating? Let us assume for the moment that Smith is correct and that sympathy is an element of the market process. According to Smith a personal bond or an ongoing face-to-face relationship strengthens the likelihood that sympathy will influence transactional behavior. The "small shops" that Commons associated with sweating—which presumably would include many Nike subcontractors and certainly would include Town Dock and perhaps also Providence College—are precisely the sorts of social locations where sympathy would be expected to be operative.[7] In such locations, a sympathetic bond would presumably develop between a worker and her immediate supervisor or, less strongly, between a worker and owners or managers with whom she comes into frequent contact. It is precisely in such locations that an impetus toward sweating motivated by naked self-interest would naturally be restrained. Thus it is

worth noticing that the increase of social distance, as I have referred to the
common element in all three of the cases, in effect renders sympathy impotent
because it eliminates or greatly diminishes the role, in the negotiation of a particular group of workers' wage bargain as well as other aspects of the employment relationship, of those who have a direct interpersonal relationship with
those workers and hence who by Smith's reasoning might forbear in bringing
their full economic power into play. In other words, even if Smith was right
about the role of sympathy in "human nature," its potentially ameliorative
function in regard to sweating is nullified by the creation of social distance between the worker and their "real" employer—the creation of which, to repeat,
is what was observed to be central to all three cases.

Can we expect the impartial spectator mechanism to be a more effective
counterforce to sweating? Nike's "engagement strategy" agreement in response
to public criticism, as well as Kathy Lee Gifford's highly publicized call for better supervision of subcontractors, suggests the possibility that moral appeals
can play a role in restraining sweating. It is worth noting, however, that by
bringing the controlling "impartial" spectator inside the economic actor, Smith
was submitting that one responds not to the judgment of an external, actual
spectator, who may have only a partial knowledge of the full context within
which a transaction is being negotiated, but to one's own judgment. In other
words, an actual spectator may render a judgment regarding what *appears* to be
the right—the moral—action, but from Smith's standpoint it is the internalized impartial spectator who judges what is *really* right. The issue, therefore, is
what is the relevant moral code or, more narrowly, the general rule of behavior
that present-day owners and managers are internalizing? Judging by the statements made by authorized representatives of the "real" employers in the cases
we reviewed, that code or rule decrees: *If someone is not a member or a citizen of
"our" firm, that is, if we have no direct wage bargain with her, "we" have no responsibility of any kind for the wage bargain under which she works.* In short,
there is no sign of moral objection to the sweating system, as a system, on the
part of the going concerns featured in the three case studies. If they are representative, then it is clear that empathic appeals to "real" employers will fail to
elicit corrective action. The sweating system itself, of course, makes it difficult if
not impossible for the actual employer—the subcontractor or labor contractor—to respond positively if moral appeals are directed at them. I return to this
issue in the final chapter when I investigate whether the recent explosion of
available information may alter the moral sensibility of other actors.

Nike's decision to create a labor practices department, to "investigate" the labor practices of its subcontractors, and to publish a list of its suppliers may appear to contradict this conclusion. I interpret Nike's action to be motivated by the goal of safeguarding the goodwill of its customers, some of whom might stop purchasing Nike products due to negative publicity directed at Nike's labor practices, rather than by a moral concern on the part of its owners for the plight of the sweated workers producing those products. It is interesting that the priests responsible for Providence College's operations apparently have internalized the same market ethos as the owners of Nike and Town Dock and hence are similarly responsive only to negative publicity potentially undermining the goodwill built up with "customers" (future students and their parents) and benefactors rather than to moral dictates—including well-known papal encyclicals! This reality would appear to establish that the market ethos preached by the Chicago school of economists has taken very deep root in America's owning and managerial classes. If my inference is on target, those championing empathic appeals as the appropriate strategy for raising labor market attainments would be wise to direct such appeals exclusively at consumers, or better yet, to support the work of those labor-based activist groups that are building organizing capacity among superexploited workers, as I discuss in chapter 7.[8] In any case, whether "naming and shaming" is likely to have *any* effect depends on what kind of moral self globalization is producing, which I take up in chapter 8.

The Nature of a Viable Remedy

The three cases provide a glimpse into a contemporary wage and working standards inequity—the sweating of developing country, immigrant, and migrant workers. This perceptible signpost of destructive competition has at its root the huge, redundant labor force now extant in an increasingly global labor market, and it is being instituted through the "old" business strategy to which Commons called attention in his American Shoemakers article and in his testimony to the U.S. Industrial Commission. That is the strategy of increasing the social distance between the worker and her "real" employer via the avoidance of a meaningful relationship with that worker. The wages and working conditions resulting from the confluence of these factors are not "reasonable." Although many commentators submit that this growing problem is capable of being corrected by voluntary action on the part of manufacturers, that is, by forbearance on their part engendered by moral and empathic appeals, the analysis in the previous section suggests that this is unlikely. In fact, under the present scheme of relatively free global trade in the context of global labor redundancy, destructive competition in the globalized labor market seems likely to persist into the foreseeable future.

Commons's remedy was adjustment of the rules governing negotiation of the wage bargain, and he saw this as the only feasible method of actually reversing destructive competition in the labor market—of which the spread of the sweating system is but a symptom.

Commons's perspective on economic policy reflects an interpretation of the capitalist market system that diverges significantly from the one presented in standard economics textbooks.[9] In contrast to the natural law conception of market activity forwarded by Smith and promulgated by the economics profession to this very day, Commons developed a legal interpretation of economic processes emphasizing the role of collective action in shaping transactional outcomes—primarily via *instituted* working rules specifying what individuals can, must, or may do or not do in their transactions with one another. These working rules confer rights and impose duties on all the "citizens" of a going concern, and by specifying "nonrights" and "nonduties," they create their exposures and liberties as well. Unlike Smith, who perceived a natural harmony of interests, Commons argued that only by virtue of such rules and the relative certainty of their enforcement does it become possible for individuals with conflicting interests to work together harmoniously and for their actions to be appropriately correlated. Working rules can be specific to individual economic concerns (a business enterprise), but enterprise-specific rules cannot transgress rules set forth by the sovereign power, that is, the rules specified in a nation's commercial and labor law.

According to Commons, the contemporary rule structure governing the negotiation of a wage bargain emerged gradually over several centuries as those consecutively authorized to settle disputes (e.g., common law judges in England and members of the Supreme Court in the United States; or, more recently and less comprehensively, the CEOs of large corporations) adjusted working rules in accordance with their conception of the public purpose (or, with respect to corporate CEOs, to the concern's private purpose). From this evolutionary perspective, social problems are understood to be "solved" by adjusting the controlling working rules to fit new circumstances, not à la conventional "natural law economics" by adjusting the rules to accord with the ahistorical requirements of competition.

With respect to the wage bargains being negotiated in his own day, it was Commons's judgment that an unfair exchange of property was thereby effected because the governing working rules were not reasonable in that they granted employers superior "power to withhold" vis-à-vis employees. Because substantial involuntary unemployment was the norm, he concluded that the wage and working conditions the weakest worker was willing to accept was the standard toward which the market would tend. This presumption lay at the core of the concept of "destructive competition" in the old Institutional economics, and it today lies at the core of the "race to the bottom" hypothesis. In part as a result of Commons's own scholarship, the "unfair" wage bargain outcomes resulting from the unbalanced power of potential employer and potential employee were remedied somewhat in the United States by the National Labor Relations Act, by social insurance mitigating some of the effects engendered by those outcomes (for example, the high incidence of poverty among the elderly), and by the creation of labor standards proscribing a broad array of wage bargain outcomes (e.g., an unreasonably unsafe workplace). Via the creation of standards, to use an old phrase, the "plane of competition" was lifted.

If Commons is right, the decisive step in instituting the sweating system—whether by subcontracting production or through labor contracting—is the legal severing of the worker from the going concern (a business enterprise) that is her "real" employer, thereby destroying her functional "citizenship." By means of this severing the owners and managers of the original enterprise are able to regard their "real" employee as a nonemployee and hence as ineligible to receive the protections or rights enjoyed by enterprise citizens. Those "real" employees are similarly regarded as having no legitimate role in shaping the working rules of the original concern.

It is not likely that a feasible method of reorganizing the realm of production—so as to eliminate the intermediate price bargains and thereby to eliminate the economic impetus for sweating—could be implemented within the existing structures of the world economy. It is equally implausible that a practicable system could be worked out ensuring that the purchasers of products (the ultimate "real" employer) are induced to forbear from negotiating agreements that result in substandard wages or working conditions for the producers of those products (their ultimate "real" employees) *and* that subcontractors or labor contractors—in actuality, middlemen for the more fundamental principals—are induced to forbear from exercising fully their market power over individual workers. One possible remedy for sweating is the creation by an overarching rule-creating entity—a state, a nation, an international organization—of mandatory minimal labor market standards making it unnecessary for anyone to forbear in order for all workers to obtain reasonable wages and enjoy reasonable working conditions. I investigate this possibility in chapter 5.

A continuing failure to implement reasonable standards will only make the sweating system—that is, from the enterprise's point of view, outsourcing and labor contracting—more prevalent as a form of organizing an enterprise's relationship with its "real" employees. Even though all three cases involved immigrant workers (as we redefined the concept), it surely is only a matter of time until the institutionalization of sweating via the creation of social distance between the worker and her "real" employer begins to impact the "native" workforce as well.

The cases bring into clear view ongoing social processes in which unregulated market forces appear to be encouraging increased use of sweated labor via the creation of social distance between workers and their "real" employers. Alerted to the possibility by these cases, I am concerned that competition among the members of the global redundant labor force, countless numbers of whom are accustomed to a very low standard of life, has already set in motion a global "race to the bottom" (destructive competition). There may still be an opportunity for individual nation-states, or blocs of such states (e.g., the European Union), to implement actions that will prove capable of shielding its own labor force from destructive international labor market competition.[10] But given the increasingly global organization of production, it seems likely that opponents will argue that doing so will cause even more firms to move their operations to foreign countries where similar restrictions are not being imposed, and that this threat is likely to undercut any legislature's will to increase protective measures for unskilled and, especially, immigrant laborers.

The sweating system approach to organizing work, and through it destructive competition, will continue to grow in significance unless a means of imposing minimum labor standards on all enterprises can be instituted by a supranational "concern" with the sovereign power to command obedience to its laws. The International Labor Organization is best suited among the already-created international organizations for moving forward with the development of reasonable minimal international standards, and the ILO is the only international body within which an appropriate set of internationally applicable antisweating standards has any possibility of being crafted.

The ILO as well as labor activists have asserted the rights of workers as a strategy to build support for such standards. But what does it mean to say that workers have "rights"? This is the issue to which I now turn.

CHAPTER 4

Are Worker Rights Human Rights
(and does it matter if they are)?

In 1999 the U.S. State Department identified human rights, along with "money and the internet" as one of the three universal languages of globalization. The implication is that the relationship between rights and economic globalization is positive, even if the causation is unclear (Ignatieff 2002).

There are two ways in which this might make sense. First, rights may be thought of as a kind of luxury good, something that societies can buy once more fundamental needs are taken care of through economic development. When globalization produces growth, then people acquire human rights. This seems to be the attitude of many repressive regimes in poor countries, which resist certain rights as incompatible with their current level of development.

Alternatively, if rights are understood solely in terms of the freedom of the individual from particular forms of political and civic repression, one could argue that globalization, by limiting the role of the state and facilitating the flow of information across national borders, directly facilitates rights. This is the connection that is often claimed by the U.S. government in promoting the globalization of the last two decades.

But what if rights are constitutive of what is necessary to lead a decent life at all levels of development? And what if such rights include economic and social conditions that go beyond the negative rights (freedom from . . .) that have been more easily accepted in and by the United States? Then, perhaps, the relationship between rights and globalization is less clear.

Economists have begun to spend more time on these issues, though there is still often a lack of comfort with normative issues in economics.[1] Less time has been put into thinking about how rights and norms are established. How, for instance, should we interpret the relationship between globalization and the reinvigoration of the international social justice movement? Is the latter simply called forth by the former, as its dialectical opposite? Does the extension of the market call forth a change in moral sensibility that could lead to a more "humane" globalization? Alternatively, are critics of corporate globalization, by highlighting a certain kind of rights, unconsciously conspiring to create a more humane *and* more efficiently exploitive capitalism?

Rights talk makes economists nervous. Not all would subscribe to Bentham's notion that this is just high-minded hot air, what he called "nonsense upon stilts." Still, the influence of the utilitarian tradition and its predilection for positive rather than normative science makes most economists want to leave the room when the subject of "rights" comes up.

Despite the easy acceptance of rights politics across the political spectrum in the United States, economists' reaction is not necessarily inappropriate. In the nineteenth century the concept of human rights was so thoroughly criticized by conservative, liberal, and socialist writers that it had little credibility in sophisticated circles. Remarkably, since World War II, "rights talk" has made a comeback in political discourse to the extent that the assertion of rights is now often the primary strategy taken by those who want to challenge (or defend) the political-economic status quo.

A politics of human rights must acknowledge that rights are conventions, purely human creations. Such rights will be neither self-evident nor eternal, and attempts to apply them beyond cultural boundaries will risk unwitting injustice. Rights need to be deeply rooted enough in social experience and aspiration to win general assent; they need to flow from social custom and common sense as the correct way to live. Such rights must be argued, articulated, and assented to, not just asserted. Any understanding of rights must be placed within historical context, including how the acceptance of particular rights affects and is affected by the exploitive social relations peculiar to the period in question.

The next part of the chapter lays out the critique of rights concepts by conservative, liberal, and socialist thinkers in the nineteenth century and discusses the reemergence of rights language in the 1940s. In the third part I argue that while orthodox economics' dismissal of the concerns of labor rights advocates is not impressive, recourse to the language of rights alone may not be any more successful than appeals to moral sympathy in promoting workers' well being. If rights are conventions, then we need a conjunctural explanation of which rights are accepted by the conventional wisdom and why. The revival of "rights talk" in our time is a specific legacy of the Holocaust and the Cold War. In the remaining sections I examine the specific kinds of rights that were certified by the intersection of class and convention in the international human rights movement, in American labor law, and by the globalization of capitalist social relations in the latter part of the twentieth century. These were, primarily, rights of the body to be free from pain and the right of the individual to equality of opportunity.

As worker rights advocates have adopted the language of human rights since the 1960s there has not been much discussion of how this language limits what they may be successful in achieving. For instance, the right to freedom from forced labor fits well with the contemporary human rights regime, whereas the rights to freedom of association and collective bargaining do not. And if the latter are the more potent tools in developing a humane and equitable globalization (or any other goal) then neglecting the discursive constitution of rights comes at a high price.

Liberals, Conservatives, and Socialists against Rights

In the early 1990s, Etienne Balibar pointed out that we hear so little about the politics of the rights of man because such a conversation would be embarrassing (1993). Since the middle of the twentieth century, "rights" as universal values and unconditional necessities have moved to the center of political discourse, but there has been very little questioning of the conditions for the formation of such rights, their forms, or their objectives.

Rights tend to function as a foundation, self-evident and not worthy of deep investigation. The American historian Thomas Haskell has noted what he calls "The Curious Persistence of Rights Talk in the Age of Interpretation" (2000). This persistence is even more curious when it comes from Socialists.

Marx's critique of rights as the basis for politics is well known. Marx was not much taken with the "rights of man," but he was very much interested in the "rights of the citizen." And in fact it has been part of the socialist tradition in many countries that civic rights cannot be fully attained without economic and social rights, that is, that political democracy can be had only when the rights of property are limited.

Economic orthodoxy creates the fantasy of a society in which individuals are free from any essential dependence on others. While a discourse of the rights of man is mostly consistent with such a vision, the right of the citizen to be involved in organizing the economic life of the community is not. Thus a politics of rights is contradictory and should be understood to have complex, not simple social effects.

For something to be understood as a "right" it must be seen as natural and unconditional, yet rights have a history; they are proclaimed at particular points in history for particular reasons. They may (or may not) coincide across societies, for example, with the timing of the 1930s Matignon Accords in France and the labor legislation of the American New Deal. To have a discussion of international rights then is to investigate how certain social processes give rise to particular rights claims across societies.

Radicals in the labor movement have been particularly interested in the idea of worker rights as a way to press a socialist agenda by democratic means. But the post–World War II revival of "rights talk" paid little attention to worker rights as human rights, and most labor organizations in the United States were reluctant to assert their agenda in such language. This began to change in the 1990s in the United States, driven largely by the antisweatshop movement that was one of the responses to neoliberal globalization. This assertion of worker rights has not been accompanied by much reflection on how rights are constituted. This is true even of the most sophisticated academic work that has come in the wake of the new organizing.

This split between rights-based politics and labor politics is in some ways particularly American. In a variety of countries going through democratic revolutions in the last several decades—Poland, Spain, South Korea, South Africa—a rights revolution and electoral democracy strengthened work-based collective organizations and agreements. The ways in which rights claims and collective politics reinforce each other in Quebec is perhaps even more indicative of the peculiarity of the American model (Lichtenstein 2002).

Why do certain claims for rights become accepted at particular times, and with what effects? Why did a "rights regime" develop in both international politics and employment relations in some countries after World War II? My explanation is conjunctural. The global reaction to the horror of World War II and the Holocaust came, in the context of the Cold War, to revive a language and practice of rights internationally that had been discredited by liberals, conservatives, and socialists alike. In the United States, a rights-based model of employment relations came to replace the discourse of collective bargaining and workplace democracy. The prevalence of "rights talk" in contemporary politics is not exactly an accident, but it can hardly be seen as a natural evolutionary move in the history of ideas.

"Human rights" are problematic as a basis for worker rights because they deal with what the individual is entitled to rather than what is in the interest of community, solidarity, or civic virtue. This was the conclusion of the most incisive conservative, liberal, and socialist nineteenth-century writers on rights.

Burke, Bentham, and Marx, in different ways, criticized the abstraction and formalism inherent in rights-based politics, and especially the abstract universalism and individualism that such a politics would promote. All thought the "rights of man" to be a thoroughly impoverished view of the functioning of human society. "The great and recurring theme in all three of these attacks is that the rights of man embody as the be-all and end-all of politics a demand for the immediate and unqualified gratification of purely selfish and individual desires" (Waldron 1987, 44). That these tensions and reservations about rights are still with us is not reason to give up the discussion but to think more seriously about what a rights-based politics entails.

The nineteenth-century writers were responding to the political theories of Hobbes and Locke and the French Declaration of the Rights of Man, itself based on American ideas as much as on Rousseau (Waldron 1987). In a sense, the American and French documents were early attempts to fill the space vacated by the Enlightenment critique of religious beliefs, in the context of the Hobbesian recognition that no basis could be found in anthropology for moral consensus. In Bentham's hands this would become a utilitarian and rational science of ethics. Bentham rejected natural rights. "A natural right is a son who never had a father." For Bentham, rights and duties are fictions whereas law and sanction are real. Building an ethical society would transform the former into the latter.[2]

The entire utilitarian framework rests on the rejection of unqualified commitment to any proposition: everything must be weighed against the calculus of the greatest good for the greatest number. For utilitarians, rights talk substitutes assertion for reason. This, in my view, is the prevalent sense in economic orthodoxy today. When Bentham and his followers opposed slavery and the slave trade they did so not out of moral concern but because these practices interfered with individual freedom of choice.[3] In fact Bentham had an expansive concept of slavery, making it a metaphor for all kinds of persistent injustices (Rosen 2005).

Bentham proposed an altruistic but self-interested humanity as the basis for reasoning about ethics. He argued not from general principle to specific application, but for an inductive process of calculating pleasure and pain to arrive at "propositions as may be capable of being given without self-contradiction as fundamental laws" (Waldron 1987, 43). Starting with general laws, he wrote, is "self-conceit and tyranny exalted into insanity" (43).

Establishing rights is both difficult and undesirable for Bentham. Circumstances of human life are too ephemeral and too varied for us to establish timeless rules for all societies. Rights excite the selfish passions of the individual, making it difficult to demand sacrifice, which he saw as a critical task of government.

For Burke and nineteenth-century Conservatism, it was the intergenerational transmission of the wisdom of tradition that was threatened by rights.[4] While Burke's thought incorporated an element of informal and implicit judgment, he was prone to rely on Aristotelian virtue rather than hedonistic calculation and rejected the idea of a tradeoff between the suffering of some and the pleasure of others. He agreed with Adam Smith that the best social results were likely to flow from people not consciously trying to produce them but preferred moral virtue rather than utilitarian calculus as the basis for the good society. But like Bentham, he criticized rights proponents for the selfishness, arrogance, and hardening of the spirit that a rights-based politics would produce, and the intoxication with abstract thought that he believed underestimated the complexity of politics and human society. There was, for Burke, no use in discussing abstract rights: the "liberties of Englishmen" were more important than the "rights of man."

If what reason tells us is how little we can know about society then perhaps it is rational to be cautious about reason. Burke and his disciples opposed wisdom to individual reason, believing that while deductive reasoning can produce clear and distinct ideas it cannot produce a decent politics. For Burkean conservatives, social stability requires awe, ritual, and honor, and if these are brushed aside all we are left with is the will to power.

For Marx and some of his followers, rights politics presents the preoccupations of the bourgeois individual as if they were human nature. Whatever positive value that rights to liberty, property, and personal security have, they are essentially oriented to the selfish desires of the acquisitive individual and are individualistic in both form and content. The abstraction of rights commits us to an artificial and legalistic utopia, neglecting real differences and inequalities that matter, especially between those who do and those who do not control the means of production. Formal equality appears to make equal what is in fact different.

In "On the Jewish Question" Marx argued that whereas the rights of man purport to be universal and perhaps even natural, they are understandable only with reference to a particular historical period, that of the bourgeois revolutions. Such rights present freedom as the liberty to do anything that doesn't harm others, making other people precisely the limit to individual freedom. For Marx, the rights of man are fences. Formal equality only secures an antisocial form of freedom.

For Marx, capitalist society fosters an impression of self-sufficient atom-
ism, but the effects of the social and technical division of labor make this an increasingly transparent illusion. The spread of the market and the shifting and
deepening (international) division of labor create increasing interdependence,
and establish the possibility for the rights of the *citizen* to be involved in the
democratic organization of economic (and cultural and political) life.

Contemporary rights theorists often present citizenship rights as serving
the more fundamental rights of man (Ignatieff 2001). For Marx this is exactly
backward. But it is perhaps not surprising that, especially since 1989, there has
been a renewed emphasis on the rights of man as opposed to the rights of the
citizen. With what are clearly transnational issues gaining in salience—international production networks, global pollutant flows, human migration, and so
on—and with governments either unable or unwilling to do much about these
issues, it is not hard to see why concepts like "the rights of humans everywhere"
have been easy tropes to adopt for those engaged in resistance to one aspect or
another of these new patterns of uneven development.

So technocratic liberalism, Burkean conservatism, and Marxian socialism
all stood in some tension with the notion of humans having rights. By the late
nineteenth and early twentieth centuries "progress" had largely displaced
"rights" as the goal of social thinkers. The second half of the twentieth century
reversed this trend. It is not hard to see why. The willingness if not desire of
states to exterminate their own citizens, the inability of states to protect their
citizens from the exterminatory tendencies of other states, and the clear connection between "progress" and exterminatory capacity all created a shift in favor of establishing transnational rights as opposed to belief in progress or reliance on national law. This was most clearly the case in the immediate
aftermath of the Holocaust and World War II, when the major contemporary
human rights documents were produced and when the International Labor
Organization committed itself to a rights-based politics in the Philadelphia Declaration. The Cold War made rights-based politics useful for state actors, and
globalization has made rights in a sense the last refuge of the Left in the current
period. But human rights arguments are more compatible with individual
rather than collective action, and it is arguably the latter that is most needed in
globalized commodity chains.

Economic Orthodoxy against Rights

Orthodox neoclassical economics adds an analytical apparatus to Bentham's
view that rights are "nonsense on stilts." The basic message is the same, though:

calculation of a utilitarian notion of marginal costs and benefits for individuals should replace the assertion of rights in almost all conversations.

It is one of the peculiarities of our time that the human rights revolution has occurred simultaneously with the growth of two intellectual currents that are diametrically opposed to that revolution. In the humanities, the variety of postmodernisms that developed in the 1970s and spread like wildfire in the 1980s and 1990s called into question any concept of transcendental rights. In the social sciences, the emergence of neoliberal thought—first in economics in the 1970s but reaching imperialistically to the other disciplines—opposes anything that interferes with the "free" choices of individuals or the activities of the market, especially when this interference is sure to involve some kind of government regulation.

Yet not only have the last fifty years seen many victories for rights and equality in the United States, but here and elsewhere growing attention has been paid to human rights concepts in foreign policy. Still, human rights advocates in the academy often feel uneasy with their colleagues in both cultural studies and economics, as well they should.

Rights advocates have tended to solve their "postmodern problem" by drawing closer to the same kind of individualism that is the foundation of orthodox economics. In other words, while battling (but mainly by giving ground to) cultural relativism, human rights theory and practice have tended to support a conception of rights that is fully consistent with the economics of capitalist globalization. Some may find this incredible, as human rights activists have been in the forefront of struggles against rapacious corporations such as Shell and Unocal. Nonetheless, the individualist approach that dominates contemporary human rights philosophy often limits human rights groups to "blaming and shaming" corporate violations of individual rights without supporting the kind of grassroots collective action necessary to countervail corporate globalization.[5]

Can one consistently support human rights and corporate globalization? The answer that neoclassical economics gives to this question is really an embarrassment, but the weakness of its answer is buried under a mountain of technique and a scientism that is disdainful of moral considerations. Unmasking this weakness is particularly important because neoclassical theory is essentially the official ideology of globalization. Global neoliberalism is the translation into policy, by the most powerful ministries and corporations at the global level, of the basic assumptions and logic of neoclassical economics. This theory promises that the market will harness selfish behavior for collective benefit. So long as countries open their borders to the movement of goods and money and guarantee private property rights, the workings of Adam Smith's invisible hand—the pursuit of self-interest disciplined by competition—will produce the good society. This was the underpinning for the Washington Consensus of the 1990s. "Balance your budget, privatize government-owned enterprise, and liberalize trade" was the mantra of both official institutions such as the International Monetary Fund and the U.S. Treasury, as well as the semiofficial proselytizers of globalization in economics and journalism. And behind these policy specifics was an almost religious belief in the invisible hand.

This belief was shaken, first by the Asian financial crisis of 1997–98 in which the world's fastest growing economies suddenly collapsed, and then by the crisis in Argentina, a country which was in many ways the poster child for international neoliberalism. And it has been shaken in a different way by the global spread of terror and the Iraq war.

Shaken, but not too much. Neoliberal true believers saw the Asian crisis as due to *insufficient* implementation of the market regime—"crony capitalism"—with undue government involvement and an immature market mechanism, not to international market forces themselves. There is an odd ritual in which the failings of neoliberalism bring forth calls for more neoliberalism, as if the patient will stop growing pale if we just let *more* blood.

We are not concerned here with the success of neoclassical theory and neoliberal policies on their own terms but with the terms that are offered. Neoclassicals make several assumptions that are critical for their ability to pass judgment on issues of trade and human rights. Most important, they assume that individuals are endowed with the ability to choose rationally among different opportunities, and in particular the various consumption choices they face. People are assumed to be insatiable, in that more of any good is always preferred to less, and people's preferences are assumed to be exogenous, or outside the theoretical purview of the economist, to be left to marketing researchers or sociologists. Agnosticism on the source of preferences is quite important. The theory holds tightly to a severe form of interpersonal relativism in which one cannot compare the satisfactions that different individuals derive from consumption.

The early utilitarians had hoped to operationalize their basic social goal—the greatest good for the greatest number—by measuring the different utilities that individuals derived from the consumption of goods. Abandoning this project forced the neoclassicals to construct a criterion of the social good that is highly limited, and unable to bear the weight of the conclusions they would like it to support: "Pareto optimality."

Neoclassical theory's celebration of individualism depends critically on this analysis of market behavior. The essential argument, which underlies all of the social policies associated with global neoliberalism, is that the market, left to its own devices, will move toward the price and output level that is socially optimal. In particular, free consumer choice leads to the Pareto-optimal situation, in which no individual can be made better off without making someone else worse off. Free markets lead to just distribution, in the sense that individuals are rewarded according to what they contribute. This also leads to progress, as the incentive structure encourages innovation and economic growth.

Market imperfections—such as monopoly, public goods, externalities, and information asymmetries—are recognized, but curative government intervention is generally thought to be worse than the disease because of government failure. In other words, while the market may sometimes fail to provide the optimality that pure theory claims for it, government provision, regulation, or redistribution encourage rent-seeking behavior. This is socially wasteful activity—like industries that incur lobbying expenditures in order to gain tariff protections. The greater the government's involvement in economic life, the greater will be this social waste.

The debate among neoclassicals concerns the relative importance of market and government failures. In the United States, conservatives tend to minimize market failure and see government failure and rent-seeking everywhere. Liberals tend to see market failures as quite common and are less concerned with government failures. For instance, Stiglitz (2002) argues that information problems are pervasive, especially in developing economies, so that the Washington Consensus, which prescribed reliance on market mechanisms in development, was (and continues to be) misguided.

What both liberal and conservative neoclassicals fail to interrogate is their more basic assumptions concerning consumer preferences and Pareto optimality as a measure of economic well being. That preferences are socially constructed and not exogenous is obvious to most people who don't have the benefit of five (or more) years of graduate economics training. Participation in market activities is one of the things that shape our preferences. Institutional economists, dating back to Veblen, have shown that consumption choices are often driven by status concerns. It is obvious that rather than serve consumers by responding to their preferences, modern corporations are actively involved in shaping preferences through advertising. Income and status powerfully influence consumer preferences, and people generally come to want what they have.

But such adjustment of preferences to expected outcomes is not limited to economics. Poor people learn to expect to feel powerless so as not to be constantly frustrated. Thus the different economic preferences of poor and rich should be seen as a *consequence* of the market process, as much as, if not more than, the foundation for it. And the same goes for politics and culture (De-Martino 2000).

The individualism that lies at the heart of orthodox economics rests on shaky ground. But without it, the familiar parables of the invisible hand fall apart. A similar problem exists in the human rights discourse because of its individualism, a problem I will come to in a moment.

If individual preferences are not sustainable as a foundation for "free trade," the Pareto criterion is not an especially useful tool for defending it. Because of the inability to make interpersonal utility comparisons, an "efficient" social outcome can only mean that no individual can be made better off without making someone else worse off. The Pareto criterion is taken to be a value-free concept of the good economic outcome when, in fact, it is quite value laden. For instance, international trade economists "know" that *who* is helped and *who* bears the costs and *who* reaps the benefits of economic integration should matter, yet they continually abstract from this question, believing perhaps that it is best left to people lower in the academic pecking order like philosophers.[6]

The solution to this problem, to the extent that one is on offer, is the so-called Kaldor-Hicks compensation principle. This presumes that an economic policy is efficient if the winners from such a policy could, in theory, compensate the losers and still have something left over. Whether compensation actually occurs is irrelevant to the basic finding. So when an orthodox economist expresses unqualified support for free trade he is really saying that of course some people will lose, but *on average* people will be better off. This is a highly normative approach in that it biases policy toward growth rather than redistribution. Issues of distribution and equality—and indeed of democracy, cultural integrity, rights, and so forth—are clearly secondary to growth and the "efficient allocation of resources." This is normative commitment masquerading as science. To say that a social situation is Pareto optimal is to say very little about its economic desirability, and virtually nothing about its contribution to building a good society. Yet the Pareto criterion and the compensation principle remain the ultimate basis for the support of "free trade."[7]

Trade economists have long recognized that while a country as a whole may benefit from "freer" trade, some people will lose. For instance, if England has a comparative advantage (relatively lower opportunity cost of producing) in wool, and Portugal has a comparative advantage in wine, it is easy to show that opening up trade will lead to an increase in total output. However, there will be competitive pressure on wine producers in England and wool producers in Portugal. According to the compensation principle, so long as the winners (wool in England, wine in Portugal) could compensate the losers and still have something left over, trade is beneficial.[8] At present, most trade agreements fail this very minimal standard, as the losers are rarely fully compensated. Even if they were, this narrowly economic approach says nothing about the impact of trade on the viability of cultures or access to resources necessary for political effectiveness.[9]

Or to conventionally recognized human rights. Neoclassicals strongly object to any interference with trade for human rights reasons because, in their view, (1) such interference eliminates legitimate sources of comparative advantage; (2) such concerns generally stem from protectionist sentiment, not altruism; and (3) even where they stem from altruism, there are other ways, besides trade policy, to deal with these issues.

In making these arguments, neoclassicals take a cultural relativist stance. Outside of a few, generally accepted rights—such as freedom from slavery or torture—they are unwilling to censure governments for allowing practices such as limiting freedom of association, the right to bargain collectively, or even child labor. These practices, they say, are acceptable as part of a country's cultural choices, and any attempt to interfere with them reeks of cultural imperialism. Neoclassical theory's relativism is simultaneously universalist: there is one correct theory for all times and places *in economics.* Thus orthodox neoclassical economists are able to portray themselves as both free traders and anti-imperialists, and attack the human rights movement at one of its most vulnerable points.

In the case of labor standards, neoclassicals acknowledge that many states have signed and ratified agreements recognizing a variety of cultural, economic, and political rights. In their view, protection of these rights goes well beyond that which should be the focus of trade negotiations, thus leading them to believe that sanctions in response to violations of labor standards stem from protectionist rather than human rights concerns. Moreover, while countries have signed such covenants, the rights embodied in them are rarely respected.

> This suggests that, at best, the rights recognized are universal aspirations, perhaps to be attained at some distant and unspecified future, though cynics may view them as empty rhetoric. . . . [I]t is worth reiterating that the claim of uni-

versality and eternity, for a subset of rights covering the so-called "core" labor standards, is overblown. (Srinivasan 1998, 230)[10]

Concern about labor standards, to the extent that it stems from altruism, is not so easily dismissed. But for Srinivasan, there are more effective measures than trade sanctions to express such concerns. Direct means of improving labor conditions in poor countries are superior to the indirect approach embodied in trade sanctions. Removing barriers to immigration is a particularly appropriate response. If this is not feasible, then direct income transfers are still more appropriate than trade sanctions:

> With higher incomes, it is reasonable to presume that the supply price (broadly defined to include labor standards) of their labor would rise and to restore labor market equilibrium, labor standards would have to rise. Indeed, a test of the depth of their humanitarian concern is the price that rich country citizens are willing to pay for translating the concern into an actual increase in the welfare of workers in poor countries. Willingness to make needed income transfers is a demonstration of the willingness to pay the price. (Srinivasan 1998, 231)

If people fear that globalization will create a "race to the bottom," they can simply stop buying imported goods. In general, the "race to the bottom" concern is dismissed as the old worry about pauper labor, a concern that neoclassicals believe is fully discredited by deployment of the Pareto criterion and the compensation principle. "Diversity in labor standards among countries is not only legitimate but also does not detract from the case for free trade" (Srinivasan 1998: 233).

Diversity of labor standards is similar to diversity of tastes or technology in that it is a source of comparative advantage and therefore of gains from trade.

> As long as there exists a non-empty set of Pareto Optima meeting the minimal standards, it is feasible to meet such standards with income transfers but without departing from free trade. As such there is no need for a social clause or to put it another way the only rationale for a social clause has to be the odious one of protection of importing competing industries. (Srinivasan 1998, 237)[11]

The right to form trade unions and bargain collectively has been identified by the International Labor Organization as a core standard. Srinivasan and other neoclassicals are skeptical as to whether the right to bargain collectively qualifies as a right in any meaningful sense. Labor unions, in their view, may promote the interests of a privileged few at the expense of the many, that is, they may create a labor aristocracy and promote corruption.[12]

Further, if collective bargaining promotes high standards inconsistent with a country's level of development they could inhibit economic growth. In the absence of market failures, and so long as the rich countries are willing to compensate potential losers in trade competition, comparative advantage that reflects differences in prevailing labor standards is legitimate for neoclassical theory. In other words, this case is no different from any other example of international trade, as in our story of England and Portugal. All that Srinivasan and other neoclassicals are adding is that it doesn't matter whether the source of comparative advantage is based on conditions provided by nature or on the fact that the Portuguese government prevents grape pickers from freely associating and forming unions.[13]

So labor standards are neither universal nor eternal, and even when the desire to enforce higher standards is driven by humanitarian concerns, trade policy is an inefficient instrument. "One is therefore led to conclude that the conventional protectionist pauper-labor type argument, rather than lofty humanitarianism, is behind the clamor for the use of trade policy instruments to enforce particular labor standards in poor countries" (Srinivasan 1998, 243).

But this all makes sense *only* within the individualist predispositions of the theory. If preferences are endogenously produced, and if they reflect more the desire for status than utility, the finding fails. And even on its own terms, to say that a policy is good regardless of its distributional effects or its effects on culture and politics is remarkably narrow and reductionist.

The Problem with Rights Talk

Neoclassical economics provides a surprisingly weak justification for putting markets first. The language of human rights does not necessarily help us make a stronger case in the opposite direction.

Some defenders of human rights have given ground to cultural relativists in order to defend a thin definition of human rights.

> People from different cultures may continue to disagree about what is good, but nevertheless agree about what is insufferably, unarguably wrong. The universal commitments implied by human rights can be compatible with a wide variety of ways of living only if the universalism implied is self-consciously minimalist. Human rights can command universal assent only as a decidedly "thin" theory of what is right, a definition of the minimal conditions for any kind of life at all. (Ignatieff 2001, 56)

When one combines this thinness with the individualist predisposition of rights theory generally, there is not all that much distance between the conventional human rights perspective and neoclassical economic theory. This, I will argue, essentially sets the borders around rights claims at the limits dictated by prevailing contemporary class interest.

For Ignatieff, "human rights is a language of individual empowerment" (2001, 57).[14] The basic documents of the twentieth-century human rights revolution were drafted in response to the unconscionable actions taken by states against (racially or politically defined and grouped) individuals. The individualism of the Universal Declaration was an understandable and admirable reaction to the barbarism of authoritarian states. But this has not always been, and is not now, the only basis for human rights work.

Ignatieff and others trace the origins of modern human rights to the antislavery movements of the nineteenth century.[15] These movements tended to downplay economic exploitation while focusing on slavery's unfortunate impact on the individual's freedom of choice. But the labor movements of the late nineteenth and early twentieth centuries drew on the *economic* moment of antislavery to construct a critique of capitalism as a system that violated the right of workers as a class to the fruits of their labor, and then to the violation of the worker's right to a living wage (Glickman 1997). In other words, there are nonauthoritarian traditions that include economic and social conditions in a core definition of rights. The thin definition of rights promoted by Ignatieff and others is a *choice* that puts them close to those in economics who are most interested in promoting neoliberal forms of globalization.

Human rights arguments can become a condition of existence for capitalist exploitation on a world scale, by highlighting some forms of oppression while obscuring others. For instance, in its important reports on the trafficking in women and bonded child labor, Human Rights Watch takes a strategy of "naming and shaming" rather than investigating the broad and global economic context within which such abuses take place. Their preferred recourse is legalistic, as if the law were neutral, rather than one that encourages grassroots organizing (Gordon, Swanson, and Buttigieg 2000; Brody et al. 2001).

For Ignatieff, moral individualism protects cultural diversity since such a position respects the various ways in which individuals choose to live. "The ultimate purpose and justification of group rights is not the protection of the group as such but the protection of the individuals who compose it" (2001, 67). For him, group rights are clearly subordinate to those of individuals and are always to be treated with distrust:

> Rights language cannot be parsed or translated into a non-individualistic, communitarian framework. It presumes moral individualism and is nonsensical outside that assumption. . . . Group rights doctrines exist to safeguard the collective rights—for example, to language—that make individual agency meaningful and valuable. Human rights exist . . . to define the irreducible minimum beyond which group and collective claims must not go in constraining the lives of individuals. (2001, 67, 69)

The list of oppressions that these thin rights doctrines oppose is notable for its absences: "Rights doctrines arouse powerful opposition because they challenge powerful religions, family structures, authoritarian states, and tribes" (Ignatieff 2001, 68). The words *class* and *property* are missing from Ignatieff's list and that of many other human rights theorists as well. Ignatieff claims that linking human rights and global capitalism misses the insurgent nature of human rights activism vis-à-vis global corporations. But just as the antislavery movement legitimated capitalist forms of exploitation by demonizing slavery, so even when it directly takes on corporate interests, contemporary human rights practice limits itself to those oppressions that are consistent with the individualism at the heart of the global neoliberal project.

For Ignatieff, liberal individualism is advantageous precisely for its thinness. In other words, it bans those activities that would make any kind of life inconceivable, yet it does not stipulate what is necessary for a good life in any kind of positive sense. This means that the primary responsibility for defining rights violations lies with the victims, and if people accept their victimization there is little that the outsider can do. Those who insist that civil and political rights need supplementing with social and economic ones make a claim that is true—that individual rights can be exercised effectively only within a framework of collective rights provision—but liberals argue that they may be obscuring the priority relation between the individual and the collective. Individual rights without collective rights may be difficult to exercise, but collective rights without individual ones end up in tyranny (Ignatieff 2001, 89–90).

> Why we must choose between individual and collective rights is unclear. The claim here would be that civil and political freedoms are the necessary condition for the eventual attainment of social and economic security. Without the freedom to articulate and express political opinions, without freedom of speech and assembly, together with freedom of property, agents cannot organize themselves to struggle for social and economic security. (2001, 90)

Ignatieff lumps the Marxist position on human rights talk together with Islamic and Asian exceptionalisms and the postmodern critique, but the former is fundamentally different. Ignatieff reverses what he takes to be the typical Marxist perspective, arguing that political and civil rights are not a bourgeois luxury but the precondition for economic and social rights.[16]

The history of African-American progress in the United States may be taken as a critique of this position, as economic and social improvement has certainly not flowed smoothly from the achievement of civil and political rights. Moreover, the right to organize and bargain collectively—one of the International Labor Organization's core labor rights and clearly a collective right—is missing from this list, and freedom of association, a closely related ILO core right, is not equivalent to freedom of speech and assembly.

There is a family of social theories, including Institutional and Marxian political economy but also the work of contemporary political philosophers like John Rawls and Amartya Sen, which provides bases for the good society other than Pareto optimality. Sen's notion of capabilities equality has been influential across a number of fields, including the discussion of worker rights.

Invoking Sen, Ignatieff argues that no country with democracy and a free press has experienced famine. Freedom, he says, *is* development. But the title to Sen's biggest selling book is *Development as Freedom,* which means something very different from, thicker than, and in some ways the opposite of the liberal human rights agenda.[17]

For Ignatieff, the lesson of Sen's work is that "a human rights perspective, focusing as it does on enhancing human agency, draws attention to the importance of unblocking individual agency as a motor for economic development itself. Human rights, like freedom of speech and assembly, as well as freedom of the press, are essential in creating checks and balances against coercive strategies by governments" (2001, 167). Again, we note the absence of the right to organize and bargain collectively from this list.

After 1945 there were two official human rights traditions. The socialist rights tradition, which emphasized economic and social rights, kept the "capitalist rights tradition" (Ignatieff 2001, 19) in check to some extent. But it would be a reach to say that the collapse of the one-party states and centrally planned economies of eastern Europe marks the end of the conflict between these traditions. Rather, the most visible official *state* representatives of one tradition are now gone. Yet the tone of Ignatieff's argument bears the same kind of triumphalism as the "end of history" narratives that were so influential in the United States in the early 1990s.

In fact there are multiple rights traditions. The one associated with the labor movement, and most effectively represented in the Charter and subsequent official documents of the International Labor Organization, clearly recognizes

the necessity of certain group rights, including and especially the right to organize trade unions and to bargain collectively.

How is such a right to be secured? The ensuing chapters answer this question in some detail. Focusing on just one aspect of this question here, the "name
and shame" strategy has encouraged the more morally sensitive (brand dependent) multinationals to adopt codes of conduct for their suppliers. When we
examine these codes we see the problem with the individualist approach. The
issues covered most frequently are safety and health, discrimination, and environmental protection. The least likely to be mentioned are overtime hours and
pay, and rights to organize and bargain collectively. The latter is the right with
the most promise for creating countervailing power to globalized capital at the
grass roots (Freeman 1998). *Thus the individualism at the heart of liberal human
rights doctrine supports the very ordering of rights promoted by the largest multinational enterprises, but not those that would be most effective in empowering
working people and popular organizations.*

We now have the technological ability—but not the will or power—to make
something like what we used to call socialism happen. If, as Marx argued, it was
capitalism's historic function to create the technological conditions necessary
for a society of associated producers, this has now occurred. However, capitalist
development has not produced the ideological conditions necessary for the
transition to such a society, nor has it created an opposition with the power necessary to challenge the entrenched interest. The new social movements that
arose in response to increased economic integration have provided a powerful
critique of orthodox globalization theory. But it is likely that the orthodoxy will
be able to reposition itself through continued appeals to science, propelled by
the power of the interests that benefit from it. Human rights language, to this
point, does not provide a deeply rooted critique of this orthodoxy.

The next section considers how a notion of rights as conventions might be
more helpful.

Rights as Conventions

What rights are, how they come about, in what sense they might be universal—
all are hotly contested questions.

There is no wholly satisfactory defense of rights or moral obligation against
relativism. Natural law theories provide a defense but the problems with such
theories are well known. Asserting rights inherent in the nature of man runs up
against not only the postmodern deconstruction of the unitary individual but

also a variety of philosophical criticisms going back to Hume concerning the limits of human understanding. Outside of a few defenders of natural law, then, rights are simply changeable social conventions. Within economics it is the Institutional approach that has the most to say on these matters, as Institutionalism sees rights as whatever legislators and especially the courts determine them to be.

Why the prevalence of rights talk now? One possibility is that the language of rights is a leftover from a time when natural law could be taken seriously, and its relevance today stems from horror over the events of the twentieth century. Those events, particularly the Great Depression, World War II, and the Holocaust, created the contemporary *human rights regime*. Yet the *worker rights regime* is older, stemming from the rapid development of labor movements in the late nineteenth century and the social solution to the "labor problem" embodied in institutions like the International Labor Organization, the New Deal, and the European welfare state.[18] Thus, even if globalization were in any sense a unified process, we would expect it to have different effects on the group rights (i.e., freedom of association and collective bargaining) characteristic of the worker rights regime as opposed to individual rights such as protection of the body and equality of opportunity characteristic of the human rights regime.

One could hope for a firmer and more optimistic foundation for rights than convention. Many people are suspicious about rights claims, and justifiably so. Rights are a cover for any number of self-interested activities, and the most horrific actions are often draped in humanitarian colors (we had to destroy that hamlet to save it, we're not going to let a country go communist because of the stupidity of its own people, etc.). It is good to remember that rights are conventions, purely human creations driven, perhaps, by a powerful post-Enlightenment drive toward rationalism in morality. We know this, but we sometimes forget it due to the horrors from which the contemporary human rights regime sprang and the continuing challenges to it.

Hume (1961) argued that our knowledge of cause-and-effect relations is radically limited, yet this did not lead him to nihilism. Social custom and common sense could, in imperfect and limited ways, lead us toward the correct way to live. Rights, then, need not be timeless or universal, but they do need to be deeply enough rooted in the human experience in any particular society to win general assent. They need to find embodiment in law and be upheld by courts in which both elites and the masses of the people have confidence. Thus for international worker rights to become "rights" there is need for an authoritative international institution, as I argue in the next chapter.

If rights are conventions, they lose some of the power attributed to rights in the natural law tradition. "They will not be self-evident or eternal. And every attempt to apply them beyond the boundaries of one's own culture will carry grave risks of injustice through the unwitting effects of parochialism and ethnocentrism" (Haskell 2000, 136).

"Rights as conventions" is particularly problematic internationally, where consensus is less likely to exist. Conventions are objects of struggle between self-interested groups but also durable assumptions about how to live correctly that resonate deeply in the common sense of the times.[19] Rights are not arbitrary merely because they are conventions. Rawls argues that to be a right, a claim must be congruent with deep understanding of our aspirations. For Rawls, moral objectivity follows from a socially constructed point of view that all can accept, as in his famous original position (1971, 131–42).

We cannot ultimately justify rights by reference to a reality outside of language and community, yet perhaps it is good for us to try. We can recognize the status of our claims while making them anyway. Just because human rights are conventions does not reduce them to "empty ritual or a devious form of the will to power" (Haskell 2000, 143).

Seeing rights as social conventions is consistent with the social psychology of Institutional economics. But Institutional economists have had less to say about why particular rights become established, or having been established, pass out of existence. I would like to develop two examples to illustrate how class and moral convention may, interactively, establish and disestablish rights. The first is the example of the antislavery movement of the nineteenth century, which is generally seen as the most important precursor of the contemporary human rights movements (Keck and Sikkink 1998, 39–78). I develop a contemporary example from the United States in the next section.

In the late eighteenth century, there was a near simultaneity between the emergence of industrialized capitalism and organized antislavery. In *Capitalism and Slavery* Eric Williams more or less reduced the latter to the former (Williams 1944). In an argument that was radical and stunning for the times—the 1940s—Williams maintained that antislavery served the interests of the rising industrial bourgeoisie. It did so by shifting political power within the British Empire from the Caribbean planters to the industrialists, and drawing attention away from the social turbulence and exploitation in the English mills. Having provided the capital necessary for industrialization, slavery and the slave trade had become a fetter on further development. Williams argued that opposition to it was also convenient in that it gave the rising industrialists a humanitarian appearance.

Williams's book has been criticized on many grounds, by Marxists and non-Marxists alike. The documentary evidence for some of his stronger claims seems weak, but the argument as a whole still has merit. David Brion Davis, the leading American historian of slavery, has produced a more complex and subtle version of this story that ties the reforming influence of antislavery to class interest.

In the work most relevant here, Davis was concerned with how ideas become social facts, "cultural attitudes, and motives and means for collective action" (Bender 1993, 2). His work on the ideology of antislavery goes beyond earlier treatments of the subject by both progressive and Marxist historians in that ideas are not *merely* reflections of material interest, but such interests, however unconscious and mediated by other social and natural forces, are tied to the hegemony of particular ideas.

His argument is that concern for the slave may have served the hegemonic function of legitimating "free" labor. While the origins of antislavery might have been primarily moral, its reception was overdetermined by class interest. Davis's subsequent debate with Thomas Haskell in the *American Historical Review* nicely illustrates what is at stake here. For Haskell, capitalism is largely defined by a market economy, not a system of class relations. Market activities, especially over a long distance, change our perceptions, or what he calls our "cognitive style." Haskell argues that Davis's attempt to preserve the spirit of Williams's argument while avoiding reductionism is not subtle but merely incoherent.

Capitalism (as Haskell defines it) has a "subliminal curriculum" that widens causal horizons and heightens awareness of remote consequences. Capitalism (i.e., the market) changes cultural perceptions, creating a new relationship between moral values and acts. The extension of the market enlarges our capacity for the recognition of remote causes and extends the chain of moral responsibility. For Haskell, all morality is conventional; capitalism, or the extension of the market, changes the conventions with which we make moral sense of the world and our responsibility in it.[20]

In response, Davis argued that while the origins of antislavery might be found in a shift in moral sentiment, it was used by the rising industrial capitalist class to single out slavery as something singularly evil, while drawing attention away from controversies over capitalist exploitation and wage labor.

But it is not quite as simple as capitalists co-opting the work of well-meaning middle-class reformers. In another response to Haskell, John Ashworth pointed out that the U.S. South was firmly connected to international markets, and yet antislavery was not the result. In order to understand why slavery and not wage labor became the focus of reform we need a definition of capitalism that includes not just markets but wage labor and an understanding of society that includes the household. In the United States, the dominant reaction to the rise of capitalism in the late eighteenth and early nineteenth centuries was a rigid separation between market and nonmarket areas of life and a turn to the home, family, and individual consciousness as respites from capitalist calculation. For Ashworth, abolitionism was a theory of capitalist morality that defined the family and the individual conscience as the bedrock of society. Because slavery denied both, it had to go, so that "the same cluster of values that made wage labor or capitalism possible made slavery impossible" (Bender 1993, 9).[21]

In chapter 7 I suggest that something similar may be occurring in the contemporary treatment of sweatshops. The antisweatshop movement, rooted as it is in a moral and often religious critique, can be used by "enlightened" capitalists to shift attention from the problem of capitalist exploitation in general and on to specific forms of exploitation that contemporary moral convention defines as particularly egregious such as forced labor and child labor. This shift is supported, in certain crucial ways, by contemporary transnational human rights networks, whose focus tends to be physical injury to the body and equality of substantive opportunity, not collective rights like freedom of association, the right to organize and bargain collectively, or the right to a living wage (Keck and Sikkink 1998, 199–217).

Worker Rights as Human Rights in the U.S. Context

In the nineteenth century, U.S. workers justified collective action by appeal to rights of freedom of association and speech grounded in the U.S. Constitution (Montgomery 1996, 16–17). Nineteenth-century judges countered with the common law doctrine of master and servant that justified employer claims to rule in the workplace. Many judges found that "a contract to deliver labor for money delivers the employee's assent to serve" (Tomlins 1993, 227).[22]

These doctrines were modified by the basic labor laws passed during the New Deal. For the most part, labor relations have developed separately from human rights discourse in the United States, and workers have "only such rights as collective bargaining contracts and specific legislation stipulate" (Montgomery 1996, 17). Because the relationship between human rights and worker rights is complex, because judicial decisions leave room for multiple paths, and because the United States differs significantly on these issues from other countries, it is worth reviewing this relationship.

My argument in this section is that so-called first-generation rights, the civil and political rights of the French and American Revolutions, have a broad but not complete acceptance in American law and culture. The second-generation rights, social and economic rights, found a limited home in New Deal social democracy but are more tenuously grounded in the United States than elsewhere. These differences in rights concepts explain many of the disagreements between the United States and both the developing and European countries, and make an international discourse of worker rights difficult at best.

The contemporary discourse of human rights was inspired both by the turmoil of early-twentieth-century capitalism and the immense human tragedy of World War II. In the establishment of the contemporary regime in the 1940s the United States insisted that the Covenant on Economic, Social, and Cultural Rights be separated from the International Covenant on Civil and Political Rights. The right to self-determination for peoples and first-generation rights like the rights to freedom of the press, free speech, freedom of religion, assembly, and due process were and have been accepted by the United States. The Reagan administration was particularly clear in arguing that these constitute the universe and limit of human rights (Meyer 1998, 58–65). The second-generation rights embodied in the Covenant on Economic, Cultural, and Social Rights such as the right to employment, the right to strike, and the right to medical care, education, and housing are seen as goals (sometimes) rather than rights in the American context.[23]

James Gross argues that the conception of human rights in the "Western tradition" has emphasized the individual's right to be protected from abuse by the state (1999b). The negative rights of individual liberty certainly fit well with the post-Smithian discourse of the "free market." Because the international human rights movement has been dominated by rich-country activists, it has tended to emphasize the individual rights guaranteed in the International Covenant on Civil and Political Rights but not those in the Covenant on Economic, Social, and Cultural Rights, which the United States has not ratified.[24]

The right to freedom of association straddles the line between first- and second-generation rights (Leary 1996). Until the 1990s, few human rights organizations had shown much interest in worker rights, and rights discourse was not a major tool of labor organizations in the United States.

For human rights organizations, the right to protection from bodily physical harm may logically and simply take precedence over the right to organize trade unions. Still, the victims of torture often are in fact those who are organizing for economic and social rights including the right to organize and bargain collectively (Leary 1996, 26). Human rights organizations often betray a profound disinterest in the structural causes of the violations of the individual rights on which they report (Gordon, Swanson, and Buttigieg 2000).[25] Since the antislavery movement of the nineteenth century, international human rights activists have tended to focus on freedom from bodily harm to the vulnerable and innocent and (more so recently) legal equality of opportunity as cross-culturally recognized "rights." Sometimes driven by a religious conviction that moral progress increases each individual's capacity to act as an instrument of God, sometimes on a purely secular basis, they have generally taken a profoundly individualist approach to rights. For instance, in the antislavery movement, slavery was seen not as a class relationship but an exercise of illegitimate power of one individual over another (Keck and Sikkink 1998, 39–51).[26]

At the same time, trade unionists in the United States are generally driven by a practical focus on the issues of most concern to their membership, which is unlikely to include internationally recognized worker rights. In the past, to the extent that rights were a concern, that concern was likely to flow from protectionist or localist concerns, which are often interpreted as illegitimate by human rights workers and developing-country activists. Added to the history of AFL-CIO complicity in repression abroad, it is no wonder that, until recently, there has been little overlap between international human and worker rights activity.

Core worker rights, as promulgated by the ILO, are not all treated similarly either in the legal case history in the United States or in the theory and practice of post–World War II international human rights. The rights to freedom from discrimination and freedom from forced labor stand well within the international human rights consensus. The right to freedom from child labor is also arguably within that consensus.[27] The right to freedom of association straddles the line, and the right to organize and bargain collectively is clearly outside that consensus, particularly in the American context. While all kinds of individual freedoms have been expanded in the United States over the last generation, workers' collective rights to freedom of association and collective bargaining have shrunk (Lichtenstein 2002; Piore and Safford 2006). On the other hand, as I show in chapter 6, the changing U.S. approach to international labor standards may be an effective way to improve worker rights domestically.

Of course, there is a subterranean tradition, both in economics and law, that recognizes the unequal relationship between employer and employee.[28] Not only Marx, but also Alfred Marshall and Adam Smith recognized the unequal bargaining relationship between employer and employee, and concluded that freedom of contract alone might not be sufficient to produce optimal outcomes in labor markets.

The overwhelmingly middle-class background of judges, however, has guaranteed that it has been the rights of property rather than the rights to freedom of association or collective bargaining that have been protected in the United States (Gross 1999b, 75). Before the New Deal especially, employment was often dependent on renouncing the right to freedom of association. Although the situation is different today de jure, it has de facto reverted to its pre–New Deal status for most workers in the United States. As James Gross, Katherine Stone, and others have argued, while the ideals of industrial democracy embodied in the Wagner Act were never fully achieved, over the last thirty years both congressional and executive branch policy has aided and abetted employers' determination to return to the world of management unilateralism.[29]

The right to bargain collectively is particularly problematic in the American context. For instance, in the 1992 *Lechmere v. NLRB* decision the Supreme Court ruled that only employees and not unions themselves (to say nothing of organizers) had collective bargaining rights. When this case was brought before the ILO's Committee on Freedom of Association the government attached the pro-management U.S. Council for International Business submission to its own. The USCIB argued that the *Lechmere* decision merely reaffirmed previous Supreme Court decisions. While the Freedom of Association committee requested remedial action, its recommendation was ignored.

Jacques Ranciere has called human rights "the rights of those who have no rights," and I think this is more or less accurate (1995). Rights talk is an ideological tool that can *sometimes* be wielded in a way that helps to secure civil rights. But such rights have no content in and of themselves. In other words their meaning and effects are less determinate than the believers in such rights are pleased to acknowledge.

To argue that "worker rights are human rights" then means that one thinks that such a slogan makes sense in the concrete circumstances we face today. We have enough knowledge now of how the "rights revolution" has affected the collective strength of workers in actually existing U.S. capitalism to be skeptical about this slogan.

Beginning with the Civil Rights Act of 1964 and continuing through the 1970s a series of federal laws established numerous rights for workers in the United States for equal employment opportunity and protection on the job. One of the major effects of these acts was to stimulate corporations to form various personnel, safety, benefit, and diversity departments to manage compliance. In time these new offices became subsumed under a human relations paradigm of employment that explained their existence in purely profit-maximizing terms and not as the necessary acts of a democratic state in an unjust economic system.

> By the early 1980s, the new human resources management movement was championing diversity as the key to expanding markets and improving innovation, safety, and health programs as the key to winning employee commitment and renovating antiquated technologies, and benefits programs as a means to reducing alienation and improving worker attitudes. (Dobbins and Sutton 1998)

Instead of defining these rights as civic rights granted to workers as a class they came to be seen as at best rights of individuals, and increasingly as profit-maximizing tools. The shift from the collective bargaining model of the New Deal Industrial Relations system to the rights-based workplace regulated the individual relationship between employer and employee while deregulating the collective relationship. And while the rights revolution in the workplace continued to spread even during the Reagan years, cuts in enforcement led employers to circumvent the law while still promoting the rhetoric of humans as resources rather than workers as rights-bearing subjects. Thus since the 1980s workers have effectively lost some of the individual protections they gained at the same time their collective strength has been eroded.

My intent is not to blame those who promoted the Equal Employment Opportunity Act, the Occupational Safety and Health Act, or the Employment Retirement Income Security Act for the lack of collective voice of the American worker or the stagnation of real wages over the last generation. But in a cultural environment in which Americans tend to have collective amnesia about the state's role in shaping capitalism and in which, since the early 1980s, organized capital has been able to nearly accomplish its goal of eliminating unions from the capitalist sector of the economy, it behooves us to think more carefully about the potential contradictory effects of promoting worker rights as human rights.

Conclusion

The major nineteenth-century critics of "human rights" did their work well. Bentham referred to most political talk as "nonsense," and human rights as "nonsense on stilts." Marx was long thought to have dismantled the concept of bourgeois rights so effectively that socialists were concerned much more with progress and power than with rights. Neither liberalism nor socialism had much use for "rights talk" until the general crisis of the twentieth century, that is the thirty years of world war, depression, and extermination of peoples between 1914 and 1945. The human rights documents of the immediate post–World War II era marked a change in the discourse, and this change was reinforced by the ways in which such talk could be put to use in the Cold War and in the postcolonial world. In other words, the language of rights became central to political discourse only with the conjunction of the horror of the Holocaust and the particular nature of the great power struggles of 1945–89. It is this very particular definition of rights that is often carried into popular discussions.

The critique of rights in orthodox economics is not compelling, but the individualism that underlies that critique is close to the vision of rights that has become most accepted, particularly in the United States. With this caution in mind, the remaining chapters investigate how the activities of the International Labor Organization, the U.S. government, and labor-based nongovernmental organizations may come together conjuncturally to create a convention for worker rights as human rights, particularly the rights to freedom of association and collective bargaining.

CHAPTER 5

The International Organization of
Worker Rights and Labor Standards

International economic integration has increased since the 1970s, as has the controversy over it. It is not surprising that integration has brought forth protest and critique. Historically, the movement of the market into new areas and aspects of social life has stimulated society to protect itself from the market's destabilizing effects (Polanyi 1980).

Integration has occurred not only among similar societies, as in Europe, but among societies whose living standards, social norms, and standard economic practices differ wildly, as in the case of Mexico and the United States. This has raised a number of problems, most especially concerning the rights of workers.

There is a fairly standard script in debating these problems. Critics of "globalization" argue that "core" worker rights should be written into regional and multilateral trade agreements. "Free traders" argue that setting standards prohibits the very differences that are the basis of trade. In this view, universal labor standards treat the "cheap labor" that is the comparative advantage of the poor countries as something to be outlawed, and if worker rights are an issue at all the International Labor Organization should deal with them, not the international trade regime. The critics find this less than satisfactory, as the ILO has no enforcement capability.

In this chapter I argue that the ILO may be the appropriate body for dealing with labor rights, though not for the reasons that the "free traders" stand on. Rather, the ILO, as an explicitly tripartite organization, embodies a set of problem-solving principles and worldview that are consistent with the problem-solving principles of institutional economics. Labor (and other) disputes cannot be resolved by reference to general principles, such as cost-benefit analysis. Resolution requires that all interested parties have a seat at the bargaining table, where they can establish "reasonable value."

There are problems in applying this approach internationally. Neither the principles of tripartism nor the legitimacy of core worker rights is well established in all member countries. The ILO lacks the economic sanctions and the ability to threaten violence that establishment of truly international norms would require. Its own processes are often so baroque that it is hard for outsiders to understand what it really does. As a nominally neutral entity it does not directly promote the kind of popular collective organization that has so often been critical to achieving social justice.

But it is possible that incorporating ILO findings in national decision making would promote the ILO as an authoritative figure. Such a figure is a necessary, though I would argue not a sufficient condition for achieving reasonable value in globalized labor markets. The ILO also demonstrates in its core values, organizational structure, and understanding of economic processes a consistently broad and interdisciplinary approach to social and labor market problems, keen awareness of the social determination of market values, and a social rather than strictly price-theoretic analysis of labor markets.

I begin here with a brief discussion of orthodox neoclassical perspectives on international labor standards and follow this with a heterodox approach based in Commons. In the next section I examine the evolution of the ILO and its relationship to the Institutional standpoint, theory of reasonable value, and analysis of labor markets, finding enough commonality to suggest the ongoing fruitfulness of an ongoing conversation between economic heterodoxy and the ILO. In the conclusion I consider some of the difficulties in creating reasonable value and authoritative institutions internationally.

Orthodox Economics and International Labor Standards

The world economy is not nearly as integrated as some of the more celebratory proponents of globalization imply: national borders still inhibit the movement of money, capital, and especially people. While formal barriers to trade have declined substantially, international price arbitrage happens slowly, investment portfolios still exhibit substantial home-country bias, and barriers to the movement of labor are the rule rather than the exception (Rodrik 2000). Still, as measured by the ratio of exports to gross domestic product, national economies are substantially more integrated today than they were in the post–World War II period.

Such integration has had a significant effect on labor market outcomes in the United States. One econometric estimate indicates that increased trade and

immigration are responsible for roughly 40 percent of the growing wage gap
between more and less educated workers (Borjas, Freeman, and Katz 1997). If
increased trade competition forces labor-saving technological change and
makes it easier for management to discipline labor, then the figure is probably
much higher (Wood 1995). International capital mobility reduces workers' bargaining power, subjects them to greater instability of employment and incomes, and forces workers to bear a greater proportion of the nonwage costs of
work, such as safe working conditions and health costs (Bronfenbrenner 2001;
Rodrik 1997).[1]

Even if we can establish that international integration has negative effects
on labor market outcomes, this does not demonstrate that labor rights have
been affected, as rights deal with process not outcome. Core labor rights as
defined by the International Labor Organization include the right to freedom
of association, the right to organize and bargain collectively, the right to refuse
forced labor, the right to freedom from child labor, and the right to work free
from discrimination.[2] In the United States at least, there is evidence that capital
mobility compromises the right to organize and bargain collectively. Kate
Bronfenbrenner has found that "the recent acceleration in capital mobility has
had a devastating impact on the extent and nature of union organizing campaigns" (2000, iv). Her examination of NLRB data indicates that plant-closing
threats are increasingly likely to deter successful organizing and that such
threats are not tied to the financial conditions of the companies involved.

Of course it is difficult to assess how much economic integration has
strengthened employers' hands and how much of this is simply due to the general deterioration of worker rights in the United States (Compa 2000). Bronfenbrenner found that unions are increasingly unlikely to file unfair labor practice complaints in response to plant closing threats during organizing
campaigns because they are so difficult to prove and relief is so limited under
existing law. She concludes that "plant closing threats are just another tactic in
their (ownership/management) anti-union campaigns, one that very effectively plays on the real fears of workers living and working in an increasingly
mobile economy" (2001, vi).

Even if increased economic integration erodes labor rights, trade policy
may not be the appropriate redress. Many orthodox economists and poor-
country elites argue that concern with labor rights in the United States is just
disguised protectionism. Gary Fields argues that the list of process rights that
are acceptable cross-culturally is actually quite short—prohibition of slavery

and child labor, freedom of association, and reasonably safe working conditions. Beyond these, economies should be judged based on "outcomes oriented labor standards—employment and wage growth—and these are most likely to occur with market wage determination and minimal regulation of the employment relationship" (1990).[3]

Jagdish Bhagwati claims that environmental and labor standards are a purely domestic matter and should not be subjects for trade negotiations. But he acknowledges that labor standards, "unlike most environmental standards, are seen in moral terms. . . . In particular, it is argued that if labour standards elsewhere are different and unacceptable morally, then the resulting competition is morally illegitimate and 'unfair'" (1998, 258).

Bhagwati argues that in the case of slavery there will be nearly universal agreement on this proposition: "If slavery produces competitive advantage, that advantage is illegitimate and ought to be rejected" (1998, 258). In this case Bhagwati would support the inclusion of a "social clause" concerning labor standards in trade agreements. But, he insists, the list of "universally condemned practices such as slavery" is quite short. It is worth quoting Bhagwati at some length here.

> True, the ILO has many conventions that many nations have signed. But many have been signed simply because in effect they are not binding. Equally, the United States itself has signed no more than a tiny fraction of these conventions in any case. The question whether a substantive consensus on anything except well-meaning and broad principles without consequences for trade access in case of non-compliance can be obtained is therefore highly dubious.
>
> Indeed, the reality is that diversity of labour practice and standards is widespread in practice and reflects, not necessarily venality and wickedness, but rather diversity of cultural values, economic conditions, and analytical beliefs and theories concerning the economic (and therefore moral) consequences of specific labor standards. The notion that labour standards can be universalised, like human rights such as liberty and habeas corpus, simply by calling them "labour rights" ignores the fact that this easy equation between culture-specific labour standards and universal human rights will have a difficult time surviving deeper scrutiny. (1998, 260–61)

That the United States could see its trading rights suspended because of violations of core labor rights is clearly correct.[4] It is also true that in practice core and other important "rights" are not treated as rights. As Bhagwati notes, the right to organize, protection for migrant workers, and guarantees against sweatshop conditions are weak or nonexistent in the United States today. As the United States (with France) under Clinton was the chief exponent of a social clause in the 1990s, there is no small amount of hypocrisy here.

Bhagwati argues that positive rights, such as the right to organize and bargain collectively, can have perverse effects in a developing-country context. Unionization could primarily benefit insiders who already have jobs at the expense of unemployed outsiders, and would primarily help the urban working class, which tends to be better off already than the landless poor. The latter group would be best aided through rapid growth, which, according to Bhagwati, might be hindered by urban unionization. For Bhagwati, it is growth alone that can pull the majority of workers out of absolute poverty.

> If so, the imposition of the culture-specific developed-country-union views on poor countries about the rights of unions to push for higher wages will resolve current equity and intergenerational equity problems in ways that are normally unacceptable to these countries, and correctly so. (1998, 263)

In this view the alleged universality of core labor standards is incorrect, except for a few special cases (e.g., slavery). The idea of including a social clause in trade agreements is faulty as it rejects the culturally based diversity of actually existing labor practices. Developing-country elites and some on the political left in developing countries share the belief that the social clause is simply disguised protectionism (Kohr 1997).

Bhagwati suggests that the more appropriate avenue for ratcheting up labor standards is the work of nongovernmental organizations (NGOs) and the International Labor Organization. For Bhagwati, the educational activities of these organizations, to the extent they have good ideas, should be sufficient: "In fact, if your ideas are good, they should spread without coercion. The Spanish Inquisition should not be necessary to spread Christianity; indeed, the pope has no troops. Mahatma Gandhi's splendid idea of non-violent agitation was picked up by Martin Luther King, not because he worked on the Indian government to threaten retribution against others otherwise; it happened to be just morally compelling" (1998, 264).

Private boycotts could also be used to create a multinational consensus in favor of labor standards. Such standards, he argues,

> should be carefully defined and formally agreed to at the ILO today in light of modern thinking in economics and of the accumulated experience of developmental and labour issues to date, and with the clear understanding that we are

not just passing resolutions but that serious consequences may follow for the signatory nations. The ILO is clearly the institution that is best equipped to create such a consensus, not the GATT/WTO, just as multilateral trade negotiations are conducted at the GATT, not at the ILO. (1998, 264)

His argument betrays a convenient naïveté about the social creation of knowledge. But Bhagwati does point out an important issue: rights are created, not discovered. Rights exist only when they are embodied in laws that can be enforced by courts.

There are orthodox economists who argue for labor standards. According to Dani Rodrik, there is "genuine discomfort . . . with the moral and social implications of trade." As evidence he points to the fact that members of Congress who cosponsored the Child Labor Deterrence Act were predominantly from districts with low numbers of high school dropouts. In other words, their interest in the bill stemmed primarily from the moral not the economic interests of their constituents. Rodrik believes that this demonstrates a prevailing norm under which it is "not acceptable to reduce the living standards of American workers by taking advantage of labor practices that are vastly below those enshrined in U.S. standards" (Rodrik 1997, 34).

The governing concept here is "blocked exchange." The Fair Labor Standards Act and the Occupational Safety and Health Act are both justified by the doctrine of blocked or "desperate" exchange, under which a market transaction will be prohibited even if the two parties agree to it, when bargaining power is wildly unequal. If someone puts a gun to my head and asks for money I may give him my wallet. A starving person may agree to sell herself into slavery. In each case, both parties have an interest in completing the transaction, but this hardly legitimates it. The Supreme Court, in the 1937 *West Coast Hotel v. Parrish* case, recognized that this concept is particularly applicable to labor markets. According to Rodrik, "U.S. laws since the 1930s have recognized that restrictions on 'free' contracts are legitimate in the case of unequal bargaining power. By generating an inequality in bargaining power globalization helps undermine 60 years of labor legislation and thus the social understanding those laws represent" (1997, 36).

These legal and normative concepts stand uneasily in the broad corpus of contemporary mainstream academic economics in the United States. But they are consistent with the Institutional labor economics of John R. Commons, and with the approach to labor problems taken historically by the International Labor Organization. Before considering the contemporary international organization of labor rights in more detail we turn to a brief consideration of the applicability of Commons's work to international labor problems.

Heterodox Economics and International Labor Standards

Heterodox economists see economic activity as inherently a group phenomenon. Individuals are engaged in a variety of groups (households, firms, unions, states), which engage in ongoing coordinated activity. Disorder, not natural harmony, is presumed to result from self-interested individuals' desire to capture for themselves a greater share of the benefits generated by the concern's collective undertaking and to reduce the share of the collective burden they individually bear. Orderly conduct is produced not by the invisible hand of the market (or of God) but, if produced at all, by rules (both legal and customary) establishing what individuals can, must, or may do, or not do. Ultimately these rules must be enforced by moral, economic, or physical sanctions.

To ensure individual compliance with the governing rules in the event it is not forthcoming willingly, every concern must have an authoritative figure, someone who is empowered to make final decisions within the concern and who has sufficient control over sanctions to obtain individual obedience to those decisions. Coercion is the dominant principle underlying activity within going concerns, and organized compulsion is a much more important source of order than orthodox economics or political liberalism admits.

Yet, despite the underlying coercive structure, "required" behavior is generally experienced as forthcoming voluntarily. Mental habits derive from the routines and practices (working rules) structuring our activities, and in institutional thought it is assumed that individual wills quickly or slowly adjust to the patterns implicit in working rules. That is, what working rules in fact require us to do comes to be seen as right or natural and is typically experienced as voluntary activity. Thus institutions, and their cultural hegemony, are where we look to "explain" the content of individual activity.

The authoritative figure adjudicates disputes and determines what the controlling rules are to be in the case of conflict. Institutional adjustment by authoritative figures, not the so-called price mechanism, is presumed to be the means of correlating the activities of economic agents. In selecting a particular rule the authoritative figure necessarily endorses one set of envisioned future consequences as superior to another. This means that human values as to what should count most—that is, ethics—are necessarily woven into the very fabric of a concern's working rules.

Rules will generally be adhered to only if there are sanctions applied to violators. Of the three principal sanctions, social disapproval, economic privation, and physical force, the latter provides the most powerful inducement. Accordingly, the party able to command superior force—in the present setting, the sovereign figure of the going concern we call the nation—has the power, outside of warfare between nations, to determine the working rules that must be adhered to under its dominion. Believing there is no such thing as the public interest but only private interests, Commons used the term *public purpose* in regard to a private purpose, arising out of private interests, approved of by the authoritative figure or sovereign.[5]

Commons coined the term *theory of reasonable value* in reference to the specific underpinnings of the American market system. He settled on this term because his research in economic and legal history led him to believe that "reasonableness" had been the dominant purpose guiding the process of authoritative dispute resolution through which English common law judges, and later the U.S. Supreme Court justices, had crafted the system of working rules structuring the price bargain, the wage bargain, and the rent bargain in the American economy of his day. By focusing on reasonableness, Commons inferred that the courts had indicated a preoccupation, first, with maintaining order and, second, with ensuring that in light of all known facts the adopted rules were as "fair to all parties concerned" as possible. In other words, Commons argued that "fairness" was a primary purpose toward whose realization the American market system had been instituted. Accordingly, by deciding that a particular working rule was reasonable and hence should be adopted, common law judges and courts had consecutively indicated a belief that market prices resulting from adherence to it would consequently be "fair" or "just" ones. As a result, Commons inferred that fairness was intended to characterize price, wage, and rent bargains. Hence he used *reasonable value* as a descriptive term in reference to market outcomes in the American economy.

The issue of what fairness entails is a deep one. Commons discerned that in the minds of justices deciding disputes over the many centuries during which the market system was gradually instituted, the word *fair* generally meant little more than "customary." Of course, disputes invariably require judges to assess tradeoffs between various established practices and the various "good" consequences they facilitate. In assessing such tradeoffs, Commons insisted, the class bias of judges, who have overwhelmingly come out of the propertied classes, has inevitably colored their judgment. Deeply committed to the idea that all humans have the citizenship potential to participate as equals in their own governance, Commons equated social progress with the expansion of the realm of representative democracy. Accordingly, Commons envisioned a future in which working-rule adjustments affecting price, wage, and rent bargains would emanate from a collective will that equally accommodates or synthesizes the conflicting private interests typical of all classes of citizens within the organization and nation. In other words, the operative meaning of *fair* should be "agreed to without coercion by all affected parties."

Thus a regime of truly reasonable market values presumes working rules that are fair in the sense that they have been agreed to without coercion by the most directly affected parties. This, of course, is precisely what is approximated by collective bargaining between a corporation and a union representing its workers. However, Commons gradually lost faith that unions could successfully organize a majority of the workforce and helped in Wisconsin to institute a quasi-corporatist statist solution to the problem. That solution was the Wisconsin Industrial Commission, established in 1911 to oversee the evolution of working rules affecting the real wage (this includes working conditions) obtained by industrial workers in Wisconsin. Viewing the Wisconsin experiment as successful, Commons proposed that the "fourth branch of government," the regulatory commission, could be similarly utilized to oversee the evolution of labor market working rules at the national level as well.

According to Commons, a regulatory commission will be able to work out truly reasonable compromises to the disputes brought before it, and thereby contribute to the production of truly reasonable market values, only if it consists of an equal number of self-selected members from the two principal opposing interests, ones who actually understand the tradeoffs involved from inside the class mentality, who in turn would be required to agree on one or more additional members who would serve as tiebreakers. To put the issue another way, no members should be appointed to represent the strictly hypothetical public interest. Needless to say, this makes Commons's proposal significantly different from the course actually chosen in the United States, even during the heyday of the New Deal.

As I argued in chapter 2, Institutionalists share with Marxists the view that competitive labor markets are plagued by "destructive competition." When there is some degree of redundancy in labor supply, competition among workers drives all toward the lowest common denominator, toward the standards of the "least conscientious" employers. Where international trade is concerned, a labor supply premised on "offer prices" tied to vastly different prevailing standards of living reinforces this downward tendency.

In the framework presented in chapter 3, it is the extension of the gap between the customer and the actual worker that tends to drive down standards. With the advent of the world market, or what Commons called the wholesale speculative stage, the producer becomes completely subordinated to the consumer, and destructive competition is generalized. Now there are three price bargains: first, between the customer and the retail merchant; second, between the retailer and the capitalist merchant organizing the distribution of a specific product; and third, between the capitalists' manufacturing firms who can only obtain a profit margin by means of sweating the worker or cheapening work. With this stage, the capitalist merchant takes on the role of the wholesale merchant but adds the function of maintaining stock in anticipation of orders from retailers. To acquire and maintain that stock, the capitalist merchant negotiates the first price in the chain, a supply price from the manufacturer who, being compelled to compete vigorously with other manufacturers, can raise its profit level only by finding ways to reduce the costs of producing the agreed-upon output, primarily by specializing in reducing the cost of its labor input per unit of output. Subsequently, the capitalist merchant negotiates a price bargain with a retail merchant but must bear the risk of being stuck with stock that cannot be sold at a price allowing for recovery of the previously negotiated price with the manufacturer and also the other necessary costs of doing business. The retail merchant, of course, is limited in his bargaining with the wholesaler by the knowledge that the consumer is ultimately the controlling party in the price bargain between the consumer and the retailer.

What is significant here is that the manufacturer profits by driving the wage bargain below that limit. That is, the manufacturer profits by advancing the process of destructive competition. Competition between producers requires that all adopt the same methods or be driven out of business.

If labor is allowed to compete "freely," that is, without restrictions, destructive competition—the gradual spread throughout the labor market of the least costly practices—is the inherent tendency if there is redundant labor. It is the role of labor standards to prevent that downward spiral and thereby to preserve socially acceptable labor market outcomes.

Equally important, at the bottom of the labor market—and, to a lesser extent at higher levels, especially in regard to working conditions—improvement of the worker's situation occurs through a raising of those standards, by "raising the plane of competition." The regulatory commission, as conceived by Commons, provides a governance structure through which destructive competition can be avoided and the plane of competition—and thereby attainments—in the labor market can be raised. Equally important, its composition allows workers, understood as citizens of their concerns with equal rights of self-determination rather than as owners offering a commodity (themselves) for sale, to participate as equals in the process of determining which working rules, that is, which labor standards are at any given time considering the trade-offs involved, the best ones attainable. In this way a reasonable compromise between the divergent interests of the employer for higher profits and the worker for higher wages and better working conditions can be worked out and objectified in the adopted working rules. And the market values resulting from adherence to those rules will truly be reasonable ones—as good as practicable for now.

The Commons branch of Institutional thought has the most developed notion of the determination of reasonable value under conditions prevailing in the capitalist world economy of the twenty-first century. It can stand accused of underestimating the differences between labor markets on the one hand and commodity, property, and financial markets on the other. Despite Commons's realism about the class background of judges, he and his followers may be excessively optimistic about the ability of law and regulation alone to moderate the excesses of capitalism (see chap. 2, this vol.). But more than any other tendency in political economy, Institutional thought provides a way to think about the international organization of worker rights.

International Organization of Worker Rights

The increased international integration of the last several decades has lengthened the bargaining chain between producers and consumers. Moreover, it has weakened the effectiveness of national systems of labor regulation. In this section I examine the extent to which the International Labor Organization might act as an authoritative institution for global bargaining chains.

My point is not to show that, in each and every instance, the ILO fits (or does not fit) the Institutional framework. Such an exercise would be both endless and pointless. Rather, I will show, based on documentary analysis and interviews conducted at ILO headquarters in Geneva, that in its chief purposes and overall organization, the ILO is consistent with the Institutional standpoint, the theory of reasonable value, and analysis of labor markets. In the closing section I examine some of the implications of this consistency.

The initial impetus for international labor legislation and an international labor organization came as a response to the perceived human costs of the industrial revolution. Its prime movers were intellectual elements of the nine-teenth-century middle class: industrial managers, politicians, public health physicians, utopian socialists, and reform economists. Three goals drove these groups: humanitarian concerns, desire for social peace, and the desire to counter destructive competition.[6]

These three motivations were reflected in the 1919 preamble to the ILO's constitution, in the 1944 Philadelphia Declaration that spelled out the organi-zation's goals for the post–World War II period, and in the ILO's current pro-grams promoting core labor standards. While the prevention of destructive competition is the most clearly consonant with the Institutional standpoint, the notion that "universal and lasting peace can be established only if it is based upon social justice" is also at the heart of Institutional thought (ILO 1919, pre-amble).

In the Philadelphia Declaration, the ILO reaffirmed and extended these concerns as its primary motivations:

> Labour is not a commodity.
> Poverty anywhere constitutes a danger to prosperity anywhere.
> All human beings . . . have the right to pursue both their material well-being and their spiritual development in conditions of freedom and dignity, of eco-nomic security and equal opportunity.
> Freedom of expression and association are essential to sustained progress.
> (ILO 1944)

The declaration goes on to enumerate conditions concerning wages, hours, em-ployment, working conditions, and other particular matters that it seeks to achieve. But these goals are all meant to be the concrete embodiment of the concerns listed here.

The third and fourth goals require some comment. By mentioning spiritual development, the ILO creates a larger conception of human activity than is common in economics. However, this is perfectly consistent with the view, widely held by many heterodox economists, that material abundance and leisure time are means to more fundamental human goals. Marx's famous line in the *German Ideology* about wanting "to hunt in the morning, fish in the af-ternoon, rear cattle in the evening, criticize after dinner, just as I have a mind, without ever becoming hunter, fisherman, shepherd, or critic" cannot simply be dismissed as a concern of the early "humanist" Marx, because interest in time runs through both his mature political economy and political writings. And while in his later work Commons called these goals "independence" and "responsibility," it is also the case that there was a significant element of Christian socialism and social gospel in the foundations of Commons's thought (Ramstad 2001).

The emphasis placed on freedom of expression and association, which clearly remain the most important of the ILO's core labor rights, is also central to heterodoxy.[7] Commons saw the regulatory commission as the preferred instrument for settling disputes over working rules that were sure to occur within the evolutionary process of social change. Without freedom of expression and association, this primary body for adjudicating disputes could not exist, at least in the way that Commons envisioned it.

These principles and practices continue to guide the ILO today in responding to the increasing international integration of our own period. In fact, in answering the question why international labor standards are needed today, the ILO's Web site starts with the statement on destructive competition from the preamble to its constitution: "The failure of any nation to adopt humane conditions of labour is an obstacle in the way of other nations which desire to improve the conditions in their own countries" (ILO 1919).

In the 1997 report, "The ILO, Standards Setting and Globalization," the then director general wrote, "This liberalization of trade carries the risk, as the Preamble to the Constitution of the ILO warns us, that international competition, by inhibiting the will of certain members to introduce progress, might be 'an obstacle in the way of other nations which desire to improve the conditions of their own countries'" (ILO 1997). This and other recent documents restate the priority given to social justice and commit the ILO to work with member states to strive for it in the new economic conditions.[8]

The designation of certain conditions as "core labor rights" by the ILO was as much a political and rhetorical as it was a philosophical or political economic choice.[9] In the 1990s it was thought necessary to designate certain rights as core rights in order to simplify the ILO's message. The *Declaration on Fundamental Principles and Rights at Work* chooses selectively from the myriad ILO standards just a few things that are now constituted as "rights." This choice was more or less arbitrary and conjunctural, designed to please what ILO and International Confederation of Free Trade Union (ICFTU) staff thought would be the chief consumers of rights rhetoric.

As argued in the previous chapter, while rights must appear to be natural to be widely accepted, they are always produced and not discovered. What is accepted as a "right" is influenced, and in turn influences, existing structures of class, culture, and power.

The rights chosen as core had two goals:

1. To appeal to liberal, Christian socialist, and social democratic concerns, these being the most important constituencies of the ILO around the world.
2. To be principles that were nearly as universal as possible, not connected to per capita incomes; already ratified by many countries; and enabling, that is, they would open the way for other things. Thus a minimum wage did not qualify, and it was thought better to go for collective bargaining and freedom of association than health and safety as the former could produce the latter.

Based on initial work done at the International Confederation of Free Trade Unions in Brussels, the ILO settled on freedom of association and the right to collective bargaining, the elimination of forced and compulsory labor, the abolition of child labor, and the elimination of discrimination in the workplace as "Fundamental Principles and Rights at Work." Having been chosen as "rights" these conditions have begun to take on a life of their own, as scholars debate whether corporate, trade association, or multiparty-negotiated codes of conduct for multinational corporations are more likely to incorporate "core labor rights," without asking the basis upon which these are the most appropriate "rights," or what it means to talk about workers having "rights" in any case.

Is the ILO then an authoritative figure in the Commons sense? It falls short on several counts. First, despite its explicit commitment to tripartism, national delegations are made up of two government representatives and one each from labor and capital. Thus the "public interest" has more weight than Commons would have given it. This is particularly the case as many poor countries sometimes find it hard to send full delegations. If public representatives are simply two more votes for the interests of capital, in what sense can tripartism really be thought to function?

The evidence here is unclear. It appears to be the case that the nongovernmental groups maintain strong separate identities because they are effectively organized by the International Confederation of Free Trade Unions and the International Organization of Employers. The employer group has been concerned with the feasibility of standards and has often desired to slow down standard setting so as to update and consolidate the existing standards. The worker group has opposed this. The government group is less homogeneous and tends to be most influential when employers and workers are split.[10]

Second, the ILO has attempted to maintain itself as both a tripartite and universal institution. But tripartism is a European concept that evolved from the particular experience of Europe's industrialization. It may have little applicability outside Europe and the industrialized countries settled by Europeans. And indeed, Commons's own views of reasonable value were developed by a reading of Anglo-American legal history. Thus what might be reasonable for Europe, Australia, or the United States may be by no means reasonable elsewhere. The notion that the ILO's principles are applicable to "all people everywhere," as the Philadelphia Declaration states, simply looks past very real differences on what might constitute reasonableness.

The ILO has handled these contradictions in theory by considering social justice as a tendency and not a state. In practice, countries have been allowed some degree of flexibility in adopting conventions. Regional standards were rejected as "sub-standards for sub-humans" (Ghebali 1989, 205). States can define the obligations of the limits they will assume within the confines of a convention. Flexibility is also sometimes achieved through general wording such as *appropriate, adequate,* or *promote.* Flexibility has not been granted in the conventions dealing with core human rights or in those instruments dealing with unfair international competition, however.

The industrialized market economies see themselves as guardians of the ILO's conscience, and their employer and worker groups are clearly influenced by Western concepts of freedom. Upon joining the ILO after World War II, the postcolonial countries argued that underdevelopment hampered the implementation of standards. For instance, freedom of association might cause expensive social unrest and political agitation. At the 1984 conference the developing countries renewed this argument, and called for looking at the structural rather than the formal causes of failure to abide by conventions. This led the annual conference to move toward allowing for the heterogeneity of its member states during the formulation rather than in the enforcement of labor standards.

These differences reflect a wider split over what constitutes rights. As argued in the previous chapter, Western countries, and particularly the United States, have been most apt to recognize so-called first-generation rights, the civil rights of the individual. Developing countries and European social democrats have tended to emphasize second-generation rights, that is, economic and social rights (Meyer 1998, chap. 1). For the ILO, as for Commons, this tension is resolved by emphasizing what we might call process rights. The rules by which the social product is produced are privileged over questions concerning ownership and distribution.[11]

Third, the process by which standards are enforced does not involve economic sanctions or the threat of violence, which is ultimately necessary for an authoritative institution. Employer or worker groups can make presentations against governments that result in moral sanctions. Most governments tend to cooperate and adopt reforms before the formal complaint process is completed, so apparently the procedure has some impact. But there is also reason to believe that many complaints are not formally brought forward, because worker organizations don't want to deter states from ratifying additional conventions, or because they do not want to embarrass friendly governments.[12]

In its core values and organizational structure, the ILO is consistent with Commons's standpoint and indeed much closer to that standpoint than any other international organization. However, it does not incorporate the full range of viewpoints necessary to succeed as a Commons-type regulatory commission, its proclaimed universality flies in the face of the presumption that core values are worked out over time through a process of judicial review, and it lacks necessary enforcement capabilities.

The ILO does present an organizational form and an attitude to social justice that might let it evolve into the kind of body necessary to regulate the increasingly long chains of bargaining in the international economy. In the following chapters I argue that the adoption of core conventions by the United States and the growth and development of labor-based nongovernmental organizations that create a desire for global justice would complement the work of the ILO. Having surveyed the institution's strengths and weaknesses here, I conclude with an evaluation of its orientation in economics and why this matters for policy.

The ILO and Reasonable Value

Contrary to Bhagwati, I do not believe the ILO would benefit much from "modern thinking in economics." Such thinking, in its purely neoclassical version, is directly contradictory to both the ILO's core values and its organizational framework. It is also deeply embedded in the other major international economic organizations, the World Bank, and especially the International Monetary Fund, organizations that directly undermine the ILO's mission in many developing countries.[13]

To see the first point clearly, consider table 3. If by "modern economic thinking" Bhagwati means neoclassicism, he might as well ask the ILO to close up shop. If, on the other hand, he means the "new information economics" or "new institutional economics" then he would have the ILO adopt an analytical framework that, at its best, has rediscovered some of Commons's insights by using neoclassical assumptions and even then is inconsistent with the economics of the other major international organizations. I investigated the strengths and weaknesses of the new institutional economics in chapter 2. But there is no question that this approach, if adopted, by the *other* multilateral institutions, can inject new life into the ILO's vision of the world economy, as opposed to those of the Bank and the Fund. This is seen most clearly in the writings and career of Joseph Stiglitz, who was fired from his position as chief economist at the Bank for questioning the conventional wisdom (Wade 2001). Stiglitz has identified an absence of attention to the connection between collective worker organization and democracy as one of the many blind spots of the Washington Consensus (2000).

In his dissent to the Meltzer commission report on reforming the international financial institutions in the wake of the global financial panic of the late 1990s, Jerome Levinson makes it clear that the World Bank and the International Monetary Fund have been actively involved in undermining the social norms behind worker rights in the recent past (2000). The World Bank recently published a widely noted report which some interpreted as passing positive judgment on the role of freedom of association and collective bargaining, thus drawing the Bank closer to the ILO position (Aidt and Tzannatos 2002). The Bank and the ILO also cooperate in a number of countries on poverty-reduction programs. The Bank has some enforcement ability in that it can choose to withhold loans. Are the World Bank and the ILO moving toward an accommo-

TABLE 3. Comparing Neoclassical and Institutional Theories

	Neoclassical Orthodoxy	Institutional Thought/ILO
Purpose of economy	Maximize individual utility	Secure economic and moral security
Price	Automatically determined by market forces	Instituted
Markets	Produce optimality and social harmony	Site of authorized practices transferring ownership, and conflict over those practices
Labor markets	Like other markets; some possibility of market failure	Prone to destructive competition
Ethics/ economics	Separate matters	Inevitably intertwined

dation that would effectively link labor and development even without a labor rights clause in trade agreements?

The ILO and the Bank have very different institutional histories, cultures, and missions. This does not mean that they cannot work together in particular cases to change the dialogue about labor rights and standards. But such cooperative ventures are likely to involve a series of institutional compromises that have different meanings to the two organizations.[14]

In designing its study of collective bargaining the Bank claimed to be "analyzing the effects" of freedom of association and collective bargaining "in order to form an opinion," a clear signal that the Bank's intellectual culture, its thought-world, is utilitarian. It also claimed that incorporating core labor rights into its decision making might insert a political dimension that is a violation of the Bank's charter (Levinson 2000). The Bank regularly encourages loan recipients to increase "labor market flexibility" and ignores the fact that this is a *political* directive, in that increased flexibility makes it easier for firms to fire workers and makes it harder for unions to negotiate on behalf of their members.

The ILO's culture is eclectically institutional, while the IMF and World Bank's is primarily neoclassical. Of course it would be foolish to reduce any of these organizations or indeed any of the people who work there to a tightly defined ideological position. Nonetheless, because each organization produces knowledges and texts that function primarily within a particular intellectual tradition or thought-world, these institutions literally mean different things even if they might sometimes agree that collective bargaining and freedom of association are positives. Walking through the buildings of these organizations or reading their most important texts, one is struck by the different feel and ethos that professionals in these organizations bring to their work.[15]

I am only concerned with establishing these differences here. In the 1990s the ILO tried to simplify its complex set of labor standards by identifying core rights out of the almost two hundred conventions that have been signed. These rights were meant to be principles that were as nearly universal as possible, not connected to income per capita; highly ratified; and enabling, that is, they would open the way for other improvements. The set of rights that eventually emerged was a political compromise designed to appeal to liberals, social democrats, and Christian democrats alike.

This eclecticism in the pursuit of core values extends to the economic arguments that ILO economists make. Thus ILO economists are perfectly comfortable saying things like "Freedom of association makes the economy more efficient" or "Collective bargaining is good because it is more flexible than legal remedies, an important advantage in an era of globalization," statements that use language that appeals to economic orthodoxy. But they begin by assuming that interests are socially constructed, that all markets are regulated, it is just a matter of how and by whom, and that it is obvious that organizations like the WTO and World Bank are as much about power as they are about economy.

This is not how World Bank economists talk. While some in the labor movement were gratified to read that the Bank had officially stated that trade unions weren't *necessarily* bad, a close reading of the report leads to a less benign conclusion. While there are statements such as "accepting that workers should have a fair share of the benefits associated with economic growth without being penalized for crises for which they are not responsible is not just another view of looking at globalization; it is the very essence of humanity" this is not the report's overall message. Instead of looking at unionization in the context of social justice, stability, peace, and combatting destructive competition, the Bank study simply reviews the literature on whether unions improve the "economic welfare" of individual workers and the profitability of firms, and the impact of union density on standard measures of macroeconomic stability. Because it is so difficult to build a consistent argument in favor of or against anything with this kind of research strategy, the authors of the study again and again state that the answers to their questions are "context specific." In the end, they cannot reject the null hypothesis that collective bargaining and freedom of association are positives in a global environment (Aidt and Tzannatos 2002).

The Bank's report does lack the immense hubris of many econometric forays. But it is rather sad relative to the broad and socially committed political economic analysis I was able to cull from my Geneva interviews. ILO economists have a strong and practical grasp of the situation on the ground in the developing world through the organization's technical assistance work. Combined with the clear commitment to tripartism and its social justice mission, this makes strengthening the ILO as much of a priority as democratizing the other multilateral institutions, which to this point has been the focus of the most prominent critics of contemporary globalization.

Beverly Silver (2003) has demonstrated that while capital mobility disorganizes working classes in the older regions it also tends to create collective worker power in places to which capital flows. Silver shows that in every case but one (Japan) the movement of the automobile companies to greenfield sites, first in Europe, then in Europe's periphery, and finally in "newly industrializing countries" such as South Africa, Argentina, and Korea, has led to a typical cycle of unrest, class formation, and resistance.

Growing strength for some collective worker-based organizations in some of the newly industrialized countries stemmed not just from the changing geographical patterns of capital accumulation but also, especially in Africa, as a legacy of the last years of colonialism, when new laws allowed for the formation of nonpolitical unions. Politics (rather than collective bargaining) became the source of trade union strength in many developing countries. But independence removed the right of appeal to colonial authority, while neoliberalism has disempowered the political friends of labor. The vibrancy of the labor movement at times in South Africa, parts of Latin America, or South Korea may be real, but for ILO economists, trade unionism does need a new political base in the developing world, to say nothing of North America. The unevenness with which such a base is developing across the regions in the early twenty-first century is particularly striking. As I will argue in chapter 7, nongovernmental labor-based organizations working in the field and stimulating a global desire for social justice are a necessary corollary to the propagation and enforcement of core labor rights.

If worker rights are to be more fully a part of the development discussion, building alliances with the other multilateral organizations is sensible for the ILO. It makes no sense for the World Bank to sponsor health education programs without also paying attention to the adequacy of employment, yet this happens. In the poor countries, the ILO generally interacts with the labor ministry, which tends to be weak, whereas World Bank/IMF rhetoric tends to be influential with the relatively stronger finance ministries; this explains the labor standards course that the ILO now runs regularly for officials of the Bretton Woods institutions. The World Bank and IMF now have an active dialogue with trade unions, and the Bank's president in 2006, Paul Wolfowitz, declared that all infrastructure projects financed by the Bank must meet core labor standards. Yet in the same year the ICFTU felt it necessary to publish *Fighting for Alternatives: Cases of Successful Resistance to the Policies of the IMF and the World Bank.* As I argue in the next chapters, there are reasons to be hopeful that a rhetoric of labor standards could become part of normal Washington discourse. But it will not be easy, and will require much translation across moral and scientific discourses.

The founders of the Bretton Woods institutions, John Maynard Keynes and Harry Dexter White, clearly saw the protection of labor's interests as a *precondition* for liberalizing trade and finance (Helleiner 1994). Indeed, the original charter for the International Trade Organization had an entire chapter devoted to labor standards and trade.

This was not the case during the days of the Washington Consensus.

Stiglitz, former Bank chief economist, wrote that "when labor issues came up at the Bank they did so mainly within a narrowly economic focus and even more narrowly through the lens of neoclassical economics; a standard message was to increase labor market flexibility—the not so subtle sub-text was to lower wages" (2000, 1).

In any institutionally and historically informed view, a "system" of employment relations is more than a process of achieving optimum efficiency in the narrow sense in which economists usually use that term. Rather, it is the result of a long history of social conflict in which political, natural, and cultural factors interact with a *variety* of economic considerations, including but not only efficiency. Social relations in the workplace are best seen as an integral component of the social compact and should not be treated as if they are the result of a blackboard-engineering problem.

For instance, just a bit of historical sensitivity might have alerted IMF and World Bank economists to the possibility that market liberalization and privatization of state assets in the 1990s would lead to social distress. Since a strong labor movement is often at the forefront of movements for social justice, Stiglitz now argues that liberalization and privatization might wisely have been accompanied by strengthening of unions and other labor market institutions (Stiglitz 2000). Stiglitz was fired for this and other violations of Washington's economic orthodoxy (Wade 2001).[16]

National and International Labor Standards

In both the World Trade Organization and Free Trade Area of the Americas negotiations, U.S. negotiators have argued for stronger action on labor rights, but they have not made this a priority. Yet Congress has already legislated that recipient countries must effectively assure core worker rights. In 1995 Congress passed the Sanders-Frank amendment, requiring the Treasury to direct U.S. representatives to these institutions to use their "voice and vote" to encourage both the institutions and borrowing countries to respect core worker rights as an integral part of their structural adjustment programs. In approving the U.S. quota increase for the IMF in 1998, Congress added the requirement that worker rights not be undermined by Fund or Bank mandates for "labor market flexibility."

Though the will of Congress is clear, these policies have never been implemented. The U.S. representatives to the Fund and the Bank have *never* voted against financing governments that are notorious abusers of core labor rights.

One problem is that the Treasury guides policy in this area and assisting the security and mobility of capital has been central to the Treasury's mission since the late 1960s (Helleiner 1994).

Jerome Levinson has developed concrete and creative proposals to strengthen the existing enforcement of labor rights by the U.S. government. In the next chapter I argue for the Senate considering and ratifying the ILO conventions on freedom of association and collective bargaining. Levinson has produced a series of compatible and practical suggestions at agency level such as giving the Labor Department a greater role in certifying labor policies under Sanders-Frank, allowing nongovernmental organizations to file Sanders-Frank petitions, and using ILO documents in findings. He also argues for amending the WTO charter to include core labor rights.

The use of ILO materials in findings of U.S. law would be helpful in promoting the ILO as an *authoritative figure*. The ILO, because of tripartism, is a preferred format for designing working rules for international labor rights. The ILO is the only international organization that is tripartite, even if its practice is not as strong as its principle. The promotion of the ILO as an arbiter of authoritative and authorized practices would serve as a counterweight to the IMF and World Bank, which are likely to remain in an economically orthodox thought-world, and more closely tied to rentier interests than is the ILO, for the foreseeable future. The ILO as a "regulatory commission for international labor problems" is a sound idea.

The ILO could become and to some extent already is the place where the meaning of organizing concepts such as "reasonable" and "fair" can be debated and confronted with other such concepts. It should, in the view taken in this book, be promoted as an authoritative institution, particularly in dealing with labor aspects of international economic activity between countries at markedly different social and economic characteristics.

Levinson's suggestion that nongovernmental organizations should be able to petition under Sanders-Frank is also a good one. This builds on experience with the North American Agreement on Labor Cooperation. Upholding a slightly broader definition of core labor rights than the ILO, NAALC and its commissions and offices have been a modest success. It has promoted a variety of cooperative activities for scholars and the social partners, which has aided cross-border solidarity in the region. It has taken and heard cases that have promoted transparency in labor law administration in all countries. Not only has NAALC helped to strengthen Mexico's enforcement of its own labor laws in some cases, it has given labor organizers another avenue to highlight declining human and labor rights in the United States. This is not to say that NAALC or the EU's social clause can substitute for other forms of international labor regulation. But the sunshine effect of these cases certainly contributes to rising public awareness and debate, and ultimately to organizing and political pressure. And by providing more examples of the possible, such cases may provide a rich pool of examples for dealing with international labor disputes in a world of uneven economic development.

Strengthening the ILO as an authoritative international institution while broadening access to decision making in regional agreements are appropriate responses to the unevenness of the development of capitalism over the last several decades. Economic life has become both globalized *and* regionalized. Globalization has not eliminated all differences between national systems, and even in Europe some form of supranational regulation is necessary. This is all the more applicable to North America and especially to FTAA should it be revived, to say nothing of the overwhelmingly difficult problem of producing agreement on reasonable value across the countries making up the WTO.

Ultimately, through the promotion of the ILO as an authoritative institution on international labor problems, the Bretton Woods institutions and the WTO may come to accept some version of ILO core labor rights into their charters. In the Philadelphia Declaration, the ILO stated that all international economic policies should be judged in terms of their impact on the right of all human beings "to pursue both their material well-being and their spiritual development in conditions of freedom and dignity."

This language is unlikely to be adopted generally without a consistent and strong popular voice pressing for change. The Commons-type regulatory commission, which the ILO resembles at the international level, may be a useful idea, but it requires a particular international political climate and a particular balance of class interests to have the chance to be effective. If U.S. international economic policy is often driven by a desire to reduce labor cost, and if the ILO lacks enforcement power precisely because it was designed to be powerless, then there is little point to the moderately reformist agenda suggested here. I investigate recent prevailing attitudes in the U.S. Congress and executive branch toward worker rights in the next chapter and the development of new grassroots organizations, or international labor-based NGOs, in the chapter that follows.

CHAPTER 6

The United States and Core Worker Rights:
Freedom of Association and Collective Bargaining

On the same day that President Clinton failed to persuade the Seattle World Trade Organization (WTO) meeting to approve a panel on worker rights and labor standards, he signed International Labor Organization (ILO) Convention No. 182 on the worst forms of child labor. It was only the thirteenth convention the United States had ratified and only the second of the eight so-called core conventions. One of Clinton's chief critics at Seattle was Egyptian trade minister Youssef Boutros-Ghali, who argued, "If you start using trade as a lever to implement non–trade related issues that will be the end of the multilateral trading system" (Greenhouse and Kahn 1999, A1). Egypt had ratified all the core conventions.[1]

By the time Clinton made his speech Seattle was under martial law. Here was the president of the United States calling for the WTO to study core rights such as freedom of assembly while leafletters were being beaten for handing out xeroxed copies of a *New York Times* article on the previous day's police riot (Cockburn, St. Clair, and Sekula 2000, 33). The most likely interpretation is that Clinton's intervention was designed to separate the labor protesters from environmentalists and self-consciously radical groups while shoring up support for Al Gore (Cockburn, St. Clair, and Sekula 2000; Sanger 1999).[2] The contradictions with the United States' own stance on ILO ratifications or with the Clinton administration's mostly uncritical embrace of globalization went not noted by the president.

A cavalier approach, studied indifference, and tortuous logic are common in U.S. treatment of international labor standards. Between joining the ILO in 1934 and the mid-1980s the United States ratified only seven ILO conventions, six of which dealt with maritime issues. Since the mid-1980s the United States has ratified seven more conventions including those dealing with the abolition of forced labor and the worst forms of child labor.

Ratification of ILO conventions alone does not guarantee the fair treatment of workers, nor does the lack of ratification mean that workers are being oppressed. A number of governments have ratified ILO conventions for show with no intention of enforcing them; others have ratified conventions in good faith but lack the resources or technical expertise to implement their requirements; and still others seem to believe they are in compliance but have standards that vary widely from international norms. On the other hand, there are nations that have not ratified conventions for one reason or another—usually constitutional constraints or other legal technicalities—but, in general, provide protections for worker rights.

The official position of the United States is that it is among this latter group: it has not ratified conventions due to legal constraints but generally complies with the broad purposes—if not the details—of nearly all ILO conventions. The reasons given for nonratification are mainly technical and legal and do not hold up to serious analysis.

The strength of employer interests is the obvious explanation for the failure of the United States to ratify the key conventions on freedom of association and collective bargaining. The prevalence of an individualist interpretation of rights in the United States is another. In this chapter I argue that these are not insuperable obstacles. My central argument is that U.S. international labor policy is contradictory in the following sense. Domestically, workers have few rights, and these are limited to a narrowly defined set of individual rights. Internationally, though, the U.S. government often projects an image of freedom and progress, and supporting certain worker rights is part of this image. What those rights are changes given the shifting nature of the U.S. international position. This contradiction at times creates the space for challenging and broadening the definition of rights both domestically and internationally.

I begin with a review of the early history of U.S. participation in the ILO from Gompers's role in its founding through the reconstitution of the ILO after World War II and the debates over the Bricker Amendment during the early Cold War. I then turn to the shift in the U.S. attitude toward ratifying conventions that took place during the Reagan administration. A consistent strain of thought, coming primarily from the State department, sees U.S. ratification as a key part of labor diplomacy. This has overcome, to some extent, the traditional legal objections of employer interests, represented especially by the U.S. Council for International Business. The ratifications since the 1980s have dealt with technical matters or issues consistent with an individualistic concept of labor rights as human rights. In the remaining sections I consider whether barriers to ratifying Conventions No. 87 and No. 98 on freedom of association and collective bargaining are primarily legal, ideological, or class interest based. While these barriers are real I argue they are not insuperable.

U.S. Ratification of ILO Conventions

The United States lags far behind other nations in ratifying ILO conventions. To date, the United States has ratified only 14 of the 184 conventions adopted by the ILO since its inception, and only 2 of the 8 core conventions.[3] Only 17 of the 175 ILO member nations have ratified fewer, and none are Western or industrialized.[4] The exact number of U.S. ratifications is shared only by the Solomon Islands, Equatorial Guinea, Sudan, and Thailand.

The eight core conventions concern "fundamental principles of human rights at work": the elimination of forced and compulsory labor, the elimination of employment discrimination, the abolition of child labor, and the freedom of association and right to bargain collectively (ILO 1998). Two conventions correspond to each of these areas. The United States has ratified only Conventions No. 105 and No. 182 concerning the abolition of forced labor and the abolition of the worst forms of child labor, respectively—with the former

TABLE 4. Core Conventions by Countries Ratifying to 2006

Core Conventions	Year of Adoption	Number of Countries Ratifying	Ratified by United States?
Elimination of forced and compulsory labor			
Convention 29	1930	161	No
Convention 105	1957	158	Yes
Elimination of employment discrimination			
Convention 100	1951	159	No
Convention 111	1958	156	No
Abolition of child labor			
Convention 138	1973	117	No
Convention 182	1999	127	Yes
Freedom of association and right to bargain collectively			
Convention 87	1948	141	No
Convention 98	1949	152	No

Note: Convention 105 was ratified by the United States on September 25, 1991, and Convention 182 on February 12, 1999.

ratified thirty-four years after its adoption. Table 4 displays information on the core conventions.

Table 5 displays information on the conventions that the United States *has* ratified. Five of the fourteen conventions were ratified on the same day—October 29, 1938—and concern maritime issues. In fact, until 1988, the United States ratified only one nonmaritime convention, a purely administrative matter (Convention No. 80) that switched the ILO's affiliation from the defunct League of Nations to the newly formed United Nations. The table also shows that no conventions were ratified between 1953 and 1988. There has been a spate of activity since 1988, but of the six conventions ratified since then half concern administrative or technical matters.[5] Therefore, outside of the maritime area, the United States has ratified only three substantive conventions: the recent mine safety convention (which affects a single industry) and the two core conventions mentioned earlier on forced labor and the worst forms of child labor.

In this chapter I examine U.S. reluctance to ratify ILO conventions focusing on the conventions concerning the freedom of association and right to bargain collectively: Conventions No. 87 and No. 98.[6] Both conventions were adopted by the ILO in the late 1940s, and while Convention No. 87 was recommended for ratification by the executive branch at that time and subsequently (U.S. Senate 1949; U.S. Department of Labor 1980), no legislative action has been taken on either.

The official position of the United States is that it has not ratified more con-

TABLE 5.   ILO Conventions Ratified by the United States (as of 2006)

Year of Adoption	Title	Date of US Ratification
1936	Officers' competency certificates	10/29/38
1936	Holidays with pay (sea)	10/29/38
1936	Shipowners' liability (sick and injured seamen)	10/29/38
1936	Hours of work and manning (sea)	10/29/38
1936	Minimum age (sea)	10/29/38
1946	Final articles of revision	6/24/48
1946	Certificate of able seamen	4/9/53
1976	Tripartite consultation (international labor standards)	6/15/88
1976	Merchant shipping (minimum standards)	6/15/88
1985	Labor statistics	6/11/90
1957	Abolition of forced labor	9/25/91
1978	Labor administration	3/3/95
1999	Worst forms of child labor	12/2/99
1995	Safety and health in mines	2/9/01

ventions due mainly to legal constraints, but that it generally complies with the broad purposes—if not the details—of nearly all ILO conventions (U.S. Senate 1985).[7] More specifically, the United States offers three principal reasons for not ratifying Conventions No. 87 or No. 98. First, our federal system, which reserves certain rights to the states, makes ratification problematic since the conventions would affect the employees of state, county, and municipal governments and others who fall outside the coverage of federal labor statutes.[8] Second, "well-established national labor policy" fulfills the broad purposes of the conventions and should not be upset to accommodate the wishes of an international agency. And, third, based on the recent *ILO Declaration on Fundamental Principles and Rights at Work* (ILO 1998), as well as long-standing ILO policy,[9] the United States has a responsibility based on its membership in the ILO—and regardless of whether it has ratified the conventions or not—to uphold the spirit of Conventions No. 87 and No. 98, making ratification largely superfluous (U.S. Senate 1985; U.S. Department of Labor 1997a; U.S. Department of Labor 1997b; ILO 2000).

I argue that the federal structure of the United States is problematic, but not an absolute bar to ratifying Conventions No. 87 and No. 98. I present evidence that the federal government has twice indicated that Convention No. 87 on freedom of association should be ratified (U.S. Senate 1949; U.S. Department of Labor 1980). Although it has not given an opinion concerning Convention No. 98 on the right to bargain collectively, I believe that most of the reasoning offered about Convention No. 87 would apply to Convention No. 98 as well.

Further, I question the assertions that U.S. policy is well-established and generally fulfills the purposes of the ILO conventions. First, I note that labor representatives, scholars, government officials, and even some employers have criticized U.S. labor policy in general and the National Labor Relations Act (NLRA) in particular (Friedman et al. 1994; U.S. Department of Labor 1994; U.S. House of Representatives 1999). Second, I provide evidence from ILO Committee on Freedom of Association (CFA) findings against the United States and comments from the International Confederation of Free Trade Unions (ICFTU), Human Rights Watch (HRW), and, indeed, the U.S. government itself under the follow-up provisions to the *ILO Declaration on Fundamental Principles and Rights at Work* that U.S. labor policy does *not* conform to international standards.

I recognize the limited impact of signing and ratifying such conventions. It is central to the argument of this chapter that concern for labor rights is generally driven by other matters, including national security concerns, and not the kinds of arguments made by economists and industrial relations scholars. But I also doubt that the supposed legal barrier to U.S. ratification of core conventions is as high as often believed and that in fact class interest is masquerading here as law. There is no reason to believe that the kinds of debates and struggles we have seen over worker rights in the last decade are about to disappear. A debate on the floor of the U.S. Senate over the ratification of the conventions on freedom of association and collective bargaining would be a highly teachable moment concerning the power of class interest and conventional thinking.

The United States and ILO Conventions to the Mid-1980s

The ILO was established under the Treaty of Versailles in 1919. At the time, and in light of the Bolshevik Revolution and social unrest elsewhere, the major powers believed that lasting peace required addressing serious labor problems. There had been several earlier attempts at developing international labor standards, particularly with regard to health and safety and women's employment, and the end of a world war seemed an appropriate time—with so many nations involved in the peace process—to revisit these issues. Support for creating some sort of international labor bureau was shared by the United States, which included AFL president Samuel Gompers in its Versailles delegation. In turn, Gompers was elected chairman of the committee that established the ILO, with Professor James Shotwell of Columbia University acting as a key adviser (Morse 1969, 3–34; Galenson 1980, 4; Lorenz 2001, 39–74; Miller 1936; Shotwell 1934, 127–198).

The United States was instrumental in establishing the ILO *and* in assuring that its constitution took into account the concerns of the United States and other federal states (Tayler 1935). After weeks of difficult negotiations, and against the wishes of several European delegates who sought a stronger body, the United States was successful in including language in Article 19 of the ILO constitution that reads:

> In the case of a Federal State, the power of which to enter into Conventions of labor matters is subject to limitations, it shall be in the discretion of the Government of such State to treat a draft convention to which such limitations apply as a recommendation only, and the provisions of this article with respect to recommendations shall apply in this case. (Tayler 1935, 62)

While this language satisfied those attending the peace talks, it did not appease isolationists at home, and the United States stayed out of the ILO until

1934. It took the Great Depression and New Deal to create the context for U.S. involvement, with members of the Roosevelt administration—particularly Labor Secretary Frances Perkins—pushing international labor standards to buttress the administration's domestic goals (Lorenz 2001, 98–101).

The congressional resolution supporting U.S. admission to the ILO states reads:

> Whereas special provision has been made in the Constitution of the International Labor Organization by which membership of the United States would not impose or be deemed to impose any obligation or agreement upon the United States to accept the proposals of that body as involving anything more than recommendations for its consideration. (Tayler 1935, 150)

In other words, the United States accepted membership in the ILO assuming that the "Federal State" proviso of the ILO's constitution would allow it to treat conventions as recommendations only, with no obligation to enact them into law.[10]

The United States was quite active at the ILO in the 1930s, quickly ratifying a series of maritime conventions. John Winant, the governor of New Hampshire, became ILO director-general, holding the post during the critical period of World War II (Lorenz 2001, 131–60). But after the war, and, moreover, after the creation of the United Nations (with which the ILO affiliated), problems with U.S. involvement resurfaced. Adding to the fears of those who thought that the UN would put the country on the road to world government were the Supreme Court's decision in *Oyama v. California* (332 U.S. 633, 1948) and the subsequent adoption of the UN Declaration of Human Rights. In *Oyama*, the Supreme Court overturned a California law (arising out of anti-Japanese hysteria) that prohibited land ownership by aliens. While the Court relied primarily on the Fourteenth Amendment for its decision, four justices also cited Articles 55 and 56 of the UN charter in voiding the law. Soon after *Oyama*, the UN Declaration on Human Rights was adopted, causing fear among conservatives that social and economic policies of the UN would, among other things, overturn segregation laws and interfere with property rights (Tananbaum 1988, 6).

Employer interests were particularly leery of the ILO, with its special responsibility for labor-management relations. The adoption of Conventions No. 87 and No. 98 by the ILO in the late 1940s, so soon after the passage of the Taft-Hartley Amendments, only increased their suspicion that the ILO could be used to undo U.S. labor law (Galenson 1980, 27; Lorenz 2001, 171). Taft-Hartley limited the legal tactics and effectively the geographic spread of trade unionism by outlawing secondary boycotts and allowing states to adopt "right-to-work" laws. Employer interests were particularly concerned—in light of *Oyama*—that portions of Taft-Hartley could be overruled if Conventions No. 87 and No. 98 were ratified. As a result, the newly appointed U.S. employer representative to the ILO, William McGrath, became one of its sharpest critics (Lorenz 2001, 167–73; Tananbaum 1988, 82–87).

During this same period, though, U.S. representatives to the conference on the Universal Declaration of Human Rights and U.S. officials in occupied Germany were *supporting* collective bargaining as the preferred solution to labor problems. In the Paris meetings on the Universal Declaration, "the struggles over the social and economic articles were mainly between representatives of liberal democracies such as the United States and the United Kingdom, who wanted to leave more room for individual initiative and collective bargaining, and delegates who thought the state should play a greater role in regulating wages and working conditions" (Glendon 2001, 156).

The postwar labor relations system in Germany was designed by the U.S. and British military governments. Wade Jacoby argues that the Allies did not simply impose an industrial relations system on Germany but did insist on a "functionally equivalent" model (e.g., one that stressed collective bargaining rather than political unionism).

The United States (particularly) wanted the unions to concentrate on wages, benefits, and working conditions, and tried to steer the Germans away from too much emphasis on economic democracy, which was much more important to the Germans. The Germans really wanted "social codetermination" at the national level, but what they ended up settling for was something less. As Jacoby writes:

> German labor envisioned it (social codetermination) as a step toward self-determination at all levels of the economy, capped by either socialization or corporatist economic management. . . . Under Allied influence, however, codetermination ultimately became an end in and of itself at the firm level. (2001, 71)

This was disappointing to the Germans, since works councils had existed before the Nazi period but had been largely neutralized by employers. The ultimate compromise was limited codetermination in basic industries (steel and coal) and work councils elsewhere. Thus the U.S. policy of arguing for *certain* worker rights internationally while circumscribing them domestically is a long-standing one.

Against the backdrop of 1950s anti-UN sentiment, Senator John Bricker, an

Ohio Republican, proposed a constitutional amendment that would have limited the executive branch's treaty-making power. About one dozen different versions of the Bricker Amendment were considered—some merely ruled out treaties that would expand the constitutional power of the federal government; others prohibited those that would take effect without enabling federal or state legislation. During hearings on the Bricker Amendment, the ILO came in for particularly harsh treatment, mainly from McGrath, who portrayed the organization as a tool of socialism largely at odds with the principles of the American people. To illustrate how truly nefarious the ILO was McGrath cited a convention that called for maternity benefits without regard for marital status (Tananbaum 1988, 84–85). No version of the Bricker Amendment passed, but its spirit guided and continues to guide U.S. policy concerning ILO conventions: no convention will be adopted that could upset existing state or federal law.

At the same time that the Bricker Amendment debates were raging, the Soviet Union rejoined the ILO. Bickering began immediately as the United States and its allies questioned the USSR's ability to send a tripartite delegation to the ILO conference (as required by the ILO constitution), since labor, management, and government delegates were all ultimately representing the Communist Party. Later, squabbles broke out concerning the position of Soviet bloc officials in the ILO governance structure and bureaucracy. As well, the United States complained that the Soviets and their allies used the annual conference to pillory the United States and Israel on Vietnam, the Israeli occupation of Jerusalem and the West Bank, and other apparently nonlabor issues. Finally, there was a general perception, based on ILO reports and articles in its official journal, *International Labour Review,* that the organization had become sympathetic to the Soviet bloc and hostile to the West. Relations ultimately deteriorated to the point of U.S. withdrawal in 1977 (Galenson 1980, 23–139; Kruglak 1980; Lorenz 2001, 189–217). Clearly, such an environment hindered the ratification of ILO conventions by the United States.

However, just two years after resigning, the United States rejoined, claiming that the ILO had corrected many of the problems that had led to American withdrawal. Whether the ILO had changed is debatable, but American posture toward it certainly had (Galenson 1980, 252–69). Prior to withdrawal, the United States had not taken its obligations seriously (U.S. General Accounting Office 1984, 16). American employers had been indifferent at best, and the AFL-CIO had become more concerned with developing its own international branch than with the ILO. For its part, the federal government had largely ceded its role to David Morse, the American who directed the organization for twenty years until his retirement in the early 1970s. But with reentry, the United States seemed to make a fresh start (Galenson 1980, 23–26).

A major move was the creation by President Carter of the President's Advisory Committee on the ILO, which is chaired by the Secretary of Labor and includes the secretaries of state and commerce as well as labor and business representatives. In turn, the Tri-Partite Advisory Panel on International Labor Standards (TAPILS) is chaired by the Solicitor of Labor and provides legal analysis to the President's Committee (U.S. General Accounting Office 1984, 16–26).[11] And while some may have predicted waning interest with the election of a Republican president, this was not the case.

The Hatch Hearings: A New Push for Convention Ratification

After ratifying no conventions for thirty-five years the United States has ratified seven conventions in the last two decades including two core conventions, No. 105, Abolition of Forced Labor, and No. 182, On the Worst Forms of Child Labor (www.ilo.org/ilolex). Particularly at the beginning of Ronald Reagan's second term, and with the strong urging of Secretary of State George Schultz, the United States, in fact, renewed its commitment to passing ILO conventions. However, Conventions No. 87 and No. 98 have received no attention.

The mid-1980s were a watershed period for the U.S. role in the ILO. Policy developed during that period continues to inform U.S. posture toward ILO conventions today. But at the time, it was the presence of the Soviet Union that largely shaped U.S. policy.

Momentum for new ratifications began with hearings by the Senate Labor and Human Resources Committee in September 1985. The first witness was then Secretary of State and former Secretary of both Labor and Treasury, George Schultz. Schultz was a key player in the 1970s and 1980s in the general shift toward neoliberalism in U.S. foreign and economic policy (Helleiner 1994, 106–19).

Unlike earlier Republican isolationists, the more internationally minded Schultz believed that the United States could not let the Soviet Union go unchallenged at the ILO, particularly in light of the Soviets' possible influence over developing nations where trade unionists often formed the core of nascent, postcolonial political movements. Rather, Schultz believed that the United States needed to be fully involved in Geneva, which required improving its ratification record at home. In congressional testimony and a subsequent State Department publication, Schultz stated:

Our leverage [in the ILO] is somewhat hampered by the fact that the United States has not improved its own record of ratification of ILO conventions over the past 30 years. Thus far, this has not proven to be a crucial impediment to achieving our goals in the ILO in any concretely verifiable way, but we believe it has taken a subtle toll. It has provided our adversaries with ready-made propaganda ammunition. It fosters attitudes on the part of third countries to equate U.S. actions and policies with those of our adversaries, and, ultimately, it is used to excuse decisions in the Committee on the Application of Conventions and Recommendations to go easy on the Soviets in individual cases under review.

He continued:

We are open to the frequent charge—and it comes not just from our adversaries—that our defense of the ILO machinery is hypocritical because we ratify no conventions and are, therefore, not subject to the machinery's operation to the same extent as others. It is also charged that because the United States does not ratify conventions we have no moral standing when urging the organization to take up the alleged transgressions of others. As a practical matter, because we have not ratified most ILO conventions we are disbarred by the ILO constitution from bringing complaints against those who violate their obligations.

In response to these charges we say that U.S. law and practice are in substantial compliance with ILO conventions . . . However, this approach conflicts with the obligations we assumed when we joined the ILO. The ILO's purpose is to raise labor standards around the globe through the process of adoption and ratifications of conventions. Every member state has a moral obligation to make a good faith effort to determine whether it can ratify conventions. But our behavior sends a message that the ILO procedures don't apply to us. The message we send is: do as we say, not as we do. (U.S. Senate 1985, 6–7)

Schultz argued that ratifications would be helpful in pressing an anti-Soviet agenda. In his view, the U.S. withdrawal had worked, and recent ILO judgments against Czechoslovakia and the USSR as well as a critical report on Poland showed that a chastened ILO was acting more "even handedly." The United States' leverage was still hampered, however, by our failure to ratify conventions: "It is my judgment that an improved ratification record would have served U.S. foreign policy interests better" (U.S. Senate 1985, 8). Although basic ILO principles are found in U.S. laws, Schultz believed that the United States was still vulnerable to criticism for not ratifying ILO conventions.

Here, four years before the collapse of the Berlin Wall, the bipolar view still dominated U.S. foreign policy, and labor standards were seen primarily as a foreign policy–national security and anti-Soviet issue. The differences between European, North American, and Asian capitalisms, already present of course, were suppressed by the cold war imagination. An exchange between committee chair Orrin Hatch and Schultz indicates just how completely the Soviet Union dominated thinking on this issue. According to Hatch (U.S. Senate 1985, 12):

> The ILO's own constitutution is predicated on the democratic and pluralistic principles of free enterprise. The Communist members, led by the Soviet bloc, have over the years engaged in a concerted effort to undermine the structure and the free enterprise objectives of the ILO. . . . Now your point is that the United States could more easily win the hearts and minds of these emerging nations and convince them of the viability of industrial democracy in free enterprise were the United States to embrace the work of the ILO, in particular a number of these conventions.

This is at best a selective reading of the ILO's purpose and history. The ILO's Constitution and its refounding Philadelphia statement are best seen as an expression of a worldview or thought-world in which collective rights and regulatory forums are necessary to make capitalism workable (see chap. 5, this vol.). The ILO, in its founding and its operation, owes as much to philosophical pragmatism, institutional economics, and Christian socialism as it does to a belief in "free enterprise." Hatch continues,

> Although we in the United States from a world opinion standpoint have very liberal labor laws and freedoms in this country, as you pointed out, we have not ratified a large number of these conventions. . . . But the Soviet Union has ratified a great number of these. I think it is fair to say that the Soviet Union's compliance with the Freedom of Association Conventions has left a great deal to be desired. (U.S. Senate 1985, 12)

Schultz responds,

> Of course, that is why, despite the fact that we have not ratified conventions, we have been able to be as effective as we are, namely because conditions in the workplace are superb compared with almost any place else that you want to look. The people are treated decently; they are relatively well paid, and so on. They have freedom of association and can form unions, and so forth. (U.S. Senate 1985, 12)

The year 1985 was more or less the high point of Reaganism, and many people were still in denial about the distributional effects of Reaganomics. Still, coming in the midst of a series of strikes in which, following the president's lead in the PATCO situation, permanent striker replacements were deployed regularly by American employers, this testimony has a bizarre flavor to it.[12]

Schultz does not present a brief for any particular conventions but argues instead for an open-minded policy that will allow us to ratify those conventions consistent with our legal arrangements and with consensus between the social partners. The logic is tortuous. We don't ratify these conventions but we live up to them. The Soviets ratify and don't live up to them. Can't we find some way around our legal problems so we can score points against the Soviets?

Much of the discussion during the hearings focused on the United States' poor ratification record. Following Schultz as a witness was Secretary of Labor William Brock, who stated:

> We have always maintained that the low number of U.S. ratifications is attributable mainly to our federal system of government. Most conventions would require legislative action by the constituent states as well as, or instead of, by the Federal Government, and the United States cannot assume a treaty obligation under a convention which might fall wholly or in part within state jurisdiction. (U.S. Senate 1985, 18)

When asked specifically about the probability of passing Conventions No. 87 and No. 98, Brock noted that "even if a country does not ratify many conventions, it is still responsible as an ILO member for complying with the basic principle of labor rights conventions, Nos. 87 and 98." He continued:

> I think the basic feeling we have is that—well, I have already expressed the caution about the state matter—the most important question is: Can we find a way to move affirmatively in these areas with a consensus? The matter of conventions has been debated in this country since the days of the Bricker amendment; it is a contentious issue. (U.S. Senate 1985, 18)

With the help of an aide, Brock went on to clarify U.S. obligations concerning the freedom-of-association conventions in the absence of ratification. In discussing charges against the United States before the Freedom of Association Committee, Brock noted: "I think they understand that we have greater freedom of association in this country than any country in the world." Nonetheless, he stated that he would take Conventions No. 87 and No. 98 before the President Committee and ask for a TAPILS review. Echoing Brock, committee chair Orrin Hatch stated: "I would like to see a way brought about where we can ratify these two controversial amendments if we can" (U.S. Senate 1985, 20).

The AFL-CIO, represented by President Lane Kirkland, argued forcefully for the ratification of more conventions for many of same reasons expressed by Secretary Schultz. In making specific mention of Conventions No. 87 and No. 98, Kirkland stated:

A former Solicitor of the Department of Labor affirmed this point [that 87 and 98 should be ratified]. His legal position was that the conventions—87, 98, and 105—raised no valid constitutional questions and would create no new rights for employees in the United States.[13] Apologists for non-ratification have argued both (1) that ratification is unnecessary because our laws and standards are equal to or superior to the terms of these conventions, and (2) that ratification would necessitate changes or improvements in our existing labor laws. As to the latter point, it scarcely affords the grounds for a refusal to submit these conventions to the mature judgment of the Senate on their merits. Surely, it strains credulity to suggest that two-thirds vote of the Senate is a weaker barrier to imprudent action than the simple majority of both Houses required for amendment to our domestic laws.

A number of legal problems concerning ratification had been laid out in an influential book by Edward E. Potter (1984)[14] a consultant to the United States Council on International Business (USCIB).[15] The principal concern expressed in Potter's book is that the ILO conventions would become the law of the land, superseding domestic labor laws. This is a problem, according to Hatch, because domestic labor laws "have been delicately drawn and have a delicate balance and which, although both sides can point to difficulties with them from time to time, still have worked rather well in our country" (U.S. Senate 1985, 11).

The substance of this point was debatable at the time and continues to be so. But the more fundamental argument made by Potter is that domestic law, no matter what its effects, should not be overridden by international conventions, as could be the case with Conventions No. 87 and No. 98: "Ratification of either convention could result in conflicts in federal and state policies with respect to . . . private sector labor activities" (U.S. Senate 1985, 96). Hatch also expressed this view in his response to AFL-CIO president Lane Kirkland: "I do not know many people who would want to have an international agreement or treaty disrupt the very difficult labor laws that presently exist, that have been arrived at with a lot of fighting on both sides all the way through these years" (U.S. Senate 1985, 66).

The business lobby's testimony, presented by Abraham Katz, president of the USCIB, leaned heavily on Potter's book. A number of separate arguments were made, all more or less concluding that (to paraphrase) "we agree with many of these conventions, but unfortunately our legal structure prevents their adoption." But at the same time the process of the drafting of conventions was criticized as allowing too much latitude to the International Labor Organization and prematurely cutting off the legislative process.

Standards are criticized for being too detailed and sophisticated and straying from the ILO's original mission.

> The subjects and content of standards have moved away from the basic body of standards that all nations can be expected to implement, toward complex instruments which attempt rigidly to monitor and control every aspect of working conditions . . . ILO standards frequently prescribe a high degree of Government involvement in labor-management relations, relative to that found in the United States. . . .
>
> The majority of ILO instruments lack the basis for universal acceptance and application. (U.S. Senate 1985, 74, 90)[16]

This is really a substantive argument, though it is mostly hidden and cloaked. In his prepared statement Katz wrote and underlined, "The practical reality in the development of ILO standards is that there is a wide diversity of points of view that are well beyond the scope of concerns of the people of the United States and the development of our own labor law."

If by this, Katz meant that in Geneva and in the most influential European countries, social democratic and (at that time often) communist labor arrangements were on the table and were discussable, whereas this was not the case in the United States, he was of course correct. Katz makes the argument, which is typically also made by orthodox economists opposed to linking trade and labor standards, that many countries adopt ILO conventions with no intention of implementing them.[17] The United States, as a nation of laws, cannot be so cavalier. So we, who supposedly uphold such standards in practice, cannot adopt them, whereas others who do not uphold them, adopt them. This is supposed to be self-evidently true.

Katz adds to this the slippery slope argument. "On broader policy grounds the business community remains opposed to ratification of ILO conventions because we are concerned that any ratification will be perceived by the ILO community as ending the long-standing U.S. policy of not ratifying non-maritime ILO conventions" (U.S. Senate 1985, 77).

So ratifying anything would subject the United States to pressure to ratify more. Better not to ratify anything. The conventions of most concern to USCIB were No. 87 and No. 98, and these are given special attention in the testimony, relying heavily on Potter's monograph. For Katz, the principles underlying these conventions are agreeable and underlie our "principle labor statutes relating to collective bargaining" (U.S. Senate 1985, 93). He lists twelve objections to Convention No. 87 and nine to Convention No. 98, summarized as follows.

- Collective rather than individual rights would be recognized.
- The classes of employees who could bargain would be broadened.
- Limitations on the right to strike would be restricted
- "Subversive groups" could not be eliminated from labor unions. Minority unions would be permitted.
- Captive audience meetings would be prohibited.
- The scope of bargainable subjects would be expanded.
- The scope of protection and discretion for union officials would be expanded.

Conventions No. 87 and No. 98 share a problem common to almost all ILO conventions according to Katz and Potter: our federal system of government.

> Because Conventions 87 and 98 prohibit strict regulation of picketing and strikes and interference in internal union affairs, ratification of either convention could result in conflicts in federal and state policies with respect to these private sector labor activities. (U.S. Senate 1985, 96)

There was the possibility of ratifying conventions on a non-self-executing basis, or of attaching reservations or understandings. The former is of doubtful legality, while reservations are prohibited by the ILO according to Katz. Understandings, which do not modify or limit the treaty but are meant to clarify domestic laws and procedures, are allowed. In fact this is the primary mechanism by which the ILO has preserved the principle of universality while acknowledging cultural difference (Ghebali 1989). But this is not sufficient for Potter.

Potter never directly confronted the president's letter of transmittal for Convention No. 87 or the endorsing reports of Secretary of State Dean Acheson and Secretary of Labor Maurice Tobin.[18] He does not address the predominant opinion at the time that the United States joined the ILO that federal states such as the United States could treat conventions as recommendations rather than obligations. Nor does he deal with the argument that the treaty power is not limited to those items directly given to Congress in the Constitution (Tayler 1935).

Katz ultimately appeals to the self-interest of Congress, and especially the House.

> Ratification of ILO conventions would deprive the House of Representatives of its constitutional role in the enactment of domestic labor legislation by excluding it from participation in the creation of labor law.... For the President, Con-

gress, labor and management to cede the development of interpretation of labor policy in the United States to an international forum, which is not responsive to the will of the electorate through their elected representatives, would be at odds with our constitutional system of government. . . . We in the business community continue to feel strongly that the establishment of labor in the United States should be the province of domestic legislatures at the federal and state level and should not be determined in the highly politicized, highly erratic forum of the ILO and its Annual Conference. (U.S. Senate 1985, 102–3, 107)

Nothing is lost by not ratifying, according to Katz. For instance, we were able to play an active leadership role in a Polish freedom-of-association case without ourselves having ratified the convention on Freedom of Association.

In the end, Chairman Hatch did not fully accept the USCIB position:

I would like you to examine my suggestion that perhaps we get everybody to agree that we ratify these conventions,[19] and then immediately re-ratify American domestic labor law, so there is no question, because there is enough in these conventions, room for interpretation, that we can conclude that we are not violating those conventions by ratifying them and yet still keeping domestic labor law the supreme law of the land in supersedance to the conventions themselves. (U.S. Senate 1985, 111–12)

This seems tortuous, even to an economist.

Hatch, in closing, referred the USCIB representatives to Kirkland's "very eloquent final statement" (U.S. Senate 1985, 113). In that statement Kirkland had linked freedom of association anywhere to freedom of association everywhere, and stated that the repression of such freedom was causing economic problems through the process of destructive competition. Tellingly, Kirkland quotes an old army expression: "Can't do it means you don't want to do it" (U.S. Senate 1985, 71).

According to U.S. Department of Labor and ILO officials interviewed in the preparation of this chapter, the present posture of the United States is to ratify only conventions that clearly conform to current U.S. law. The job of TAPILS, therefore, is to make sure that conventions under consideration do not interfere with any current statute. Hence, Conventions No. 87 and No. 98 are off the table for many of the reasons cited in Potter's book.

Nonetheless, the State Department has taken the position that some conventions could be ratified without creating legal problems, as shown in the report of the secretary accompanying President Bush's letter to the Senate urging consideration of Convention No. 105, the abolition of forced labor, in 1991.[20]

This remains the case even now that the State department's agenda is dominated by the war on terrorism. In its second report to the secretary and the president, in December 2002, the Advisory Commission on Labor Diplomacy argued strongly that the promotion of internationally recognized core labor rights supports all key U.S. foreign policy goals including stability, security, democracy, and prosperity. This is seen as having the utmost practical impact.

> Trade unions exist in varying degrees in Muslim countries and have a role to play in the struggle against terrorism and for democracy. However, there is often little protection in law or practice for trade unionists. The Middle East stands out as the region where the right to organize trade unions is least likely to be protected by law. Where unions do exist, their independence is often threatened by authoritarian governments on the one hand and Islamist political factions on the other. A policy that aims to cultivate union leadership at the enterprise and industry levels represents a promising approach to inculcate modern economic incentives and democratic political values among workers in Muslim countries. (U.S. Department of State 2001)

Among its suggestions, the committee includes revisiting the ratification of ILO core labor standards.

> The United States has one of the worst records of ratification of ILO conventions of any member state of the ILO, especially of the core labor conventions. This failure to ratify the core conventions undermines U.S. efforts to lead the international campaign to eliminate child labor, forced labor, and discrimination. (U.S. Department of State 2001)

But despite the presence of AFL-CIO president John Sweeney and executive vice president Linda Chavez-Thompson on the commission, there is no evidence of a sustained discussion of the rights to freedom of association and collective bargaining. There is a recommendation to consider Convention No. 111, on discrimination, which President Clinton had forwarded to the Senate in 1998, but merely a suggestion to look for "innovative ways to make ratification [of other core conventions] possible" given the legal problems inherent in the federal-state relationship and other aspects of the U.S. legal and political tradition.

To sum up, the interests of the State Department in using ILO conventions to promote national security goals seemed to trump USCIB objections to ratifying anything since the 1980s. However, only certain kinds of conventions can be ratified. These include those dealing solely with the rights of the individual and his property in himself. Collective rights, as are embodied in the rights to freedom of association and especially collective bargaining, are off the table because (1) such rights are not recognized in the American cultural context and (2) the United States would in fact be found in violation were it to ratify Conventions No. 87 and No. 98. Rights to freedom of association and collective bargaining as these are internationally understood are not protected in the United States. The silences and tortured arguments in these documents and hearings are symptoms of the need to dance around this. The next two sections establish these points in more detail.

In light of the historical record, it is clear that the primary reason for the United States' failure to ratify Conventions No. 87 and No. 98 is the class interest of employers. The other ostensible concerns can be classified as (1) issues that could be dealt with if the political will to ratify the conventions were present or (2) complete subterfuge.

The federal structure of the government and certain peculiar aspects of U.S. labor law matter, but these problems are surmountable. It is hard to accept that U.S. labor law provides a "proper balance" of employer and worker rights. Nor does U.S. labor policy fulfill current U.S. obligations to uphold the broad principles of Conventions No. 87 and No. 98 as required as condition of ILO membership. In the next section I present evidence from the International Confederation of Free Trade Unions, Human Rights Watch, the ILO Committee on the Freedom of Association, and the U.S. government itself indicating the variance between current U.S. and ILO standards.

As to the structure of government and current U.S. labor law, neither should constitute an absolute bar to ratification. In fact, in certain cases, the legal barriers are precisely what need to be changed in order for the United States to come into compliance with ILO standards.

Freedom of Association in the United States Is Not in Conformance with International Standards

The current U.S. position against ratification of ILO Conventions No. 87 and No. 98 is based largely on three assertions: that well-established national labor policy fulfills the broad purposes of the conventions and should not be meddled with; that under the recent *Declaration on Fundamental Principles and Rights at Work,* as well as the ILO constitution, the United States has a responsibility, based on its membership in the ILO, to conform to the spirit of Conventions No. 87 and No. 98, and that it generally does so; and that our federal system, which reserves certain rights to the states, makes ratification problematic since the conventions would affect employees who fall outside the coverage of federal labor statutes (U.S. Senate 1985; U.S. Department of Labor 1997a, 1997b; ILO 2000).

None of these assertions holds up to serious scrutiny.

First, I address the assertions that current labor policy is well-established and generally conforms to the spirit of Conventions No. 87 and No. 98 as required by the *Declaration* and membership in the ILO. The former is easy to dismiss. While current labor policy has its roots in statutes that are approximately seventy to eighty years old, age cannot be confused with acceptance.[21] Organized labor, in particular, has long fought for changes in labor policy. In the late 1940s and early 1950s the labor movement pushed for Taft-Hartley repeal (Dulles and Dubofsky 1984, 343–62); some years later, the AFL-CIO sought substantial changes to the NLRA through the unsuccessful Labor Law Reform Act of 1978 (Dark 1999, 99–124), which would have provided greater protections for union activists and organizers. In the 1990s the labor movement spent considerable resources in trying to pass legislation to prevent the use of permanent strike replacements (Gould 1993, 181–203; Weil 1994, 93), and in the early twenty-first century on preserving the right to organize.[22]

Employers have also signaled their displeasure with certain aspects of labor policy, most notably the NLRA's restrictions on employer-dominated labor organizations, which might restrict the establishment of employee-involvement programs. The TEAM Act attempted to amend the NLRA to allow employers greater latitude in establishing such programs (U.S. Senate 1995). Narrower issues such as the use of salting as an organizing tactic by building trades unions and the so-called garment industry provisos, which provide exceptions to the NRLA's "hot cargo" proscription, have also been criticized by employers (Bodah 1999; U.S. House of Representatives 1999).

The reports of two government commissions in the 1990s—the Commission on the Future of Worker-Management Relations appointed by President Clinton (i.e., the Dunlop Commission) and the American Worker at a Crossroads Project, led by Republican representative Peter Hoekstra—are filled with both labor and management complaints about U.S. labor policy (U.S. Department of Labor 1994; U.S. House of Representatives 1999).

This lack of consensus is also reflected in the decisions of the National Labor Relations Board (NLRB), which has been criticized by both scholars (Cooke and Gautschi 1982; Cooke et al. 1995; Estreicher 1985) and the federal courts (*Mosey Manufacturing v. NLRB* 701 F2d 610, 1983) for its oscillations based on political control of the board. Indeed, over the years, Congress has held a number of hearings concerning abrupt changes by the Board in the application of legal standards (see Bodah 2001, for a list of such hearings). James Gross in an article entitled "The Demise of the National Labor Policy: A Question of Social Justice" writes:

> This country needs a definite, coherent, and consistent national labor policy. That requires more than changing NLRB case doctrines or amending Taft Hartley to tighten or loosen government regulation of the labor-management relationship. The re-crafting of a national labor policy must begin with a precise and certain statement of its purposes and objectives. Fundamental questions must be confronted and answered. (1994, 53)

The second argument against ratification of these core labor standards is that ratification is unnecessary since the United States must already comply with Conventions No. 87 and No. 98 as a condition by ILO membership and to comply with the ILO Declaration on Fundamental Principles and Rights at Work and its Follow-up. A June 19, 1998, press release from the USCIB called the Declaration "a major achievement for the ILO" and stated that the "USCIB and its colleagues on the IOE have been instrumental for some years in advocating a Declaration of Principles with an effective follow-up mechanism." The USCIB's enthusiasm may, in part, arise from a belief that the Declaration provides another reason why Conventions No. 87 and No. 98 are unnecessary. But there is ample evidence that present U.S. labor standards do not conform to the ILO principles.

The U.S. government itself admitted to a lack of conformance in the *Review of Annual Reports under the Follow-up to the ILO Declaration on the Fundamental Principles and Rights at Work.* After beginning on a positive note in stating that "the United States recognizes, and is committed to, the fundamental principle of freedom of association and the effective recognition of the right to collective bargaining" (ILO 1998, 144), the report later states: "Nonetheless, the United States acknowledges that there are aspects of this system that fail to fully protect the rights to organize and bargain collectively of all employees in all circumstances" (ILO 1998, 153). It went on to cite evidence from the Dunlop Commission's *Fact-Finding Report,* including the frequent firing of union activists, the failure of many newly organized units to achieve a first contract, union organizers' lack of access to employees, and generally insufficient remedies available to the NLRB. The report also cited the United States' lack of protection for economic strikes.

In the same report, the observations submitted by the ICFTU were even more critical. Too lengthy to summarize adequately, the ICFTU's indictment contained at least two dozen specific shortcomings of U.S. labor law at each stage of the collective bargaining process (ILO 1998, 160–63). The ICFTU noted the harsh treatment and insufficient remedies available to union activists; employers' union avoidance strategies, such as the frequent use of antiunion consultants; the failure of new units to get first contracts; and the restrictions on certain types of concerted activities. The ICFTU was also critical of U.S. labor policy in the public sector, noting the severe limits on bargaining subjects in certain jurisdictions and broad restrictions on striking.

Yet another source of evidence for the shortcomings of U.S. labor policy is the ILO Committee on Freedom of Association. All members of the ILO have a responsibility to respect the freedom of association and right to bargain collectively (*International Labour Review* 1949; Hodges-Aeberhard 1989; Gernigon, Odero, and Guido 2000). In 1950, the ILO set up a special tripartite committee to monitor compliance. Unlike other ILO committees, complaints can be lodged with the CFA even if a country has not ratified the requisite conventions (Freeman 1999b). Since its establishment, the CFA has issued forty-nine decisions involving the United States.

Focusing only on cases since reaffiliation, the CFA has found U.S. labor policy at variance with ILO standards in many instances.[23] In Case 1557 (1993), the CFA requested the U.S. government to "draw the attention of the authorities concerned, and in particular in those jurisdictions where public servants are totally or substantially deprived of collective bargaining rights, to the principle that all public services workers other than those engaged in the administration of the State should enjoy such rights." In Case 1543, the CFA stated (1991) that "recourse to the use of labour drawn from outside the undertaking to replace strikers for an indeterminate period entails a risk of derogation from the right to strike, which may effect the free exercise of trade union rights." In Case 1523 (1992), the CFA "requests the Government to guarantee access of trade union representatives to the workplace, with due respect for the rights of property and management, so that trade unions can communicate with workers, in order to apprise them of the potential advantages of unionization." In Case 1467 (1989), the CFA indicated its "regret" over the "excessive length of appeals procedures" for unfair labor practices. Case 1467 also includes: "the CFA points out with concern that this is the fourth recent complaint lodged—by different complainants—against the United States on the grounds of anti-union tactics and unfair labor practices." In Case 1437 (1988), the CFA wrote that "subcontracting accompanied by the dismissal of union leaders can constitute a violation of principle that no one should be prejudiced in his employment on the grounds of union membership and activities." In Case 1074 (1982), the CFA stated that it was "of the view that the application of excessively severe sanctions [i.e., the termination of air traffic controllers] against public servants on account of their participation in a strike cannot be conducive to the development of harmonious industrial relations."

The 2000 Human Rights Watch (HRW) report *Unfair Advantage: Workers' Freedom of Association in the United States under International Human Rights Standards* provides extensive evidence on the shortcomings in U.S. labor policy (Compa 2000). The HRW report contains fifteen general findings of variance between U.S. and international labor standards, and several more concerning the rights of immigrant and agricultural workers. Most of the charges against U.S. labor policy concern limits on the freedom of association resulting from inadequate protections for union activists during the organizing process. Specifically, HRW notes, among other things, discrimination against union supporters, a lack of access to employees by union organizers, and imbalances in communication power between employers and unions.

Finally, I take issue with the assertion that the United States' federal structure is a bar to ratification of Conventions No. 87 and No. 98. First, note that there are two streams to this position. Some argue that the ratification of Conventions No. 87 and No. 98 would (or could) override certain aspects of current federal labor law and the prerogatives of the states; others argue that ratification would not be self-executing and, therefore, the United States would be out of compliance with conventions unless the federal government and many states changed their current statutes (Bradley 1998; U.S. Senate 1985; Potter 1984).

Starting with the latter, the United States *could* be criticized for not being in compliance with ratified conventions based on the actions (or inactions) of the states—in fact, this situation has arisen elsewhere. For example, there have been a number of cases brought against Canada for the actions of its provinces (see, e.g., CFA Case 327 [2002]; CFA Case 324 [2001]). However, typically, the Canadian government has forwarded the CFA's charges to the provinces for their response. The U.S. Department of Labor could do the same for the states.

If the ratification of either Conventions No. 87 or No. 98 were self-executing, the United States could still be found out of compliance if the federal government or the states did not take effective action to see that the provisions of the conventions were, in fact, put into practice. Potter (1984, 81 n.258) notes that

Mexico continued to be criticized by the ILO for not truly operationalizing the requirements of Conventions No. 87 and No. 98 after ratification. But a larger fear seems to be that Conventions No. 87 and No. 98 would effectively override or void contrary federal or state statutes in the eyes of the courts. In contrast, consider the comments of the secretary of labor in recommending to President Truman in 1949 that he seek ratification of Convention No. 87 by the Senate:

> It is our view[24] that the subject matter of this convention [No. 87] is appropriate under our system for federal action . . .
>
>   It is our view that this convention should be ratified by the United States, and we recommend that the President of United States transmit this convention to the Senate of the United States with a request for the advice and consent of the Senate to its ratification. It is also our view that no new Federal legislation or revision of existing Federal law is necessary to effect compliance by the United States with the terms of this convention. (U.S. Senate 1949, 9)

In 1980, the Solicitor of Labor wrote:

> Although it is our conclusion that Convention No. 87 (freedom of association) may unequivocally be ratified by the United States without entailing any undertaking to enact legislation or to modify existing law, we recognize that some parties may still anticipate that ratification would unwittingly nullify domestic legislation through creative judicial construction. (U.S. Department of Labor 1980, 1)

The solicitor went on to suggest two strategies that "would absolutely preclude such a result":

> First, the Convention could be ratified with a declaration that it is non-self-executing. Second, the Convention could be ratified with an understanding that "all necessary and appropriate measures" as provided by Article 11 means, in the context of the United States, that the obligations contained in the Convention have been acceded to only to the extent of the Commerce Power.

Although Convention No. 98, on the right to organize and bargain collectively, was never subjected to such analysis by the federal government, such provisos could also be used to avoid upsetting existing statutes.

It has been noted (Potter 1984, 78–82) that it is the ILO and not a member state that ultimately determines whether a nation has met its obligation. The Committee of Experts, Committee on the Application of Conventions and Recommendations, and the CFA could all continue to find fault with the United

States' implementation of Conventions No. 87 and No. 98. However, as mentioned earlier, Conventions No. 87 and No. 98 are unusual in that member states are subject to criticism by the CFA whether they have ratified the conventions or not. Hence, the United States cannot escape international rebuke (and has not) by simply refusing to ratify the conventions.

The current powers of the CFA do not, however, mean that ratification is superfluous. Article 19 (5) of the ILO Constitution requires member states to seek ratification of approved conventions.[25] Conformance is not a substitute for ratification. This remains true even after adoption of the *Declaration on Fundamental Principles and Rights at Work*. Further the United States is clearly not in compliance with international standards of freedom of association or the right to bargain collectively as I have shown. Ratification of Conventions No. 87 and No. 98 would be a positive move by the United States toward meeting its international obligations and could be used to pressure both the federal government and the states to gain the needed regulatory and statutory changes. It could provide the "definite, coherent, and consistent national labor policy" called for by James Gross.

Social and Economic Rights Are Tenuously Grounded in the United States

The ILO reporting system is designed to make sure that countries are effectively guaranteeing rights within national space. If we see the 1944 Philadelphia Declaration as part of the infrastructure of the embedded liberalism of the post–World War II period, this makes perfect sense. The problem is that governments may simply refuse to enforce such rights while simultaneously claiming their own labor relations system to be superior. In the United States, collectively defined rights such as the right to bargain collectively have a particularly tough go. ILO conventions are likely to be adopted only when the government has an overriding foreign policy concern that forces management and ownership to compromise. Before 1991 this was the need to combat the Soviet Union. More recently, it has been the great power struggle with China.[26] The United States is more or less clearly in violation of Conventions No. 87 and No. 98. If in fact, the United States cannot ratify these conventions for legal reasons—and I do not consider this fully established—then the ILO cannot be the preferred adjudicator of international labor rights, as those who are opposed to trade-based labor standards argue.[27]

Even if the government were to change its interpretation and the legal barriers could be overcome it is not clear the traditional ILO approach is feasible in the current environment. Increased capital mobility has diminished the ability of states to regulate economic conditions while at the same time the accompanying ideology of neoliberalism rejects such regulation in the first place. In other words, whether we think of globalization as a structural shift in economic conditions or a political-ideological project, the kind of nation-based economic regulation envisioned by the ILO's Philadelphia Declaration is now problematic at best.

On the other hand, the ratification of Conventions No. 87 and No. 98 would positively affect U.S. labor policy (see also Bellace 1999; Gross 1999a; Adams 1999a; Freeman 1999a), and it would be good to see the conventions reintroduced in the U.S. Senate. As with the child and forced labor conventions (No. 182 and No. 105) this would be most likely to happen if either were to fit into the broader foreign policy goals of the U.S. government. Conventions No. 182 and No. 105 were ratified in large measure as a U.S. response to perceived abuses in China. Similarly, the convention on Tripartite Consultation (No. 144) was ratified in 1988 with a view toward embarrassing the USSR.

In the absence of broader foreign policy objectives it remains difficult to convince American policymakers that labor standards—particularly those relating to organizing and bargaining—are truly human rights issues. Indeed, this problem can be located in the legal history of the United States and the preference for individual over collective rights. First-generation rights—the civil and political rights espoused in the American and French Revolutions—have a broad acceptance in American law and culture. But second-generation rights—the social and economic rights of the New Deal—are more tenuously grounded.

Gross (1999b) argues that the conception of human rights in the Western tradition has emphasized the individual's right to be protected from abuse by the state. Hence, the negative rights of individual liberty certainly fit well within the post-Smithian discourse of the "free market." But Conventions No. 87 and No. 98 stand (to varying degrees) in differential relationship to the development of legal theory in the United States. The right to freedom of association in the workplace could possibly fit within this tradition, but the right to bargain collectively is clearly beyond consensus in the American context. That Convention No. 87 was twice recommended for ratification, while Convention No. 98 was not, may suggest that the freedom of association is easier to fit into the American context than the right to bargain collectively. One may both support the ratification of Conventions No. 87 and No. 98 and be cautious about the efficacy of the traditional ILO approach in the current environment of increasingly mobile capital and neoliberal ideology.

Some writers have argued for an emerging transnational vision for the regulation of labor relations (Trubek, Mosher, and Rothstein 2000). Such a vision finds a place for traditional nation-based regulation woven together with the activities of transnational actors and advocacy networks, both public and private. The basic idea is that such networks can create an overlapping consensus on normative goals. The ILO would be one part of such a consensus—and a key part indeed—as virtually all actors refer to the core labor rights established by the ILO. But the creation of an overlapping consensus requires also the activities of internationally oriented labor organizations, national governments, and NGOs. These groups would be active in regional arenas such as NAFTA and EU, international arenas such as the WTO, and through their direct influence on multinational corporations through the promulgation of codes of conduct. Examples of norm construction and mobilization include the EU social dialogue, the North American Agreement on Labor Cooperation (NAALC), and the activities of the Fair Labor Association and the Worker Rights Consortium, the subject of the next chapter.

Such networks might create and enforce rights through what Keck and Sikkink (1998) call the "boomerang effect." When governments are unresponsive to the desires of their own citizens, activist groups can put pressure on their home country governments, which in turn put pressure on the offending state. Trudek, Mosher, and Rothstein (2000, 1187–1211) present the activities of the Support Committee for Maquiladora Workers and the Campaign for Labor Rights in the Han Young strike in Mexico as an example of this boomerang effect. Even more successful was the transnational organizing campaign to guarantee the rights of Coca-Cola bottling workers in Guatemala. This campaign succeeded without any overarching legal framework such as NAALC or EU.

It is easy to overestimate the impact of these often isolated successes. I will investigate the activities of one organization, the Workers Rights Consortium, in the next chapter to explore the uses and limits of transnational labor rights action networks. Moreover, even if U.S. law can be mobilized to support organizing campaigns in poor countries, this does little for U.S. workers whose rights to freedom of association and collective bargaining are being systematically violated. Focusing on these developing country struggles orientalizes oppression to some extent, as it makes it seem that violation of basic rights is something that happens "over there" or at worst also in the barrios and China-town sweatshops in New York and Los Angeles. Yet the evidence is clear that the violation of U.S. worker rights is long-standing and systematic.

A reasonable argument can be made that the United States should take a unilateral approach to the enforcement of worker rights (Levinson 2000; A. Freeman 1999b). Jerome Levinson would have the Labor Department certify that countries requesting trade preferences are actively enforcing internationally recognized labor standards and would direct the U.S. executive directors at the World Bank and International Monetary Fund to vote against loans to countries that violate such standards. The Sanders-Frank Amendment of 1995 already provides a mechanism for this; Levinson would change the process by making the Labor Department rather than the Treasury responsible for examining such violations. Labor would be directed to use ILO reports and standards in their findings.

This would be a significant change in that the Treasury has been the locus of support for neoliberal globalization since at least the late 1960s.[28] While it presumes a consensus in favor of the rights to freedom of association and collective bargaining, a consensus that does not in fact exist in the United States, this proposal would go a long way toward creating the conditions for such a consensus. The proposed use of ILO findings would also promote the ILO as an authoritative institution.

In the U.S. context, worker rights are unlikely to be promoted because of decisions made in Geneva. While this is particularly true under Republican presidents, it is generally the case that attempts to use international human rights language to create change in American practices have failed. As Michael Ignatieff has written in a different context,

> The very idea that American justice should be brought before the bar of international standards seems, to many Americans, to be impudent, unpatriotic, or irrelevant. If abolition of the death penalty eventually prevails, it will not be because it offends against the International Convention on Civil and Political Rights, but because Americans conclude that the manner by which it is inflicted violates American constitutional norms, chiefly due process and equal protection. (2002)

Still, ILO conventions form the context within which an overlapping consensus on labor rights might be created and enforced. A debate over freedom of association and collective bargaining could galvanize the forces of democracy and social justice against corporate-led globalization. The ILO's Committee on

Freedom of Association as well as U.S. self-reporting to that body refers over and over again to the fact that no in-depth tripartite analysis of Conventions No. 87 and No. 98 has been performed in recent times. It is time for such an analysis.

The record of the Clinton administration suggests the difficulties of going beyond individualism in worker rights. The need to secure labor backing led Clinton to support the labor side agreement to NAFTA. However, at the urging of both the Mexican government and the Business Roundtable he removed language from the NAALC that would have allowed trade sanctions and monetary penalties for countries' failure to enforce their own labor laws. Thus while the National Administrative Office has been both brave and candid in its reporting, there is no enforcement mechanism.

One can perhaps accept such compromises as necessary in a tripartite system. But the problem is deeper and is illustrated by Clinton's general approach to human rights. During his trip to China in 1998 the president made a number of speeches on rights, including especially his remarkable nationally televised debate with President Jiang Zemin. He declared that certain rights were universal—"the right to be treated with dignity, the right to express one's opinion, to choose one's own leaders, to associate freely with others, and to worship or not, freely, however one chooses" (Border 1998). Throughout his remarks he confined his discussion of rights to the political and cultural spheres.

This is characteristic of both the dominant American approach to rights and much of the contemporary international human rights movement, in which economic and noneconomic aspects are often widely separated, even when in practice they are not.

International labor policy moved closer to the center of the foreign policy agenda under Clinton. Clinton's apparel industry partnership was a particularly clear example of the attempt to channel the social movements responding to the contradictions of neoliberalism toward an accommodative stance with the particular constellation of capitalist interests—especially internationally oriented financial and industrial capital—that played such a prominent role in that administration. The partial success of this strategy is shown by the now commonplace adoption by corporations and industry associations of corporate codes of conduct. Its limits are shown by the case study of the contemporary factory inspector movement in the next chapter.

The different interests represented in the George W. Bush administration and the remarkable change in the international position of the United States after September 11 led to a change in the U.S. practice and discourse of human rights. The Bush administration's political coalition incorporated much of the military-industrial complex, energy, agri-business, and the millennial vision of fundamentalist Christianity. David Harvey characterizes this "neo-conservatism" as having as its primary objective

> the establishment of and respect for order, both internally and upon the world stage. . . . To the neo-conservative movement, adherence to moral principle is also crucial. . . . Though recognized as distinctive American values, these principles are presented as universals, with terms like freedom and democracy and respect for private property, the individual, and the law bundled together as a code of conduct for the whole world. (Harvey 2003, 190–92)

Bush's international labor policy was clearly influenced by these interests. These particular groups of supporters have less of a need to distance themselves from sweatshop abuses, and the moral component of Bush's appeal is particularly important in the rhetoric of international relations. This led to diminished attention to the sweatshop issue and more attention to child labor.

For example, the State Department's Partnership to Eliminate Sweatshops saw its funding cut in half and in fiscal year 2005 was folded into the Human Rights and Democracy Fund. Of the four substantive "frequently asked questions" on the Web site of the Department of Labor's Bureau of International Labor Affairs in 2005, three dealt with child labor. (The fourth dealt with the North American Agreement on Labor Cooperation.) The majority of press releases from the Bureau under the Bush administration were concerned with child labor, in strong contrast with the Clinton period. Funding for the International Child Labor Program was increased.

Conclusion

International labor rights conventions are unlikely to be adopted, regardless of the legal issues, when such rights are breached at home and seen as unrelated to our major foreign policy goals abroad. But rights are created, they are not given by God. A thorough, tripartite review of U.S. ratification of ILO Conventions No. 87 and No. 98, in the context of globalization, can help to define what rights mean today. Clearly, the United States is currently in violation of 87 and 98. Employer opposition is most likely to be overcome if committed national political leaders and civil society organizations can argue effectively that ratification serves important foreign policy goals that trump narrow management interests. A debate over international labor rights might be the best path for improving domestic labor rights.

CHAPTER 7

The New Factory Inspectors

In the preface to *Capital,* vol. 1, Marx states that he will deal with individuals as mere personifications of social categories.

> To prevent possible misunderstandings, let me say this. I do not by any means depict the capitalist and the landowner in rosy colors. But individuals are dealt with only insofar as they are the personification of economic categories, the bearers (*Träger*) of particular class relations and interests. My standpoint, from which the development of the economic formation of society is viewed as a process of natural history, can less than any other make the individual responsible for relations whose creature he remains, socially speaking, however much he may subjectively raise himself above them. (1981, 92)

Yet on the previous page Marx seems to violate his own stricture when he discusses the English factory inspectors.

> We should be appalled at our own circumstances if, as in England, our governments and parliaments appointed commissions of inquiry into economic conditions; if these commissions were armed with the same plenary power to get a the truth; *if it were possible for these purposes to find men as competent, as free from partisanship and respect for persons as are England's factory inspectors.* (1981, 91, emphasis added)

The reports of the factory inspectors are the source for much of the analysis in the critical chapters on the length of the working day and on large-scale industry in *Capital,* vol. 1. Marx quotes from the reports extensively and presents the work of the inspectors as heroic, although this is mostly inferred rather than stated. Perhaps Marx did not treat the inspectors as personifications of social categories because they, like Marx, had a middle-class background.

Beginning in the electronics and apparel industries in the 1970s, and gaining momentum with the opening of vast new spaces for capital accumulation after the opening of China and the former Soviet bloc in the 1980s and 1990s, factory production is now beyond the regulatory reach of any particular national authority. I have described the extension of social distance that this involves in chapter 3 and 4, and argued that a particular effect on moral behavior has been produced by the lengthening of commodity chains. In chapter 4 I demonstrated how attempts to correct for or ameliorate particular forms of exploitation and oppression often give implicit support to other forms, and how the concept of rights itself brings with it some not altogether innocent baggage. In the previous two chapters I looked at how labor rights are differently defined by the International Labor Organization, other multilateral organizations, and the U.S. government, and how this creates a conflicting macro rhetoric of worker rights and labor standards.

This chapter focuses on the micro rhetoric of rights by studying the history of the worker rights movement, from the early agitation over the Factory Acts in England through to the present-day "new factory inspectors," nongovernmental organizations that certify conditions inside the new global commodity chains. I begin by surveying the early nineteenth-century struggles, showing the complexity of class alliances and the importance of the state bureaucracy in the dramatic improvement in working conditions in England. In the second part of the chapter I focus on the contemporary activities of the Worker Rights Consortium (WRC), which certifies factories producing logoed apparel for colleges and universities. My central point is that by focusing on the enabling rights of freedom of association and collective bargaining the WRC helps to foster a community of fate between workers in the poor countries and in the rich ones, creating cross-border standards of accountability and directly empowering poor working people.

I link the historical and contemporary discussions by looking more closely at the uses Marx made of the factory inspectors reports, the tension between his self-conscious structuralism and the lack of structural analysis of the factory inspectors themselves, and how this relates to possibilities for reform within capitalism. I then locate the WRC and other labor-based NGOs at the intersection of labor, religious, and anti-imperialist organizations that developed partly in response to the globalization of capitalist employment relations. Through a close reading of their factory reports, I argue that the WRC, while certainly reformist, and mildly reformist at that, is engaged in creating a desire for class justice, and a practice of thinking locally while acting globally.

The "Middle Class" Origins of Worker Rights and Labor Standards

The modern story of international worker rights and labor standards usually starts with the English Factory Legislation of 1802 and the writing and agitation that led up to it. Sponsored by the Conservative prime minister Robert Peel, this legislation was understood as an attempt to deal with the social costs of what came to be called "industrialization" (Engerman 2003; Hutchins and Harrison 1903).

The 1802 act did not deal with wage labor. Notably, it was titled The Health and Morals of Apprentices Act. The employment of children on a large scale was characteristic of the British factory system from the beginning, but it was only with the introduction of steam power toward the end of the eighteenth century that a system of "free labor" developed. This euphemism initially covered more or less the same people as in the pre-steam factory—children and some women—but under different assumptions about their relationship to their employer.

The mills of the first wave of the industrial revolution employed "apprentices," pauper children who were theoretically under the care of the mill owners. Parish authorities were glad to reduce their expenses through this practice, and mill owners were happy to access this abundant supply of cheap labor, even if owners sometimes had to agree to take "one idiot with every twenty sound children supplied" (Howard 1975, 58).

Dr. Thomas Percival was arguably the first effective crusader for labor standards. In 1773 he published a study of mortality in Manchester and its environs, finding that the death rate in the city was 1 in 28 whereas just a few miles away it was only 1 in 68. He then began to argue that improving public health in the towns required improving conditions in the factories.

In 1784 there was an outbreak of typhus in the cotton mills at Radcliffe Bridge, including in the factory owned by the elder Robert Peel. This so alarmed local landowners that they brought it to the attention of the magistrates, who called on Percival and his colleagues at Manchester infirmary to investigate. Percival used this opportunity to not only make specific recommendations for changes in mill practices, including improvements in general cleanliness, sanitary arrangements, ventilation, and lighting. He also called for more and longer breaks and a shorter working day. The magistrates passed a resolution refusing indenture of "Parish Apprentices" in any situation including night work and longer than a ten-hour working day.

Peel's mills were considered good compared to most, but he himself admitted he had little direct knowledge of conditions in them. "Having other pursuits, it was not often in my power to visit the factories" (Howard 1975, 61). He stated that he later found that his own mills had been mismanaged but because of the press of other activities "he had it not in (his) power to put them under proper regulation" (61).

"Once he faced up to the appalling conditions in his mills he took steps to remedy the situation" (Howard 1975, 62). Peel joined the Board of Health soon after its establishment. This pattern of lack of attention, denial, acceptance, and reform has repeated itself again and again in the history of labor standards and rights. In his film *The Big One,* Michael Moore confronts Phil Knight, the Nike CEO, with a challenge: a free ticket to Indonesia, accompanied by Moore, to directly inspect the factories making Nike apparel. Knight begs off, saying he doesn't have the time. This scene occurs at the height of the negative publicity Nike received in the late 1990s over conditions in Indonesian and Vietnamese factories. As demonstrated in chapter 3, the initial reaction of Nike spokesmen was denial that this was their problem. In just a few years Nike would become a key player organizing "reform," eventually publishing a list of its worldwide supplier network.

Beyond documenting the health effects of conditions in the mills and writing a report leading to the first effort by any public body to limit the working day for children, Percival called for a deeper change in the way the social relations of the workplace were understood. He advocated some form of inspection of the workplace. In testimony to the Manchester Board of Health in January 1789, after further documenting continuing and deplorable conditions in the mills, he proposed "an application for Parliamentary aid (if other methods appear not likely to effect the purpose) to establish a general system of laws for the wise, humane, and equal governance of all such works." Though he got little immediate response, Percival's efforts became the basis of the Factory Acts.

The younger Peel was influenced by Percival and drew upon his advice in writing the 1802 act. This act passed with virtually no opposition. Its only method of inspection was voluntary enforcement, which in practice proved to be no inspection whatsoever. The act became a moral exhortation that mill owners believed they could largely ignore. And indeed for a time they could, but changes in technology—the introduction of steam especially—were undermining the apprentice system. The new "free labor" was totally unprotected, but the principle of parliamentary aid in governing the workplace had been established. The 1802 act, however ineffective in directly accomplishing its goals, was a wedge that could be used against the dominant laissez-faire doctrine.

Liberal and Social Democratic Rights

Since the first Factory Acts, the worker rights and labor standards discussion has included issues such as wages and hours of work, the acceptability of particular working conditions, and the permitted "range of arrangements" within the labor contract including rights to association, union status, bargaining rights, dispute settlement, and apprenticeship conditions. An important aspect of each of these categories of rights is the differential treatment of workers categorized by age, sex, and race. Here we can make a distinction between liberal arguments for rights for certain kinds of workers based on them not meeting the classical liberal standards for free agents and social democratic arguments that construct rights on the basis of a concept of collective entitlement.

The opponents of the acts that followed the 1802 law argued against them on the basis that "free workers" did not need such protection. While academic opponents of labor standards today are more likely to argue against them on the basis of their unintended negative consequences, or their ineffectiveness, or, remarkably, *both*, more popular antistandards views question standards on the basis of individual freedom of choice.

As it has evolved this debate has covered a wide array of "rights" and forms of argument. The official and academic discussions have a complicated relationship to more popular rhetoric. For instance, the ILO notion of core labor rights makes no mention of wages or hours even though these have been most prominent in the press and in organizing circles.

The early labor standards movement drew on many of the same social sources as did the antislavery movement, that is, middle-class reformers and agitators as well as some "enlightened" conservatives such as Peel. As government bureaucracies developed in the nineteenth century these came to be another influence defining and disseminating ideas about standards, as did international agencies like the ILO in the twentieth. Trade unions and nongovernmental labor-based organizations have formed a third important influence.

The outlines of the argument over standards are long-standing. Moral claims are typically made about protecting the poor and those without social voice, as well as the possibility of enhancing economic growth, which itself has desirable moral consequences. Economic arguments are made about correcting for externalities, improving efficiency, or offsetting unequal bargaining power. Those concerned with international standards especially emphasize that labor markets are prone to a race to the bottom in the absence of standards.

Opponents of standards have typically emphasized the effects of standards on competitiveness, the unanticipated effects of standards, and the stigmatizing effects of standards on particular groups. The main nineteenth-century argument about the extension of standards to adult males was the freedom of contract cherished by classical liberalism, but in general those opposed to labor standards have adopted what Hirschman calls the "rhetoric of reaction" arguing that such standards will be either ineffective, will come at the expense of other social goals, or will hurt those they are intended to help. Often opponents argue that standards will both be ineffective *and* have negative effects.

The continuities in this discussion have led some scholars to see it as static. According to Stanley Engerman, within any country

> The introduction and extension of standards depends more on shifts in political power, effective rhetoric, changing attitudes regarding the role of men, new empirical data, or the attempt to apply standards to a broader group of nations, rather than upon the introduction of new justifications or new claims for what the policies will achieve. (2003, 29)

Engerman makes a similar claim for the debate over international standards. Since the French Revolution, the difficulty of achieving broadly acceptable standards across countries and whether we should have different application of common standards have been debated without answer. "Almost 200 years of discussion has left such questions unanswered" (2003, 30).

I would like to destabilize this notion of a continuous debate, so as to highlight how and why class interest and conventional knowledge have produced different understandings of rights at different times. Indeed, Engerman recognizes that the terms of the discussion have not been so continuous when he writes immediately after the preceding quoted passage that "changing legislation regarding male labor required a change in society's underlying belief system" (2003, 30).[1] The development of trade unions and the philosophy of social democracy in the late nineteenth and twentieth centuries shifted the terrain of debate over labor standards, as did the end of colonialism in the second half of the twentieth. Arguably, the current moment, with the collapse of the state capitalisms of the Soviet Union and Eastern Europe, the proletarianization of vast numbers of people in the formerly planned economies and the former Third World, and the growth of international civil society organizations, marks a third turning point in this discussion.

Industrialization and ideas about morality and economic well being seemed to spread together in the nineteenth century. At first only women and children were to be protected, but liberal economists like Mill and Senior found separate legislation for women unacceptable on feminist grounds. But of course things were never really that simple. The inclusion of men in France in 1848 legislation is one example, but so is the complexity of the situation in the United States, with Massachusetts continuously leading the way from 1836 on but no successful national labor standards regime becoming law until 1938. So to the extent that the growth of standards is coincident with industrialization it is best understood as the product of uneven development within particular societies with an overlay of international causation, rather than an emergent tendency within a unidirectional process of development.[2]

Engerman writes that "it seemed politically inevitable" that standards would spread to men and across industries and nations with "the spread of the basic ideology accompanying industrialization" (2003, 59). But what was this ideology? Wasn't it in fact the change in philosophy that Engerman also mentions, the rupture in thought represented by social democracy? What was inevitable about it?

Engerman seems to deploy a soft economic determinism that recent work in labor history has moved beyond. Rather than economic change simply producing paradigmatic shifts in thinking, causality can just as easily flow in the other direction. For instance, Gareth Stedman Jones (1983) has demonstrated that the Chartist movement was not a response to economic change but rather developed out of the language of political radicalism. Michael Sonenscher (1989) found that the language of class in mid-nineteenth-century France developed not in reaction to economic disruptions but as a new way to voice old grievances given the disruption of the corporate structure of the ancien régime. Jacques Ranciere has established that the language of class developed by French artisans in the 1840s was not a direct reflection of their lived experience but was rather a myth fashioned by workers who wanted to be something else (1991). Joan Scott's work (1988) shows how representations of family and gender have overdetermined workers' understanding of occupational identities.

In other words, the "postmodern" labor history of the late twentieth century casts doubt on the notion of any unified ideology necessarily accompanying industrialization. But whether we see the development of worker rights and labor standards as flowing from a unified and universal process of economic growth accompanied by changing preferences or a shift in language related to social norms resulting in legislation that raised standards, after legislation was passed hours decreased, wages rose, child labor declined, female labor force participation rose, and industrial accidents declined in one country after another. The emergence and evolution of rights is likely to be place- and time-specific rather than a general story that is essentially the same everywhere, even when we can find similiar effects.

My main concern is to understand how certain standards become conventional, that is, how whether they are legislated or not they become accepted as a normal part of a civilized society. In England, the original 1802 factory legislation was modified many times over the course of the nineteenth century, generally with expanding coverage and enforcement. The movement toward *international* standards can be dated to Robert Owens's "Two Memorials on Behalf of the Working Class" in 1818. International conferences were held through the late nineteenth and early twentieth centuries, and both the International Workingmen's Association and the more traditional trade unions also pressed for international standards. But outside a few very specific agreements it was not until 1919 with the founding of the ILO that a general international standards regime became possible. Before World War I the achievement of uniform standards even in Europe was quite limited as were internal standards for male workers. Enforcement was weak, especially internationally.

The ILO grew organically out of the nineteenth-century worker rights and standards movement, but, particularly after its reorganization in Philadelphia in 1944, the ILO shifted attention toward broader political and social goals and began to treat labor rights as part of the more general issue of human rights. This concern with labor standards as rights became more explicit in 1998 with the Fundamental Declaration of Rights at Work, but this is best seen as a consolidation of the "worker rights as human rights concept," not something radically new.

What is new in the last two decades is the attempt to embed labor rights in trade agreements. Not entirely new of course—England had a differential tariff for free- and slave-produced sugar in the 1830s and 1840s, and the United States has prohibited the importation of convict-made goods since 1890—but this trade-labor standards linkage has now moved to center stage in the debate, as at least some rights in the workplace for all and the desirability of avoiding a race to the bottom have become broadly accepted claims.[3]

In the earliest days of the labor standards debate, ethical arguments tended to draw on religious beliefs and soul-searching over slavery rather than the humanitarian–human rights rhetoric of today. Arguments in favor of standards for women and children were easier to make because they drew on both this moral framework *and* a kind of protoexternalities argument within political economy. Having a variety of arguments (both moral and economic) and including self-interested groups has always been needed to build a successful coalition in favor of standards and conventional knowledge about those standards (Humphries 2003).

Opponents argued then and now that intervention would be both inefficient and ineffective. But again, for all the continuities there have been disjunctures in this debate. The early discussion of worker rights and labor standards in England was colored by the very high rates of child labor force participation in England in the eighteenth and early nineteenth centuries (Humphries 2003). This was partly due to the rapid growth of labor-intensive industry, the low cost of child labor, and the organizational leap provided by the factory revolution. However, the use of children in factories occurred in an environment where sending children to work was already considered normal. Children were already working in households. In agriculture they held jobs as shepherds, plowboys, crow scarers, and so on. The social acceptability of preindustrial child labor made industrial child labor acceptable. It was only later that sending children to school became part of bourgeois respectability.

It is, of course, quite difficult to disentangle the effects of ideology, law, and economics in changes in child labor or any other aspect of the labor standards debate. As Humphries writes, "Whether social norms changed in advance of declines in child labor . . . or whether they changed in line with the decline in child employment is less certain" (90–91). However, she cites evidence from both England and Japan indicating an important and autonomous role for ideas about childhood and poverty.

Many child workers in the industrial revolution were orphans or had one parent. Both urbanization and empire had increased bastardy. As these children entered industrial labor their entrance lowered standards for those in poor but intact families. Poor-law officials, apparently overwhelmed by the rising cost of relief, tended to collaborate with manufacturers.

Both orphanage and abandonment are rising today and could overwhelm efforts to impose labor standards in poor countries (Polgreen 2006). As with many other aspects of this debate, the chief difference today is the *international* nature of the discussion, and the changed nature of the ideological framework within which it is taking place. Because of the proliferation of single-issue NGOs, there has sometimes been insufficient emphasis on the multidimensionality needed to address the multiple problems of working people. In the case of child labor, standards have needed and still need to be packaged with other social and economic reforms such as health care, schooling, and training.

Thus we need a framework that takes economics, ideology, and law seriously. I have argued that concepts of class and convention provide such a framework. Despite the predation that increasingly characterizes economic life, there is still reason to believe that a shift can occur in the very concept of labor standards, in the way that Amartya Sen has changed the way we think about development. Thus, we seek labor standards, and argue that "worker rights are human rights," not as the humanitarian payoff of economic growth, nor because they may eliminate externalities in the labor market, but because eliminating forced labor, protecting children, ending discrimination, and, especially, providing workers with freedom of association and the right to bargain collectively constitute human development themselves. And we should look to humans, in all their complexity, not just social structures, to produce this change.

Marx, the Factory Inspectors, and Reform

Marx's praise of the factory inspectors is more implied than stated, but in certain places he is very clear. For instance in a footnote in the chapter entitled "The Rate of Surplus Value" in *Capital*, vol. 1, he writes the following about Leonard Horner, one of the factory inquiry commissioners in 1833 and Inspector (or "Censor") of factories until 1859:

> His services to the English working class will never be forgotten. He carried on a lifelong contest, not only with the embittered manufacturers, but also with the Cabinet, to whom the number of votes cast in their favor in the House of Commons was a matter of far greater importance than the number of hours worked by the hands in the mills. (Marx 1981, 334, fn10)

In the chapter entitled "The Working Day" Marx describes the factory inspectors as opposing the "pro-slavery" rebellion of the cotton manufacturers (1981, 401). In the same chapter Horner is described as being "ruthless" and "on the spot" and his description of "nefarious practices" is quoted approvingly (393, 397). In the chapter "Machinery and Large Scale Industry" Marx approves the factory inspectors' description of capitalist complaints about obstruction of business as a mere sham, and the investigation of the Child Employment Commission is described as "thoroughly conscientious" (609). Horner is portrayed here as "the tireless censor of the manufacturers" (538).

In several places in these chapters Marx takes long extracts from the factory inspectors' reports, surrounding them with some of his most thunderous and powerful language. *Capital* really becomes a new kind of book beginning with chapter 10; an abstract, exhaustive, and heavily dialectical specification of the source of the social surplus in the capitalist mode of production in the early chapters gives way to a mix of analysis and drama as Marx surveys the struggles over the length of the working day, the effects of mechanization, the growth of corporate giantism, the powerful impulse to inequality endemic to the capitalist mode of production, and the origins and fate of capitalism itself.[4]

Marx seems not to have thought or had the time to think about the particular class relations and interests borne by the factory inspectors themselves. They, and Horner in particular, stand out as an intriguing exception to Marx's self-imposed rule in *Capital* of treating individuals "only insofar as they are the personifications of economic categories, the bearer (*Trager*) of particular class relations and interests" (1981, 92).[5]

I will return later to this conundrum in *Capital*, but here I would like to examine some of the rhetoric of the factory inspectors themselves and the "literature of the factory" that emerged around the same time, because these together created a particular imagery of what was wrong and what could be fixed in factory production. When first appointed, Horner held meetings with the factory owners in his district, who received him politely and told him that despite their distaste for such legislation they would do their best to conform to it. In a letter to his daughter Horner wrote, "I have no fear but that in a short time the greater proportion of mill owners in my district will view the act not only without dislike but will even admit it to be in many respects highly beneficial" (Djang 1942, 32).

Horner was being optimistic. The rethinking of poverty that occurred with the rise of the dismal science of political (as opposed to moral) economy in the early nineteenth century recast hardship and deprivation as a learned habit rather than a condition brought about by low wages and irregular employment. Ure and other early "philosophers of manufactures" naturalized the historically strange world created by factory production, consigning critics such as the Luddites and William Morris to the romantic category of protesters against the inevitable (Garraty 1979).

Marx's "model" of production has been characterized as "market despotism" by Burawoy (1985), by which he means competitive product markets, the real subordination of workers to capital, workers being more dependent on the capitalist than capitalist on workers (because of the reserve army), and the state being unwilling to regulate conditions inside the factories. But the prominent place given to the history of the Factory Acts and the inspectorate in *Capital* highlights the complex nature of social struggle, involving not just the workers (and their organizations) and the masters, but the state, middle-class reformers, and aristocratic landlords. If this was indeed despotism, it was resisted almost immediately, and it was through middle-class reform as much as the class struggle between workers and capitalists that change came.

In the central chapters of his most important book, Marx's views are consistent with those of Polanyi and other Institutional economists: that the Factory Acts were "required to protect industrial man from the implications of the commodity fiction with regard to labor power" (Polanyi 1980, 132, 165–66, 234) and were the initial step in protecting society from the devastation of the "self-regulating" market.[6]

The 1802 act (The Health and Morals of Apprentices Act) was the first instance of factory legislation (Djang 1942; Engerman 2003), but for Marx the repeal of the Combination Act in 1825 marks the beginning of the definitive shift away from the ideology of free individual contract. The sharpest divide occurs with the act of 1833 when there became some hope of enforcement. But it was not until after the "civil war" of the late 1840s that regulation of the factories was generally secured, underlining Marx's point that "it is a mistake to regard the first empirical form of appearance of a thing as its cause" (Marx 1981, 527), an important caution for those impatient with the (relatively more rapid) pace of reform today.[7]

The key aspect of the 1833 act was the funding of the factory inspectorate. The vast majority of inspectors were children of lawyers, physicians, schoolteachers, engineers, the clergy, military officers, and so forth, in other words the bourgeoisie of the university and the professions. Armed with legal authority, and demanding at-will admission to inspect factories, the inspectorate was chronically underfunded and underpaid.

The class barriers between proletarians and inspectors were hard to overcome, especially as many of the inspectors shared the outlook of the more paternalistic mill owners, and at least initially there were few prosecutions. The Home Office instructed the inspectors to treat owners as friends rather than potential violators, and while the educational background of the inspectors gave them some advantage with owners, it did not make cooperation with workers easy.

Initially, many adult workers opposed the factory inspectors because they were more interested in limiting their own working hours than the hours of their children.[8] Working-class parents, especially fathers, clearly benefited from child labor, and while the child-oriented, affectionate family was a bourgeois ideal this was not the case for workers. Children were understood to be family wage earners hired out by their parents, so that parents functioned as hiring agencies or even as slave owners (Marx 1981, 519–20, 613, 620, 795). A regularized working day was often seen by adult males as a hindrance, interfering with their preference for night work and work late in the week to offset earlier loafing and drinking (Reid 1974). The main victims of this preference were women and children (Marx 1981, 607).

The 1844 Act prohibited children from cleaning self-acting mules while the machines were in motion "but most employers merely hung a copy of the clause in every workroom," not much help with a largely illiterate workforce (Macgregor, 229). Still, the 1844 law reduced the working day for children under thirteen and protected women. Horner saw it as a step forward from the 1833 law, which he thought had been constructed so as to prevent the attainment of its stated goals. Significantly, the 1844 act was supported by those manufacturers opposed to "immoral competition" (Marx 1981, 393). Antipathy between landlords and industrial capitalists was also critical as the former sought to punish the latter for their support of "free trade," which would hurt British agricultural interests.

The 1844 law was unreservedly praised by Marx (1981, 394–95) as the official recognition and proclamation by the state of the rights of workers, and as the overcoming of the ideology of free contract. Despite the weaknesses of the 1833 Act it can be argued that it created a momentum that led to further reforms, especially once the inspectors were exposed to real conditions in the factories, and a class alliance for further reform was created. A bad law may be better than no law at all. The "alliance for further reform" played on the contradiction between paternalism and laissez-faire conservatism on the Tory side and the tendency of middle-class liberalism to leak over into the social question on the Whig side.

Some feminists have argued that the Factory Acts represented a victory for men over women and capital, whereas others have argued that while it enforced the sexual division of labor by enhancing the family wage it improved material conditions for all. Horner conducted surveys to determine the attitude of women and men to the law, and his evidence does not support the notion that the acts were a defeat for women. Roediger and Foner in their history of the working day argue that women were burdened by more work in the home but had some control of the pace of work there and so may have been especially sensitive to the value of time and thus also to the negative aspects of capitalist labor discipline (1989, 165). Female workers were at the forefront of the shorter hours movement in the United States not on the basis of biology but on women's double oppression and subjection to sexual harassment in the workplace (276).

The education clauses of the Factory Acts did not always have the whole-hearted support of workers. Eventually the inspectorate could count on significant worker support in limiting the working day but not for an effective system of education. For Marx, though, these clauses were important in that they "proclaim that elementary education is a compulsory precondition for the employment of children," and this represented a revolutionary alteration in the conditions of the working class (Marx 1981, 613–14; see also 411–12, 619). The Factory Acts undermined capital's "free contract" with labor but also gave children protection from their parents.

Marx argued that the experience of large-scale industry would revolutionize people's minds, and Horner certainly agreed. Horner's own views shifted radically after the first few years of inspecting experience. He remained aware of the dangers of coming down too hard on owners, which would lose him both the support of his political superiors and possibly his own credibility. "He rarely neglected to mention law abiding manufacturers who supported the principles of the factory acts" (Macgregor 1996, 243). But after his survey, and capitalists' vociferous reaction to the proposed ten-hour law in 1847, he began to shift his position, publicly abandoning belief in the validity of the free contract, unless this was legislated and enforced by the state (Macgregor 1996, 243; Marx 1981, 538).

Employers as a class did not welcome regulation as a way of stabilizing economic conditions. Instead, and especially in 1847–48, they engaged in what Marx called a "pro-slavery rebellion" asserting their "rights" vis-à-vis the state and Labor. "Capital in general would have resisted the regulation of the workday until doomsday" (Macgregor 1996, 250). By this time Horner believed that few owners "have genuine sympathy for the employees." Whereas workers celebrated the 1847 Factory Act, owners opposed it in all ways. With the collapse of the Chartist movement in England and the failure of the revolutions on the Continent the time was ripe in the late 1840s and early 1850s for a wave of bourgeois reaction. The "false relay" system was developed to meet the letter of the regulation on children's hours while grossly violating the spirit. Factory inspectors were attacked as revolutionary commissars, and inspection itself as "one of the delusions of communism." Owners petitioned the Home Secretary to suspend the act even as Horner began publishing advertisements warning owners against violating it.

The National Association of Factory Occupiers—which Marx called the "Association for the Mangling of Operatives"—was the first organized expression of employer class interests. The costs of membership in the association exceeded the expenditures necessary to install legally mandated safety devices but as Marx noted, killing is not murder if it done for the sake of profit (Marx 1993, 183).

After 1853 it was the inspectors rather than working-class organizations or the threat of revolution that were critical in promoting regulation. Parliament was still controlled by the landlords and the industrial capitalists, but the bureaucracy they had spawned was now difficult for them to rule. Eventually, by 1860, the employers had been beaten back. Horner and his associates carried the day through a shifting set of alliances with working-class organizations, middle-class reformers, the landed aristocracy, and, to a limited extent, progressive industrialists.

Marx's judgment on the Factory Acts was clear, and it is one with which most historians agree.[9] Once the principle of a regulated working day had been established the working class was regenerated, opposition weakened, and the alliances with working-class allies opened up multiple avenues of attack on Capital, even if conditions did not improve so rapidly outside of textiles. Indeed one could argue that the success of the Factory Acts movement was the beginning of over a century of working-class success and uneven progress in eliminating some of the worst aspects of capitalism, a period that lasted until the tide turned in the last third of the twentieth century.[10]

In *Capital* Marx seemed to believe that regulation would naturally spread and become conventional in the sense used in this book, once established in textiles. But resistance was just as bitter in other industries even given the apparent rationality of reform.

The most dangerous obstacles to improving conditions in the factories had been the class loyalty of the owners and the ideology of classical economics. Vulgar political economy never admitted defeat but proclaimed the Factory Acts as a characteristic achievement of modern economic science, despite repeated countering of the principles of classical economics in the factory inspectors' reports (Marx 1981, 688, 703–4, 1076). The interests of capital as a whole may actually point in the direction of a regulated working day, so as not to wear out exploitable labor power, but there was nothing in the capitalist organization of production or politics that guaranteed that result (380–81, 532–33).

Horner's work is not well known in the contemporary movement for international labor rights. But he certainly inspired the leading communist, who was also the most important political economist of his time. Marx and Horner were men of both thought and action, widely and deeply read, with female children but no surviving sons. They shared intense hostility to exploitation of both children and adults, and contempt for the narrow spirit that dominated political economy. While they were critical of both capitalists and economists, they were harder on the economists who they thought should have known better. Over time, Horner came to appreciate the structural position of Capital as an obstacle to his goals, and Marx made an exception to his generally structuralist account of individuals in the case of the factory inspectors. In making a moral argument that is not naive about the structural power of Capital, certain contemporary labor-based NGOs may be considered the contemporary analogue of Horner and his allies.

The New Factory Inspectors

A variety of groups have developed a factory inspection practice over the past quarter century in response to the new international division of labor. Some of them are more or less corporate, such as Social Accountability International, and appeal to the sensibility of the corporate accountability movement. Others have a mix of corporate, political, and popular roots, such as the Fair Labor Association, the offspring of the Clinton Administration's Apparel Industry Partnership. Some have roots in religious organizations and international solidarity work, such as the National Labor Committee, which has publicized celebrity connections to sweatshop labor and pioneered the investigation of sweatshop conditions in China. Still others are closely tied to student and labor organizations, such as the Worker Rights Consortium.

The growth of this global network of factory inspection has been astonishing (Rodríguez-Garavito 2005). The proliferation of corporate codes of conduct indicates a newly produced need on the part of global corporations to at least be seen as doing the right thing. And despite the obvious asymmetries between the small, not quite shoestring operations of the various monitoring and transnational support groups and the global reach of the major multinational corporations—to say nothing of the contrast of these fragile international labor-based NGOs and the repressive power of the ideological and military state apparatuses—a sweeping dismissal of the potential of these organizations seems premature. To the extent that they are successful in changing the conventions within which globalized labor markets are thought about and normatively evaluated they are effective.

All of the groups just mentioned differ from the nineteenth-century British factory inspectors in that they are nongovernmental organizations. Thus they take on as their charge the work of supporting the enforcement of the laws of the countries they work in, as well as the core rights of the ILO.

The Worker Rights Consortium is particularly interesting in that its constituent members are university groups. Robert Ross and others have criticized the Worker Rights Consortium for trying to deal with the sweatshop problem one factory at a time (Ross 2004). While the WRC approach is unlikely to reverse the historical tendency toward superexploitation *on its own*, it does make a unique contribution. More than the other verifier or vigilante groups the WRC is concerned with building local organizing capacity. While this is not explicitly part of their mission, and WRC staff is reluctant to talk about it, WRC investigations are clearly oriented toward increasing the capability of working people themselves to monitor and report on working conditions.

The late 1990s resurgence of the "labor problem" in the United States surprised many commentators (French 2002). The social science consensus that labor movements are in severe and general crisis may just be wrong, once we move our gaze away from the United States and a few other rich countries. In important recent books, Beverly Silver (2003) and Jefferson Cowie (1999) have argued that while deindustrialization and management opposition have created such a crisis in the US, working classes have also been created and strengthened in favored new investment sites such as South Korea, Brazil, Mexico, and South Africa. Journalistic evidence exists that a tide of protest and dissent is now rising in China (French 2005). While one can not take seriously the structural argument of the *Communist Manifesto* that through capital accumulation the capitalist class creates its own grave diggers, it is in fact the case that simultaneous industrialization and deindustrialization provokes organizing in new industrial centers as well as by those trying to defend the hard-won gains of the past. The trick is to document the existence of a community of fate between the geographically dispersed and racially and economically diverse groups of workers, something that the WRC has begun to do.[11]

That the WRC represents colleges and universities also puts them in a unique position. Certainly universities have become more like corporations, especially as public funding has dwindled. And certainly identity rather than class politics have been prevalent on university campuses in the last two decades. But as Naomi Klein writes, university campuses "with their residences, libraries, green spaces, and common standards of open and respectful discourse—play a crucial, if now largely symbolic role: they are the place left where young people can see a genuine public life being lived" (2000, 101).

Ross distinguishes between the turn-of-the-century student activists and those of the 1960s. While expressing sympathy with and sometimes identification with a socialist vision, the members of United Students Against Sweatshops that Ross interviewed preferred to identify themselves as anticorporate, finding the word *socialism* to be too much of a historical burden. Though less inclined to see the labor movement as "part of the problem" than their 1960s forerunners, their politics is so closely linked to local and communitarian concerns and to identity politics that socialism—the traditional politics of the left wing of the labor movement—really does not capture their consciousness. "If the socialists of the 1960s were sociology students with economic ideas, this decade's radicals are international studies students with vegetarian anarchist culture" (Ross 2004, 261–62).

But the actual effects of USAS and the WRC are not necessarily explained by political consciousness either. However anarchist the more radical students may be in spirit, the result of their work is to allow some progress on the more traditional goals of the labor movement. The WRC and USAS are in no way a global challenge to "corporate capitalism." They do challenge the dictatorship of the global factory, but they do so as reformers not revolutionaries. As one sympathetic critic puts it:

> The proximate goal of the WRC is thus to involve corporate universities in negotiations with corporate behemoths such as Nike and Reebok, so that the billions of dollars worth of consumer goods marketed by these corporate behemoths in our consumer society can be produced under marginally less exploitive labor conditions. (Isaac n.d., 6–7)

The WRC is not a mass movement, nor are its constituent organizations. Were the WRC to achieve its goals, mass production and consumption of overpriced branded products would still exist, as would the corporate exploiters that sell them. Sweatshop conditions might be lessened, but exploitation (if not superexploitation) would still exist. In other words, not only is this not revolutionary, it is not even revolutionary reform.

It *is* a small effort toward developing a moral response to human indignity. It is a partial response to a global problem, and it can, in some times and places, concretely improve the material living standards, solidarity, and freedom of some of the most exploited people on the planet. In doing so, because of its unique base in the radical students of the millennium generation, the WRC and USAS may encourage both capacity to act in the poor countries and a greater desire for class justice in the United States.

Labor relations scholars are just beginning to deal with these issues. In *Workers Rights as Human Rights* editor James Gross gathered together a variety of viewpoints on the current U.S. and international labor rights situation. But while Gross titles his lead chapter "A Long Overdue Beginning: The Promotion and Protection of Workers Rights as Human Rights," he provides no theoretical argument as to why worker rights should be considered human rights. Lance Compa, the author of the Human Rights Watch report on labor rights in the United States, provides a chapter in Gross's book that summarizes that report, in which the human rights–worker rights connection is everywhere asserted but never explained. On the last page of his article he writes, "So long as worker organizing, collective bargaining, and the right to strike are seen only as economic disputes involving the exercise of power in pursuit of higher wages for employees or higher profits for employers, change in U.S. labor law and practice is unlikely. Reformulating these activities as human rights that must be respected under international law can begin a process of change" (Compa 2000, 52).

Just so. But merely reasserting the core labor rights of the ILO as basic human rights is not going to accomplish this goal. Another chapter in the Gross book demonstrates why. Emily Spieler writes a detailed and compelling case for occupational health and safety as a core right. Why are these other "rights" raised to the level of the core, and this is not?[12]

As I argued in chapter 5, the promulgation of the core rights—freedom of association and collective bargaining, freedoms from discrimination, child labor, and forced labor—in 1998 was meant to simplify a dizzying array of ILO conventions. These four core rights were designed to incorporate liberal, Christian socialist, and social democratic concerns so as to appeal to the most interested parties. It was thought that rights that were based on already highly ratified conventions, enabling of other rights (thus collective bargaining might get you a better minimum wage and health and safety but not the other way round), and appealing to these core constituencies would garner more support.

And this is exactly what has happened; the spread of this language of core labor rights in the years following has been remarkable, even when only lip service is being paid. But note that these conditions have been designated as rights on a purely conventional and political basis. Perhaps labor rights theorists believe that by designating something as a human right they are resting on a firmly established body of theory and research, but they are not.

As I argued in chapter 4, since the middle of the twentieth century, "rights" as universal values and unconditional necessities have moved into the center of political discourse, but there has been very little questioning of the conditions for the formation of such rights, their forms, or their objectives. Rights tend to function as a foundation, self-evident and not worthy of deep investigation.

Socialists have consistently argued that civic rights cannot be fully attained without economic and social rights. In other words, political democracy can only be had when the rights of property are limited, and when workers "can be prevented from selling themselves into slavery and death by voluntary contract with capital" (Marx 1981, 416).

I have argued throughout this book that a politics of rights is contradictory, in that such a politics assumes a foundation it does not have (consensus on rights) and that some rights fit well within liberal capitalism while others challenge it. The discourse of the rights of man is mostly consistent with neoliberalism, but the right of the citizen to be involved in democratically organizing the economic life of the community is not. Moreover, the fetishism of commodities hides the *increased interdependence* between peoples that accompanies the growing social and technical division of labor that we call globalization. It is precisely by playing on these contradictions and tensions that the student antisweatshop movement has the potential to open up something beyond reformist reforms.

The post–World War II revival of "rights talk" paid little attention to worker rights as human rights, and most labor organizations were unwilling to assert their agenda in such language. In the United States this began to change in the 1990s, largely driven by the antisweatshop movement. But this assertion has not been accompanied by much reflection on how rights are constituted.

Workers have few collective "rights" in the United States, although there is an expanding set of rights granted to individuals. As shown in the previous chapter though, the U.S. government and important corporations often need to project an image of freedom and progress internationally, and supporting certain labor rights is part of this image. What those rights are changes given the shifting nature of international economic, political, and cultural conditions. This contradiction at times creates the space for challenging and broadening the definition of rights both domestically and internationally.

Can the antisweatshop movement, in concert with other elements of the alter-mondialist/global justice movement, play on this contradiction to advance workers' collective power in the free trade zones of the poor countries and in the United States? One way to think about this is to look at the practice of the antisweatshop movement as this is embodied in factory reports and campus events. I turn to the factory reports here, and campus events in the next chapter.

Global Class Justice

The Worker Rights Consortium produces factory reports and publishes them on their Web site. There is an unwritten understanding that there is at-will entry for the plant visits necessary for these reports, but this is ambiguous as factories are not members of the WRC (universities are) and there is no prior agreement. Sometimes visits are arranged ahead of time. WRC staff believes the best source of information is from workers, especially when such information is gained through off-site interviews.

Let us consider two typical reports. The first, for the "Easy Group," was filed on September 20, 2005 (WRC 2005a). The companies that had contracts with Easy Group worked with the WRC, but Easy Group itself did not cooperate honestly. In the end the WRC recommended that its constituent member universities not source from Easy Group. Typical violations in Easy Group factories included mandatory overtime (forced leave as punishment for refusal, frequent failure to properly compensate, day swapping without consent), misuse of the contract labor system (using contract employees for some positions that are effectively regular positions), discrimination in compensation, and violation of other employee rights such as seniority and freedom of association. "The Assessment Team found overwhelming evidence supporting the conclusion that Easy Group management has engaged in a range of acts that violate worker rights under applicable codes of conduct and Filipino law to associate freely and bargain collectively without interference or reprisal from factory management" (11). Easy Group

> engaged in a pattern of threatening workers with job loss if they chose to affili-
> ate with the union, placing workers on unpaid forced leave, and ultimately ter-
> minating workers en masse in retaliation for their decision to join the union. In
> doing so, management repeatedly justified its actions by claiming that buyers
> had reduced orders from specific facilities, rendering forced leave and termina-
> tions unavoidable. Overwhelming evidence indicates that these claims by Easy
> Group were false and were made deliberately to mislead workers and other
> stakeholders in this case. (WRC 2005a, 12)

Findings of violations included intimidation and harassment of union supporters (also home visits and captive audience meetings), surveillance and isolation of union leaders, use of forced leave as punishment for union activity, attempted bribery of union officers, illegal disqualification of workers, factory closure and mass termination.

> In many instances, the reasons behind a plant closure involving a unionization
> effort are contested and it is difficult to disentangle legitimate reasons from il-
> legitimate anti-union animus. In this case, we are provided with rare circum-
> stances resembling a controlled experiment, in which we can evaluate the re-
> sponse of a parent company to events in two of its own facilities. In one facility,

a unionization effort was successful and the facility was closed. In the second facility, a unionization effort was unsuccessful and the facility flourished. Claims that the closure was made necessary by economic forces are belied by the facts that the facilities differed in no discernable ways relating to production capacity and that the parent company could have easily adjusted business levels in each of the plants to prevent the closure. (WRC 2005a, 15)

In the case of the Easy Fashion subsidiary, according to substantial worker testimony, during the year leading up to the closure of the facility, plant management persistently told workers the factory was experiencing a sharp reduction in orders from buyers that did not approve of the unionization effort and that management would likely be forced to close the facility. Despite these messages, the election results indicated majority support for the union, and the union was certified as the workers' bargaining agent.

Roughly two months after collective bargaining began in earnest in September 2004 management closed the factory and terminated the workforce, citing a loss of orders. Within three months of the closure, Easy Group announced plans to reopen the Easy Fashion facility under a new name, Allen Garments 2. Workers in the "new factory" are not represented by the union.

In the case of another subsidiary, Kasumi Apparel, in February 2003, prior to the union election there, plant management likewise frequently told workers that the union activity was causing a reduction in orders from buyers and that, as a result, the factory might soon close. In this case, the union lost the election. "In contrast to the case of Easy Fashion, following the election management immediately ceased making such statements about a loss of orders and Kasumi's orders and production levels have remained stable since" (WRC 2005a, 15–16). Easy Group management privately acknowledged that the closure threat was related to the unionization effort. Management made the claim that buyers opposed unionization only to the workers but did not try to make such claims to the WRC inspectors or the government. Thus their claims are not particularly credible.

The WRC analysis is generally based on specific aspects of national labor law. The reports in general and this one in particular make extensive use of "substantial (or highly credible), mutually corroborative worker testimony." The one-on-one interview is the basic technique. In each case the WRC provides recommendations, in this one that universities should terminate all orders from Easy Group factories. The rhetoric in these reports is striking in that there is lavish praise for any corporation that cooperates with the WRC. Like Leonard Horner in his early days, the WRC has appealed to the conscience of the brands even as it tries to build organizational capacity in the free trade zones.

A report on Far East Textile and First Apparel was filed on February 8, 2005 (WRC 2005b). The investigation was carried out by a WRC Assessment Team composed of experts in Thai labor and employment law and occupational health and safety during October and November 2004. This investigation included extensive interviews with employees and managers, an occupational health and safety survey, a review of relevant documents, and discussions with several "pertinent buyers."

This exercise was more successful, and the report claimed this assessment "has thus far resulted in substantial improvements in working conditions at both Far East and First Apparel." The WRC credits the management of these facilities for working constructively with the WRC and several key buyers—the Gap Inc. and Levi Strauss & Co.—to realize these improvements in an unusually short time-frame.

Despite the improvements, several issues remained outstanding or required ongoing monitoring to ensure that commitments to remedial action are carried through. "The WRC looks forward to working with buyers and management to see that all three facilities meet our shared standards" (Ibid, 3).

The WRC received cooperation from Levi Strauss and the Gap but not Vanity Fair (VF). The latter company claimed no production at these plants though they had listed them for the Collegiate Licensing Company. Workers recalled seeing Vanity Fair apparel but could not determine whether or not it was for the collegiate market.

> The WRC has also requested that VF accept some level of responsibility for having provided universities with flawed disclosure information over a period of years and to correct problems in their disclosure process. To date, VF has remained unwilling to participate in any way in the remediation process, and has only made vague suggestions as to how it might correct problems in the way it discloses data on supplier factories. (WRC 2005b, 5)

In contrast, Levi Strauss and the Gap

> helped facilitate meetings between the WRC and management, and have lent substantial technical expertise and given insightful input into the development of recommendations for corrective action. Both brands have pledged to continue monitoring the situation, working with management, workers, and the WRC to assure that the recommendations set out in this report are carried through. . . .

> The results of this collaboration in monitoring efforts have been overwhelm-
> ingly positive. All parties, including the WRC, Gap Inc, LS&CO, management,
> and employees, shared in developing the comprehensive remediation plan
> reflected in the recommendations of this report. The collaborative approach
> has streamlined the monitoring process and minimized conflicting recommen-
> dations. The remediation plan is well understood by all parties and its imple-
> mentation will be monitored collectively. (WRC 2005b)

For this report, sources included interviews with employees, management,
brands, collection of relevant documents, and assessment of Thai labor law. In
each case factories were found to be in violation of laws on freedom of association, hours and wages, harassment and abuse, and occupational safety and
health.

Evidence produced in fieldwork conducted by César Rodríguez-Garavito
indicates that the WRC approach, emphasizing direct empowerment of workers, can supplement national labor laws to allow sustainable improvement in
both protective rights and wages. Rodríguez-Garavito (2005), during interviews in Guatemala and Mexico, found a general consensus that the state was
not a reliable enforcer of its own labor laws in either country, because of the
more or less complete cooptation of the official labor movement within corpo-
ratist structures in Mexico, and the state's inability or unwillingness to control
antiworker violence in Guatemala. Collective, concerted, and often violent opposition to organizing by managers and owners, blacklists, and preemptive
codes of conduct have made the boomerang effect necessary, that is, transnational organizing with Northern groups (like WRC and FLA) pressuring their
home country governments and transnational corporations who in turn pressure in-country suppliers and regulators (Keck and Sikkink 1998). As part of
sustained cross-border political pressure, corporate codes, when they are understood by and grievable by the workers themselves, can play a role alongside
national law and the ILO in creating a desire for and practice of class justice.[13]

If behavior is best understood as conventional, the possibilities for ideological as well as economic and political victories should not be idly dismissed.
Of course this may all be seen as a decentering of power in which certain kinds
of exploitation are normalized whereas others are destabilized.

This is certainly part of the effect of the new labor rights discourse as a
whole, but again, this discourse has multiple effects depending on the different
practices that are embodied in it and the different contexts within which these
practices are inserted. My own reading of the cases along with Rodríguez-Garavito's fieldwork indicates that a practice of promoting worker rights that puts

"countervailing pressure and empowered participation" at the center will have quite different effects from the more cosmetic impacts of corporate codes directed primarily at consumer guilt (Rodríguez-Garavito 2005, 210).[14]

Ethical consumerism and investment are not bad in and of themselves, but without the information campaigns and organizational capacity building that the WRC engages in, a different ethic will not produce the kind of countervailing power that can create meaningful shifts in the bargaining position of workers both North and South. The most widely used corporate codes, those of industry groups like Social Accountability International and the Worldwide Responsible Apparel Certification Program, are the least protective and conducive to worker empowerment. Commercial auditing firms dominate these organizations, producing analysis that one of Rodríguez-Garavito's interviewees described as "getting at the tip of the iceberg" at best.

The cutting edge of factory monitoring work until recently was in relationships between U.S. and Latin American organizations.[15] Both the WRC and Fair Labor Association (FLA) include freedom of association and the right to bargain collectively as part of their code. The major differences between the WRC and the FLA are that the former makes it relatively easy for workers to file complaints, uses independent monitoring in collaboration with local workers and support groups, and continuously monitors a small number of cases. FLA monitoring is more complete but does not build local or independent capacity for monitoring, and it has no systematic process for workers to file complaints. The WRC is more stringent, less systematic ("trying to change the world one factory at a time"), and more transparent, and it has much greater worker involvement.

The WRC's use of joint investigative teams is a form of popular education and organization building that includes constructing important ties to both transnational networks and local workers' support groups that are themselves often organized around the complex needs of often mostly female workforces. Working training, popular education, and channeling of complaints are particularly important activities. The importance of training and education can be seen in that often when workers are first exposed to the idea of "codes of conduct" they think these refer to *their* conduct, not that of the owners and managers (Rodríguez-Garavito 2005).

The first two collective contracts signed in Latin American global factories producing for North American brands with codes of conduct came from WRC investigations. More recently FLA investigations have also led to contracts, and these two organizations are sometimes complementary, with the WRC pulling the FLA further in the direction of worker empowerment. The WRC approach of sustained pressure in particular locations seems to be a better form for promoting worker self-organizing, but there is a small number of cases so far.[16]

So while limitations on state capacity may indeed be the reason for the rise of collaborative systems of governance, the usefulness and desirability of various governance networks are contextually specific. At the microlevel, building workers' countervailing power through popular education and training and regularized grievance procedures while constructing umbrella transnational organizing campaigns not only leads to concrete improvement in working conditions and material standards of living but allows workers to build new social identities while learning they are part of a broader movement.

Still, the structural power of capital and the ability of brands to massage global human rights rhetoric are increasingly seen as problematic by those with deep experience both on the ground in the poor countries and in Washington. While Wal-Mart's ethical sourcing report is seen as a joke, it is considered only marginally worse than those of Reebok and Adidas.[17] The increasing cynicism of the new factory inspectors contrasts with the optimism of the brands and their allies in multilateral organizations who see rights violations as regrettable but incidental even though they locate in those countries because of those violations!

From the point of view of labor-based NGOs like the WRC, the ILO appears singularly ineffective by design, and the other multilateral organizations just uninterested. The ILO's lack of enforcement capability looks like a bigger issue from the viewpoint of a Guatemalan sweatshop than it does from a Geneva hearing room. There has been some joint work between the WRC and the World Bank in Haiti following the latest coup, but according to WRC executive director Scott Nova, "if there were 1% as much interest in worker rights as in intellectual property rights there would be no problem."

Nova agrees that while there are weaknesses in ILO standards these are still useful in establishing an international rhetoric of worker rights. Given what the WRC is trying to accomplish, the lack of a consensus on a wage standard is a big gap in the ILO system, because minimum wage enforcement within countries is generally weak or nonexistent.

In its short life, the WRC has followed a trajectory similar to Horner's, from fear that companies will reject standards, to hope that they might accept them and praise for them whenever they do, to recognition that other alliances must be built because most brands, most of the time are hopeless.

WRC's relationship with corporations has been changing. According to Nova, even the best corporate programs are nearly bankrupt. Cooperation and multistakeholder coalitions have not been particularly valuable. From his perspective the brands are not serious about improving conditions in any sustainable way. Cooperation may make sense on a case-by-case basis, but as a basic strategy it does not seem to work. While cooperation is the rhetorical strategy of the Fair Labor Association, Nova points out that "the FLA is the brands themselves."

The WRC has developed its new Designated Supplier Program (DSP) in response to this perceived bankruptcy. Rather than waiting for complaints, the WRC will now designate particular factories as having achieved basic standards on freedom of association and living wages, and colleges and universities will be encouraged to gradually shift production of their logoed goods to those factories. DSP is a response to the contemporary economics of supply chain management.

The brands have generally followed the Nike lead—"in the past we were lax, now we are involved." The line is that countries don't do a good job, and factories need to be educated. Corporate spokespeople tend to deny that the *prices* they offer to factories are part of the problem. It took the WRC a while to recognize what it now sees as the hypocrisy of the brands. In the first wave of engagement, WRC assumed that prices would be raised to allow standards to be met by "engaged" brands.[18] But the system is set up to produce goods very cheaply, fast, and with reasonable quality, and it reflects those priorities. Worker rights were not a concern when this system was developed. Constantly setting one factory off against another and maintaining temporary supply relationships, especially in apparel, with three to thirty customers per factory, forces prices down.

Retailers' primary interest with regard to worker rights is public relations, and they prefer low-cost solutions to worker rights issues. According to Nova this is why the brands have found complaints about child labor the most important and also the easiest to handle. It is the labor rights violation that most offends individual-liberal rights and is not that expensive to fix. In most lines of footwear and apparel at least, using child labor does not significantly reduce costs. Forced overtime, more prevalent and more costly, does not get the same attention.

This is only partly because brands increasingly rely on essentially their own social accounting standards. It is worth quoting Scott Nova at length here:

> Labor costs are a small issue for brands. They could operate models but choose not to. Brands want to solidify private codes of conduct and (private) monitoring as the gold standard, the best that can be established "given economic backwardness and unscrupulous factory managers." But a good brand would establish long term relationships, reasonable pricing, and give the bulk of a factory's business. Instead they externalize the risks and costs associated with the industry. Outsourcing externalizes, not just lowers costs.

Cooperating factories tend to be criticized by peers. Any factory recognizing a union will be ostracized. Factories know brands aren't serious. Software is available to keep triple books, and there is a whole culture with dialogue among producers around "how do we fake it?" According to Nova, "People doing inspections are often sincere but corporate people have to know it's bullshit."

In the previous chapter I advocated for a debate on the floor of the U.S. Senate over the ratification of ILO Conventions No. 87 and No. 98. Such a debate would take place in front of and shed light on new networks of class and social power and convention that are active but not often seen or discussed. This would not be a partisan debate in the American sense. On the philosophical issues concerning labor rights there are few substantive differences between most Republicans and the Clinton wing of the Democratic Party. Individual Democrats may raise important issues of class and morality in international economics,[19] but the Clintonite approach—sign trade deals that are just awful and then talk about labor rights—has been the winning one in the 1990s and 2000s. Bill Clinton's appeals on this issue in Seattle and after were often for domestic political audiences. According to Nova, "Clinton's anti-sweatshop initiative was a pittance. Bush is the awfulness without the pittance."

Conclusion

The effectiveness of factory inspector groups, whether of the old or new type, depends on their ability to forge cross-class alliances, the extent to which workers themselves are organized, and the ability to establish a bureaucratic presence at least somewhat autonomous from the power of Capital. There is no simple recipe for success, and the tactics that work in one time and place may not work in others.

Worker rights and labor standards were originally and to some extent are today issues pushed primarily by middle-class reformers. One's class background does not fully explain either the intentions or the effects of one's actions however. Still, the temptation to accede to a purely liberal version of worker rights might be expected to be strong, particularly as it is the rights of the individual that corporations find it easiest to accept. But the experience of employer resistance both in Horner's time and ours has had the effect of pushing reformers toward more structural and collective forms of resistance. The prospects for such resistance depend critically on the forms of moral valuation that globalization is producing, and this is the subject of the final chapter.

CHAPTER 8

Think Locally, Act Globally

For much of my adult life I have straddled the popular and academic worlds. I have a *Jobs with Justice* bumper sticker in my office that says (in Spanish and English) "Worker rights are human rights." A valued colleague, a Latin American historian, signs all her e-mails with Amnesty International's slogan: "Human beings have human rights, whatever label they are given and wherever they are."

I am made nervous because I don't understand what either of these slogans means, yet I want to support them. Outside of a religious context it is not clear to me what it means to say that *human* rights exist. Civil or citizen rights are clear, in that they are grounded in law and the power of the state. But, as I have shown in this book, the contemporary human rights discourse is better explained as a product of a peculiar conjuncture of social forces, and it rests on not very much *philosophically*. So I fear that my politically engaged friends think that when they say "labor rights are human rights" or "human beings have human rights" they have grounded these "rights" in something solid when they have not.

It is awkward to say this because the late twentieth-century human rights movements produced many social victories that I support and see as conditions for any kind of decent society. But these movements were and are diverse and have been most successful when notions of rights have become attached to mass organizing and been translated into enforceable laws. Moreover, "human rights" is a big tent concept, and the failure to closely examine the content of these rights and their possible effects can lead to unexpected results. Antislavery reinforced exploitive industrial capitalism, the social movements emerging from the 1960s contributed to the individualization of the employment relationship, and today corporate codes of conduct tend to focus on child labor to the exclusion of freedom of association and collective bargaining.

Using concepts of convention and class drawn from the Institutional and Marxian traditions in economics I have argued that an important and imminent tendency in the world economy today is the creation of social distance through various techniques that dissolve the moral responsibility of the employer for his employees. There is strong reason to doubt the effectiveness of appeals to the moral conscience of company management or consumers in combating the effects of the sweating system of production that has resulted from this increase in social distance.

The pursuit of worker rights through labor market regulation and worker organizing may be more promising, but if the assertion of rights claims is colored by class interest then the individualism of most human rights work today is not a sufficient basis for pursuing the most important rights goals in the workplace. The antislavery movement's tendency to idealize "free labor," the displacement of the New Deal system through the growth of individual rights in the contemporary U.S. workplace, and corporate codes of conduct that emphasize child labor while avoiding mention of freedom of association or collective bargaining are examples of the ways in which capitalist class interest can capture the language of human and worker rights.

I documented that the International Labor Organization and the U.S. Senate are important places where the laws and conventions governing the workplace might be discussed as rights. In the last chapter I showed that some groups documenting conditions in the new global factory, however middle class their origins, contribute to the assertion of worker rights by building workers' own organizing capacity and by challenging the fetishism by which the endless stream of commodities flowing from the global factory seem to fall from the sky rather than being produced under definite conditions by particular workers in specific places.

During the cultural revolution of the 1960s people were encouraged to "think globally, act locally," to consider the global effects of the way we live while being active in our local communities. Today it is the opposite that seems most important, to "think locally and act globally," to shrink the social distance that corporate globalization has created, so that the person who made the sneakers you are wearing is actually your neighbor, while acting through global networks to challenge the material and ideological conditions that continue to exclude workers from the most important decisions affecting their lives.

In emphasizing the possibilities in international organizations, domestic politics, and NGOs I do not want to seem like a Pollyanna. The massive defeat of the organized working class in the United States and the increasingly disconnected lives of so many people in the rich countries as well as the poor is a real-

ity that must be contended with. While the new factory inspector movement
suggests that the establishment of worker rights and labor standards can happen with a broad-based coalition for change, the extension of the market can
lead to backsliding, and the moral effects of globalization are not always as simple as its proponents seem to believe. I will illustrate these two points through
a brief consideration of Wal-Mart's supply network and employment system,
and some evidence on moral changes associated with globalization and neoliberalism, before concluding with a discussion of how and why one can, indeed,
think locally and act globally.

Sweating and the Dictatorial Factory

> A woman arrives at a cash register in a Wal-Mart store at 6:45 A.M. two days
> before Christmas. The man running the register appears to be in his seven-
> ties. He looks at the twenty people waiting in his line, turns around to notice
> again that he has no bagger, and looks across at the only other cashier on
> duty.
>   "This is ridiculous, only two cashiers," he says to no one in particular, but
> loud enough for the woman to hear him. "Yes it is," she says. "Why do you
> think they only have two cashiers on?"
>   "Because Wal-Mart management are pricks," the man says, now looking at
> his customer. Pretty strong language, she thinks, then asks, "What do you
> mean?"
>   "They just want everything for themselves and don't give a damn about
> the people who work here. They're like communists."
>   "That sounds like capitalism to me," the woman says. "The idea of com-
> munism is to share everything equally isn't it?"
>   "Yeah, they're capitalists all right," the cashier responds. When the woman
> mentions that the only way things will change is for the workers to get to-
> gether the cashier continues to mutter about the "pricks" in management as
> he bags her items and turns to the next customer.[1]

It seems evident that the shift toward a sweating system of organizing the employment relationship is a key element in creating a race to the bottom (or at
least a downward spiral) for a significant segment of the American labor force.
Unfortunately, there appears to be a second tendency evident within the contemporary American labor market, namely, the transformation of the "factory
system" back toward the dictatorship of capital model that predominated a
century ago. Wal-Mart combines both of these tendencies.

Wal-Mart's famed supplier network, in terms of the labor system intrinsic to it, is an external sweating system analogous to that I associated with Nike and Town Dock in chapter 3. Similarly, Wal-Mart's widely condemned system of procuring janitorial services is an "internal sweating system" analogous to what we see in many hotels and universities but perhaps more nefarious as it depends on a workforce of illegal aliens. At the same time, Wal-Mart maintains a factory system in its stores, with direct employment practices of the sort critically analyzed by Marx and others.

I wish to briefly sketch some essential elements of the factory system to justify my claim that this devolution to the dictatorial factory is partly produced by a moral shift in American capitalism.

In any labor process, workers may be made to do some things but cannot be required to do others. Ethical considerations may make the distinction between "reasonable" and "unreasonable" demands obvious, but ethical standards are subject to erosion by the competitive process and so require both legal sanction and ongoing education to reinforce their normality. In the first two-thirds of the twentieth century in the United States, employers were increasingly restrained and employers and workers collectively liberated through child labor laws, fair standards legislation, recognizing the right to freedom of association, and establishing occupational health and safety standards. This transformed factory-type workplaces from dictatorships to (limited) democracies, or what we might call social contract factories.

The master-servant relationship originally guided the construction of the employment relationship in the United States (Tomlins 1993). Accordingly, the owner (master) assumed responsibility initially for the wages (negotiating the wage bargain) of the workers doing the owner's substantive work. That is, a central element of factory production is the presumption—discarded under the sweating system—that compensation for and fair treatment of the employee is the owner's responsibility.[2]

Just as it uses its superior bargaining power to negotiate miserly wage bargains, so Wal-Mart implements callous managerial transactions to maintain rigid, dictatorial control over its employees. These were both hallmarks of the early stages of factory-based industrial capitalism.[3]

Department stores, the ancestor of today's Wal-Mart, arose shortly after the industrial revolution, evolving out of the dry goods stores of the 1830s and 1840s in both the United States and France that emphasized rapid turnover of product (Bensen 1988; Miller 1981). They originated as anchors of a new and openly commercial urban culture. As opposed to earlier retail shops, the new department stores of the second half of the nineteenth century set uniform prices, provided refunds for shoddy merchandise, allowed free access without the obligation to buy, and provided a previously unimaginable variety of goods. These stores defended themselves against allegations of unfair competition by pointing to their low prices and better service to the public.

The early department stores employed floor walkers to greet customers and to supposedly assure they were well served. In the 1920s they developed a specialized (and mostly female) labor force to more directly manage the customer. Wal-Mart is in a sense a return to the early days of the department store, with the customer free to walk the aisles with little chance of being approached with an aggressive sales pitch but also with little chance of receiving any help.

Mechanization came slowly to the department store. Even now, retail sales workers are not, like many workers in manufacturing, engaged in a single repetitive task. Instead, their work is dictated by the flow of goods from the back of the store to the front and the flow of customers from the front of the store through various departments and back to the checkout counter. Both of these flows are uncertain, so that the labor process is dictated not by the assembly line but by direct management supervision. Floor managers are generally given a budget less than what is necessary to fully staff their stores so that "they have an idea of how much extra work they must try to extract from their workforce" (Head 2004, 85). That Wal-Mart is ruthless in exercising its bargaining power is indisputable. For example, Wal-Mart starts its textile buyers at a salary significantly below the industry standard salary. The average salary for store "associates" is below the federal poverty level for a family of three (Monbiot 2004). Wal-Mart managers ruthlessly force down prices in the supply chain, leading to systematic abuses of worker rights and giving more and more business to the gigantic Chinese factories that turn out schlock goods with "always low prices." Meanwhile the collapse of retailing alternatives means that Wal-Mart increasingly occupies a monopsony position with respect to its suppliers, and this collapse along with the destruction of domestic manufacturing employment means it is provided with an ever-growing reserve army to choose from for its "associates."

Wal-Mart has changed the nature of managerial transactions, in its own stores, and as the leading edge of a new type of employer. Common practices at Wal-Mart include illegal doctoring of time cards (time theft), extensive violation of child labor laws, unequal pay and treatment of workers, illegal use of undocumented workers, violation of state regulations governing time for breaks and meals, and violations of the Americans with Disabilities and the Occupational Safety and Health Acts (Greenhouse 2004a, 2004b; Miller 2004). Using Wal-Mart as the model for retail success, other stores are now following Wal-Mart's lead both in using labor subcontractors who employ undocumented workers and consistently violating labor law (Schneider and ElBoghdady 2003).

According to the *Random House Dictionary*, to exploit is to "use selfishly for one's own ends."[4] According to Simon Head, "The exploitation of the working poor is now central to the business strategy favored by America's most powerful and, by some criteria, most successful corporation" (2004, 89). That is, exploitation in this sense of the term lies at the very heart of Wal-Mart's system of labor relations, whether implemented indirectly through the sweating system approach or directly through the dictatorial factory system. If it is indeed true that Wal-Mart is now considered to be paradigmatic of how a company can succeed, exploitation of labor has become enshrined as an explicit business principle.

Grab as Much as You Can Any Way You Can

While Wal-Mart has become a lightning rod for critics its successful business strategy is symptomatic of larger social shifts. Of central concern here are (1) the *norms* or the limits imposed by the formal and informal rule structure, or "conventions," that spell out what we can, may, or must do in relation with other economic agents; and (2) *sovereignty*, by which I mean our anticipation of limits that the state will in fact impose via law and violence. The state's likely interpretation and, equally important, its will to enforce enacted law is a central element in determining individual behavior.

In the case of informal rules—values, mores, norms, that is, internalized mental habits and ethical beliefs drawn from social experience—the sanction of social disapproval limits the individual's aims beneath what may technically be legal.

One's values, or more broadly one's ethical principles, obviously are the root cause of forbearance. Values or ethical principles also lie at the very heart of working rules, not one's individual values but those of the authoritative figures who have consecutively decreed that specific working rules shall be applicable. Working rules, whether incorporated into law and generally applicable or an enterprise's (or, for that matter, labor union's) specific policy pronouncement, were all authoritatively adopted at some point in the past. At such time, their selection was motivated by their utility in advancing some public or private purpose. Thus values or ethical premises infuse every element of the work-

ing rules that together in interrelated fashion dictate the logic of what economists know as "market forces."

Wal-Mart's organization of its labor process, partly via adoption of the
sweating system and partly via implementation of a dictatorial version of the
factory system, has implicitly enshrined exploitation of labor as a valid business
principle. There is of course nothing new about individuals being driven by a
value premise that might pejoratively be described as "it's OK to grab as much
as you can, any way you can."

All major religious systems throughout history have promulgated standards of personal behavior condemnatory of the "grab as much as you can, any
way you can" ethic, yet it has also been long recognized that the spirit of Mam-
mon—an "unhealthy" proclivity to pursue wealth for oneself irrespective of the
consequences for others—is always a possibility. Social theorists have worried
whether it is possible to constrain the influence of this unhealthy proclivity in
an environment where individuals are left free to pursue their self-interest in
unregulated markets. As we have seen, Adam Smith's advocacy of "the system of
natural liberty" was premised on his determination that, via "sympathy" and
the "impartial spectator," individuals generally possess an internal mechanism
that brings their conduct into line with established moral principles.[5]

During the Progressive Era, many students of capitalism argued that, unless
minimum standards are enforced, competition inexorably drives all producers
in the direction of the "lowest common denominator," that is, *requires* them to
abandon any moral strictures that might prevent them from adopting the standards of the low-cost competitor or, alternatively, with an eye toward the capital market, the high-rate-of-return competitor. The Commons wing of Institutional economics, with its emphasis on market regulation, grew out of and with
the Progressive movement. Commons perceived that the business system at any
point in time generally contains a mix of "good" (high standard) and "bad"
(low standard) enterprises. The objective of regulation, he argued, should be to
force the "bad" up to the workable standards already shown to be practicable
through their previous adoption by "good" concerns.

In the middle decades of the twentieth century it continued to be presumed
that regulation helps ensure that market outcomes remain within morally de-
fensible bounds. During the 1970s and 1980s, however, a clear shift occurred in
the guiding philosophy espoused by capitalism's defenders. Milton Friedman
can be seen as the most visible public spokesman for this new view, which insisted that business principals and agents have no moral responsibility other
than to maximize the interests of business owners and, furthermore, that gov-

ernment has no useful role to play in supervising business behavior or in providing for a social safety net (Friedman 1962; Friedman and Friedman 1979). If Smith's normative ideal can appropriately be designated "moral capitalism," then Friedman's must be deemed "amoral capitalism."

The race to the bottom is widely used in public discourse in reference to an anticipated downward spiral of wage outcomes, environmental standards, and so on, as a result of globalization via "free" markets. The case of Wal-Mart alerts us to another manifestation of this phenomenon, namely, a *moral* race to the bottom, with the bottom of course being the ethic of "grab as much as you can, any way you can."

In recent years we have witnessed within the United States the seemingly inexorable spread of "grab as much as you can, any way you can" excesses previously kept in check by working rules enforced by reasonably vigilant regulators. The scandals of Enron, Worldcom, the California Energy Crisis, subprime lending, and that prominent symbol of crony capitalism, Halliburton all exemplify this. I want to be clear that *this kind of behavior—"grab as much as you can, any way you can"—now is the rule not the exception.* Wal-Mart has essentially transported the same ethic into its labor policies, writ large.

In capitalism, most individuals depend on their success in negotiating appropriate outcomes to two discrete types of bargains. As consumers, they negotiate a large number of price bargains allowing them to gain access to the many items that provide them with their material standard of living. Policymakers conditioned by the Friedman vision have focused single-mindedly on improving the economic system's ability to deliver goods and services to consumers at the lowest possible costs, that is, via ever more favorable price bargains. Wal-Mart, with its "low prices always," is a creature of, and indeed epitomizes, this tendency.

Attaining an adequate standard of living presumes those individuals who might be capable of negotiating favorable price bargains must previously have succeeded in negotiating an adequate wage bargain. Most people negotiate few of these. Hence sound public policy requires that the policymaker balance the desirability of low consumer prices (price bargains) against the equally compelling desirability of higher money wages and better working conditions (wage bargains). That is, the market place works well only if it balances the goal of "cheaper goods" with the goal of "equitable incomes and working conditions."

During the 1950s and 1960s, the nation's largest and most successful companies—IBM, U.S. Steel, General Motors, and so on—while often viewed as "monopolists," were also viewed as "good" employers providing American citi-

zens with "good" incomes and reasonable working conditions. To be sure, the
Wagner Act and its subsequent case law along with a National Labor Relations
Board prepared to enforce the established law were ever-present background
factors exerting their influence upon the behavior of these employers.
Nonetheless, those companies provided the nation with its normative model of
appropriate wage bargains (in some cases, negotiated with union representatives). This was the model that business schools prepared their industrial relations students to emulate.

In large part the capitalist class in the United States never accepted the New
Deal settlement, but they were prevented by law and prevailing moral standards
from violating its terms. Milton Friedman and other neoliberals argued against
that settlement right through the 1950s and 1960s but it was not until the 1970s
and 1980s that they began to achieve ideological hegemony.

Reaganomics was the means by which the Friedman vision became public
policy. Workers' collective organization was attacked in theory, law, and everyday practice. Regulation, in general, was dismissed as counterproductive or ineffective. Regulatory bodies were subverted, foremost among them the National Labor Relations Board (Gross 2003a). Productive efficiency and low
prices for consumers came to be regarded as the sole beacons by which economic policy should be directed. At the same time, the "grab it" ethic was freed
to operate in a more naked form. Indeed, "grab it" shows many signs of having
already attained the status of an institution, a settled habit of thought, one generation after Reagan's victory.

If selfishness is part of human nature, then "grab as much as you can any
way you can" has always lurked in the background, as an instinct or a propensity. But a propensity is not the same as an institution. It is this transformation
that the neoliberalism of the last thirty years has accomplished.

Wal-Mart is now increasingly regarded as providing retail business with its
paradigmatic model. Terms such as *growth, competitiveness, efficiency,* and *low
prices always* are generally employed in providing a reason why Wal-Mart is ac-
corded this status. But the fact is that exploitation of its implicit and explicit
workforce is at the base of these achievements. And "Grab!" is the controlling
ethical principle.

The preceding anecdote of the Wal-Mart cashier captures worker alienation
in the new retail factories as well as the low level of political consciousness so
common today in the United States. Caught in a set of social relations that they
know are exploitive, these workers feel powerless to change their situation.[6]
Workers striking a Kroger supermarket were quoted as saying they would never

work at Wal-Mart, but most of them admitted to shopping there (Schneider and ElBoghdady 2003).

While some Americans might feel guilty about shopping at Wal-Mart, a consumerist response, so easy to think of in American life, may not be particularly helpful. Above and beyond the obvious elitism of such a response, the identity of consumer, by displacing that of citizen or worker, is supportive of Wal-Mart because what Wal-Mart offers above everything else is "always low prices."

In this book I have attempted to discern the likelihood of creating a normative consensus in favor of certain rights, and the likely effectiveness of existing and prospective laws and organizations in securing those rights. I recognize that social change always requires effective political leadership and organization.[7] But it also takes an honest recognition of how changes in the economy are interacting with systems of moral valuation. To the extent that I am right about the "grab it" ethic the news is not good. What kind of person is globalization producing?

What Kind of Moral Self Is Globalization Producing?

Since the 1970s there has been a massive extension of the market both geographically and into new areas of social life. More and more things take the form of commodities, and more and more people have become wage laborers. How has this affected dominant moral conventions? How have these changes been influenced by class interest?

Some of the organizations that are currently most active in the area of worker rights have their origin in the international solidarity networks built to combat U.S. Central America policy in the 1980s. Often with religious roots, these organizations make what is primarily a moral critique of contemporary multinational capitalism. One of these groups, the National Labor Committee (NLC), succeeded in putting the sweatshop issue in the mainstream through its exposure of Kathy Lee Gifford.

It is possible that consumers are more aware of the sweatshop problem through the work of the NLC and other groups. Richard Freeman and other economists have shown that people are willing to pay more for "sweat free" goods but that there is an information problem. "The problem is that unlike the brick maker who knows whether he works in a sewer or palace, the consumer does not know directly if the t-shirt he bought was made under good or bad work conditions" (Freeman 1998, 10). The cost of gaining this information is simply too high. Various organizations now exist to provide and disseminate such information, but they face their own inability to monitor conditions in the literally thousands of factories that might be servicing even one retailer. So consumers are willing to pay more, but there is no obvious way to tap this willingness.

For Freeman, progress in labor standards could occur rapidly if an effective way were found to use consumer pressure and willingness to pay. Since labor costs are low in developing countries, and since labor costs typically account for a small percentage of total costs, a small increase in price has a big potential payoff. For instance, suppose consumers were willing to pay $1 more for a t-shirt currently selling for $20, and that labor costs represented 10 percent of the price of the shirt. This would increase the funds available to labor by 50 percent ($1/.1^*20$), which could be used to increase wages, improve working conditions, raise nonwage compensation, and so on.

One approach to solving this information problem is the sweat-free labels that were developed first in the Rugmark campaign in Germany but that have also become part of the Fair Labor Association (FLA) program in the United States. However, there is currently no single and sufficiently funded labeling organization or body regulating exist labeling organizations, meaning that labels are likely to be subject to their own race to the bottom.

Adverse publicity such as the National Labor Committee's campaign against Kathy Lee Gifford has some impact, but again, absent widespread monitoring, such campaigns are more successful in embarrassing rich-country media celebrities than they are in actually improving conditions in the poor countries or, especially, empowering workers and their organizations.

Corporations have developed their own codes of conduct, mostly in response to the risk they face to the millions of dollars they have spent developing brand recognition. The content of these codes is heavily influenced by class interest, as I argued in chapter 7. Moreover, the companies that have developed such codes are often already the most socially responsible and are targeted in the first place because they have brands that can be stained and management that is likely to respond. This is similar to the way in which human rights activists have been successful in shaming countries like Argentina that aspire to Enlightenment norms, but less effective with countries like China that do not. Government-sponsored initiatives such as the FLA seem best suited for firms that want to make marginal improvements while maintaining low wages and absolute control in the workplace.[8]

The issues covered most frequently in corporate codes are safety and health, discrimination, and environmental protection. Those least likely to be mentioned are overtime hours and pay, and the right to organize and bargain collectively. As Freeman argues, the latter is the right with the most promise for creating countervailing power at the grassroots. Yet not only does it run up against the interests of the corporations, it finds less than ringing support in the human rights world because these are collective, not individual rights.

If the recent period of globalization has led to a shift in moral sensibility of the kind that Thomas Haskell (1985) discusses, it has been a very particular shift. People in the (over)developed world are more aware of remote suffering, and in some cases are aware of ways they might alleviate that suffering and are prepared to do so. But the suffering that tends to appeal most broadly, that the media focuses on, and that corporations find relatively easy to accommodate is physical pain of the body and inequality of opportunity. Neoliberal globalization teaches us to think as equals, and as individuals.

Rather than an ethical self, one can argue that globalization is producing an "investing self." As the welfare state is rolled back individuals find themselves thrown into a world that offers fewer institutional supports. This engenders feelings of both widened freedom to construct one's own life *and* uncertainty about the result of one's choices. Left without traditional authorities and securities, one is now more than ever "condemned to be free." What has been at the core of the neoliberal project, the freeing of the "enterprising spirit," is now being extended to the private sphere. The remarkable spread of the word *capital* to include all kinds of human characteristics and relationships—human capital, social capital, cultural capital—is a sign of this transformation.

The substitution of electronic and digital media networks for human interactions also affects what Haskell calls humanitarian sensibility. Haskell argued that the abolitionist movement effected a real transformation in moral sensibility "through changes the market wrought in *perception* and *cognitive style.* And it was primarily a change in cognitive style—specifically a change in perception of causal connection and consequently a shift in the conventions of moral responsibility—that underlay the new constellation of attitudes and activities that we call humanitarianism." What links the capitalist market directly to a new sensibility is "the power of market discipline to inculcate *altered perceptions of causation* in human affairs" (Haskell 1985, 342, emphasis in the original).

The spread of market relationships encourages a particular kind of humanitarian sensibility. In other words, the workings of the market as product and producer of social conventions allow for some forms of moral responsibility to occur and not others. These social conventions, filtered through the culture of the market, enable the individual to maintain a good conscience even when doing little about most of the world's suffering and injustice. Because transactions happen at arm's length, we alleviate very few human sufferings without feeling that "we have thereby *intended,* in any way, or *caused,* in any morally significant way, the evils that we leave unrelieved" (Haskell 1985, 352).

As Haskell points out, technology plays a part in what we think is caused by our actions and what is not. The example he uses is that of the starving stranger. We all know that every day people starve in places like Ethiopia or Bangladesh, yet we do nothing about it. They are strangers, and all we know about them is that they will die. In the eighteenth century there was literally nothing that we could do. Today we know that we actually could sell our cars, get on a plane, and save a stranger's life. Our sense of responsibility does not extend far enough to consider this action. Still, our feeling of responsibility for the stranger's death, albeit not strong enough to move us to action, is most likely stronger today than it was before safe and fast air travel was an option, and information so easily available.

This suggests that new technology—using that word broadly to refer to all means of accomplishing our ends, including new institutions and political organizations that enable us to attain ends otherwise out of reach—can change the moral universe in which we live (Haskell 1985, 356).

Interview evidence supports Haskell's assumption of markets as a driver of what could be called "enlightened capitalist rationality" while at the same time underscoring how globalization contributes to the erosion of ethical standards. What sounds inconsistent might not be so. The investing self has a heightened interest in global events and thus a larger moral universe than before the age of digital communication. Harm to the body and nature, and violations of equality of opportunity are particularly obnoxious to the investing self, and consumers and investors are sometimes able to act, and often do, on this repugnance (Zwick, Denegri-Knott, and Schroeder 2007).

I argued in chapter 4 that liberals, conservatives, and socialists have all thoroughly criticized the concept of human rights, and that human rights have almost no standing in neoliberalism, which is the translation of neoclassical economics into the policy realm. The robustness of "rights talk" then must be found in the conjuncture of the Holocaust, the Cold War, and now neoliberal globalization, and this talk has little use for collective rights like freedom of association and collective bargaining. This is especially true in the United States.

In evaluating labor standards, orthodox economists would generally start by calculating the cost of meeting those standards and the next best options available to those who might lose their jobs if improved standards raise costs. But even holding aside the enormous measurement problems here, it is likely that the one standard that has the most potential for empowering workers— guaranteeing workers the right to freedom of association and collective bargaining—is also the most controversial and costly. It changes the balance of power in both the workplace and in politics. Unionization raises costs, and it challenges management power on the shop floor and in the government. Freedom of association threatens the stability of repressive regimes in the enterprise and the state.

This is the place where the worker rights and labor standards debate is most closely connected to the kind of globalization we are going to have. While Freeman believes that "what is necessary is economic growth," another conclusion flows just as easily from his analysis: "what is needed is increased power and participation for ordinary people." Freeman himself says as much: "If only capital is at the table devising the rules of the game, the rules will be set to benefit capital. . . . representatives and advocates of labor must be at the table that set the rules of any new world financial system" (1998).[9]

Thus, in the end, the campaign for labor standards is not purely about labor standards but about creating a wedge for bringing the concerns of working people to the tables where the great issues of globalization are decided.[10] That we have so much difficulty doing so must be attributed both to contemporary moral convention and class interest. If the impact of class interest and conventional morality is to be turned aside in favor of a worldview incorporating collective rights like freedom of association, the starving stranger must seem like a neighbor. People must be able to think locally and act globally.

Think Locally, Act Globally

Labor rights NGOs have been sponsoring tours by sweatshop workers from poor countries in the United States for some time now, and I have had several visit my classes. The International Labor Rights Fund recently sponsored a tour that made a stop at my university to speak to international economics students. The group included three workers, two translators, and an ILRF staff member. The class was a typical public university mix of business, economics, and political science students. Teaching at a small state university where most of the undergraduates are themselves part-time wage workers, political consciousness is not particularly high.

Damaris Meza Guilen makes and inspects jeans at the Mille Colores factory in Nicaragua. These jeans are produced for labels selling exclusively at Wal-Mart, and her quota is checking 1,000 pairs a day. The factory is located in a free trade zone and is owned by a North American company Her wage is $0.30 per hour. The normal working day is 9.5 hours. The dining area is dirty as are the bathrooms, which the workers are not allowed to use during work time. These workers are mostly women between the ages of eighteen and thirty. Older workers and pregnant women are openly discriminated against in work assignments and pay. Damaris is twenty-eight years old though she looks older.

The Wal-Mart supplier code was displayed in the plant, but only in the manager's office and only in English, which none of the workers reads. Workers are openly threatened with firing for joining a union. The government of Nicaragua at the time refused to respond to the workers' claims that Nicaraguan labor laws were being violated, claiming the free trade zones are good for all.

Flori Averato works in a shirt factory in the Philippines owned by Koreans that also produces some exclusively Wal-Mart brands like White Stag. She is thirty-seven years old. Her wage is $0.40 per hour with what she describes as a high quota. She brought a memo posted in her factory prohibiting water breaks during work time. Unlike Damaris's plant, Wal-Mart representatives did occasionally visit Flori's factory, in fact one had visited the previous Friday, but visits were always known about in advance. When a labor dispute occurred, Wal-Mart asked for an amiable settlement or they would pull out. While the other women said that their employers knew they were touring the United States, and Damaris's was actually encouraging, Flori told hers that she was on vacation, for fear of retribution.

Estelle Inez Orgeulo produces bouquets of roses and carnations at a cut flower plantation in Colombia. She has done this work for eight years and has four children. The normal working day is eight to nine hours but rises to fifteen before Valentine's Day. Because Wal-Mart is squeezing the company, a quota system has been established that has forced lots of Sunday work. There are no bathrooms and no water available to the workers, and there are various occupational health problems including carpal tunnel syndrome. Estelle showed a bouquet that she had bought in a U.S. Wal-Mart for $9.92. It would take her 2.5 days of work to earn enough to buy a bouquet.

The students paid close attention to the presentation and asked questions. Many of them had previously said things that implied they were aware of but bored by these issues. The discussion in the next class was particularly lively though. And while only a few students had the time or inclination to become more active on this issue as a result of this presentation, there was a noticeable softening of their skepticism and tone of voice. Shortly thereafter, the university administration agreed to affiliate with the Worker Rights Consortium under pressure from an undergraduate student organization.

Such visits present opportunities to shorten the social distance that globalized production has created. The students do not come to care for these workers as they might for members of their family, friends, neighbors, or compatriots, but they are now real people, not faces on a television screen. They become local in a sense, and it becomes clear that a community of fate exists between them and us, a community that can only be developed and secured by acting globally.

One of Marx's more powerful concepts was "commodity fetishism," by which he meant the ways in which the social aspects of exchange come to be understood as properties of the commodity itself. A shirt is evaluated for its texture, material, and style, but not for the conditions under which it was produced. We might understand such fetishism today as the set of processes through which the logic of commodity exchange is expanded and normalized in ever more aspects of social life, producing subjects that see smaller and smaller slices of a bigger and bigger social whole. The division of labor contributes to the fragmentation of knowledge, as does the geographic division of labor across global commodity chains.

It is not lack of knowledge or false knowledge that is the problem but its fragmentation and our inability to gather the pieces together into a system. What we call "objective knowledge" is always and everywhere conventional, the product of a common social symbolic structure that we call language. It is this symbolic structure that is in play in the tensions between transnational corporations, transnational action networks, and state actors in the labor rights debate. We could characterize the student antisweatshop movement and its allies in part as demystifiers of commodities. It is not that there is any reality outside of theory that has been mystified and is now clearly visible because of the activities of the new factory inspectors. It is that new images of the social whole and new subjectivities are produced in their work (Zizek 1994). One exercise I have borrowed from the new factory inspectors is to have students examine the tag on the shirt of the person sitting next to them. Having them call out the country of origin is a consciousness raising exercise.

In May 1831, Alexis de Tocqueville visited the Sing-Sing prison in New York on his grand tour of America. He was also working at the time on another project: a report for the French government on the American penitentiary system

(Beaumont and Tocqueville 1964). He was deeply impressed with a scene outside the prison walls: hundreds of prisoners cutting stone, unshackled and with only a few guards. Tocqueville noted in his diary that these men, unchained and with serious tools, could easily have escaped or at least worked less hard had they banded together. Yet they worked as hard as paid laborers. Marcus Jiborn summarizes the conclusion of Tocqueville and his companion:

> The secret, they find, is *silence.* All communication between prisoners is strictly prohibited, 24 hours a day, and any transgression of the prohibition immediately and severely punished. Hence discipline is preserved, they conclude, because the keepers communicate freely with each other, act in concert, and have all the power of association; while the convicts separated from each other, by silence, have, in spite of their numerical force, all the weakness of isolation.[11] (2006)

The history of the factory inspectors and the contemporary international organization of worker rights point to the importance of freedom of association and collective bargaining in creating a decent society. The assertion of these conditions as rights does not now find general assent, and for them to become standards requires political organizing and increased acceptance of international labor law. The extension of the market may be a real but fickle ally in achieving such international labor standards.

A more pessimistic view is that the modes of subjection in contemporary capitalism are part of a shift from exterior to interior sources of social control, and indeed, following Foucault, we may see the current moment as part of a long history going back to the antislavery movement in which such a shift has occurred. That we acknowledge that new forms of discipline are developed within transnational production networks is not to deny the real gain in human freedom that the establishment of rights to collective bargaining and freedom of association can produce.

NOTES

1. I do not explicitly develop Keynesian or Feminist views here, but Keynes and the Institutionalists overlap in important ways as Keynes himself noted. Recent Feminist economists and historians have emphasized how gender is embedded in and not simply determined by the economy (Fraad, Resnick, and Wolff 1994; Scott 1988).

2. Fighting forced and child labor is not *necessarily* a bad thing, but the focus on these issues is not innocent and will be interrogated here.

3. See, for instance, Resnick and Wolff 2006; Gibson-Graham 1996.

4. In drawing primarily from the Institutional and Marxian traditions in political economy to make my argument I risk making the proponents of each unhappy, but in my view concepts from each are necessary for an adequate explanation of the emergence and evolution of worker rights, and the still real differences between these two schools of thought are relatively unimportant for my purposes. These differences are discussed briefly at the end of chapter 2.

5. In his summary statements and prefaces Marx generally paints a picture of history marching in a single direction in all countries, such as in the prefaces to *Capital*, vol. 1, and the *Contribution to the Critique of Political Economy,* whereas in more discursive and popular writings, such as in the historical chapters in vol. 3 of *Capital,* his journalism on French politics, the Amsterdam speech to the International Workingmen's Association, his late writings on Russia, etc., he sees many paths for the development of capitalism. It is the latter approach I am invoking here. For more detail on this distinction within Marxian political economy see McIntyre and Hillard 2008.

6. Throughout this book I will refer to *worker rights* as a set of beliefs and *labor standards* as the enactment of such belief into law. By both *worker* and *labor* I mean something like the social category posited by the classical economists, especially Smith and Marx, and adopt this usage to more clearly distinguish the evolution of beliefs from that of law.

CHAPTER 2

1. As Piore and Safford (2006) point out, there is no guarantee that conventions will spread even where they are arguably efficient. Their example is the failure of high-performance work organization to spread through the American economy. One could make the same argument for worker rights.

2. A more complete discussion would focus also on the political coalitions behind various ideas. In the United States, an alliance of workers, farmers, "enlightened" industrialists, and internationally oriented bankers was able to take control of the Democratic Party as a vehicle for promoting a mild version of social democracy. See Ferguson 1984 and Helleiner 1994. For international comparisons see Hall 1989.

Debrizzi (1983) argues that Commons's version of Institutional thought became the most influential because his theory incorporated much of the common sense of his day. Even Commons's followers often complained of the lack of coherence in his theoretical remarks, but in fact it was just this that provided for the wide appeal of Commons's work, as different social groups could make what they wanted of it to suit their own purposes.

Commons's version of Institutional thought was distinctive in that it most clearly expressed the common sense of the old middle class of small owner-operators. Society was portrayed as a balance of different class groupings, with an independent and thriving middle class of small business owners and professionals as the guarantor of social stability.

Commons's thesis of American exceptionalism was a major target of the new labor history of the 1960s and 1970s, yet it lives on. What was more important in the middle two quarters of the twentieth century in the United States was that some businessmen who shared this middle-class common sense could accept his reformism. Commons showed how capitalism could be moderated to blunt the challenge of militant socialism and the dangers of unfettered individualism.

The labor movement only accepted Commons's ideas after it had been greatly weakened by the repression of the immediate post–World War I years. Ironically, Commons could not save the social group he set out to protect, the old middle class. Rather, the next generation, the neoinstitutionalists, appropriated some of Commons's apparatus to promote a state-guided form of corporate capitalism that Commons certainly could not have embraced. The absorption of certain aspects of Commons's thinking by the New Deal and the effectiveness of some of his students, especially Perlman and Taft, explain the persistence of Commons-style thinking into the 1960s.

3. Some of the students of this group formed a third phase of institutionalism in the 1960s. Interested in urban labor markets and influenced by the civil rights and antiwar movement, these economists developed theories of dual and segmented labor markets in an approach that sometimes attempted to combine institutional and Marxian ideas. For the more strictly institutional part of this third generation see Doeringer and Piore 1971. For a more combinatory example see Edwards 1979.

4. Boyer and Smith 2001; Kaufman 2004a; Kaufman and Hotchkiss 2005.

5. There is a school of analytical Marxism that seeks to integrate some Marxian insights with methodological individualism, but we leave that aside here.

6. See, for instance, Resnick and Wolff 2006, chap. 17.

7. Women of course were engaged in producing surpluses within the household,

which they then delivered to male patriarchs. Social restrictions on women in the wage labor market far exceeded those of men. These surpluses freed men to become capitalists in much the same way that Northern slave labor did (Boydston 1990; Melish 1998).

8. See also Kaufman 2004a.

9. In fact, Kaufman gives a summary of the capitalist employment relation that is very close to Marx's, but without citing Marx (2004b, 22–24). "What the employer buys with the wage is a certain amount of time of the employee; however, it is not time that produces output and earns a profit but the amount and intensity of physical and mental effort (or work). The amount of work provided by the employee, however, is to some degree discretionary."

Kaufman goes on to say that this requires management to motivate labor to be performed, the same point that Harry Braverman makes in the first chapters of his neo-Marxist classic *Labor and Monopoly Capital*. Finally, the establishment of capitalist employment relations establishes an "asymmetric authority relation" that in nineteenth-century industrial workplaces took the form of "industrial autocracy."

10. See Kristjanson-Gural forthcoming for a clear introduction.

11. For North, the uncritical absorption of neoclassical theory into economic history was intellectually devastating because neoclassicism focused on frictionless transactions at a moment in time, precisely the opposite of the appropriate concerns of economic historians.

12. On Samuelson lurking see Perelman, http://www.mail-archive.com/pen-l@galaxy.csuchico.edu/msg47749.html. For his acknowledgment of Marx's importance see Hymer and Resnick 1971.

13. For a critique of the essentialism of some links between proletarianization and working-class formation see the essays in Berlanstein 1993, especially 1–54. That proletarianization and the response to it still explains a lot is illustrated by Silver 2003.

14. An outstanding example of this kind of argument is Bluestone and Harrison 1982.

15. The notion comes from the Webbs and was picked up immediately in the United States by Commons in the late 1880s. For a critical discussion of this view, see Montgomery 1993 and Staughton Lynd, "The Webbs, Lenin, and Rosa Luxemborg," in Lynd 1997.

16. Even where the state acts against those interests it is not therefore anticapitalist. For example, a long-run effect of the creation of the NLRB—for which Roosevelt was called anticapitalist—was to quell and suppress militant expressions and radical politics in the labor movement.

CHAPTER 3

1. The Dartmouth team performed no qualitative analysis or cultural analysis, and it made no mention of the repressive role of the Indonesian state. No meetings were held with prolabor nongovernmental organizations. While the project's coordinator states

that the Indonesian manpower ministry takes worker rights very seriously, it was in fact at the time notoriously antiworker and paid almost no attention to workplace safety issues. The fact that Nike contractors mainly employ young women, who often are the weakest participants in the labor market, was not mentioned in the Dartmouth study.

The correlation of wages with productivity is questionable at best. There are many well-known institutional critiques of the marginal productivity theory (Lester 1946; Thurow 1975; Simon 1979). Productivity and wage growth have diverged dramatically in the United States over the last several decades (Mishel, Epstein, and Allegretto 2001, 151). The ratio of value added to labor cost is much higher in China and Indonesia relative to Korea (or the United States), and there is no sign that these ratios are converging, which is a prediction of the orthodox model. For the Nike data see Spar and Burns 2000, 19. For the orthodox argument see Krugman and Obstfeld 2000, 25.

2. Similarly, the debate over NAFTA focused largely on the number of jobs that might be lost or won. But the major effect of NAFTA has been on social relations in the workplace, especially workers' rights to organize and bargain collectively. See Bronfenbrenner 2001.

3. For a succinct statement of the main argument, see the editor's introductory reading in Heilbroner 1986, 57–63.

4. My interpretation of Smith's concept of "sympathy" has been influenced by Ginsburg 1994 and Stabile 1997.

5. It is clear, however, that Smith did not consider self-interest to be the only means of eliciting a desired action. Indeed, it is worth noting that Smith's oft-quoted passage "It is not from the benevolence of the butcher, the brewer, or the baker, that we expect our dinner, but from their regard to their own interest" is embedded in a discussion in which Smith makes obvious his contention that there is a benevolent tendency in people. Cf. Smith 1937 [1776], 14.

6. Commons assigned no direct role to sympathy in his "transactional psychology" and proceeded by assuming that self-interest alone motivates the competing wills pitted against each other in transactional negotiations. Commons did discern a role for moral principles, however, which he understood to exert their effect via "habitual assumptions" woven into the fabric of the "institutionalized mind" giving direction to an individual's "will" (power of self-direction). By the term *habitual assumption,* Commons meant a reflexive criterion of judgment formed by repeated participation in the practices of the going concerns—the nation, the family, the school, the club, the business enterprise, and so on—into whose orbits an economic actor enters. In the main, Commons insisted, what is repeated, especially if it is consistent with one's self-interest, tends eventually to become "right"—moral—in the institutionalized mind. This suggests Commons probably would have rejected the sharp separation of "morality" and self-interest at the root of Smith's conception of the impartial spectator.

For a discussion of Commons's social-psychological conception of the individual, see Albert and Ramstad 1997, 1998. Marx's approach is discussed in the next chapter.

7. I emphasize that I am here engaging in a what-if exercise. If the charges of Town Dock's former employees about workplace conditions are accurate, one might question whether the facts allow for the existence of any sympathetic proclivity at all on the part of its owners.

8. A fully Smithian strategy would appeal also to the sympathy and moral feeling of the capitalist. In this sense, the strategy of groups such as the National Labor Committee in exposing working conditions in factories producing goods for Kathy Lee Gifford and Disney and then appealing to the latter on a moral basis is Smithian, as is the appeal that the filmmaker Michael Moore makes to Nike CEO Phil Knight at the end of the movie *The Big One.*

9. For a concise overview of Commons's theory of an instituted market system, see Ramstad 1998. For an overview of Commons's analytical system as an integrated whole, see Ramstad 1990.

10. See Ramstad 1987 for the argument that a system of tariffs levied on products produced in countries where "reasonable" labor standards have not been implemented would serve the public interest in the United States. DeMartino (2000) proposes a flexible tariff system based on countries achieving "capabilities equality" as measured by UN Human Development Indicators.

CHAPTER 4

1. For an important recent exception, see DeMartino 2000.

2. This distinction is important for what follows, but note that the ILO's Universal Declaration seeks to turn law and sanction into rights and duties. In other words, in the current context, the task is as much about transforming laws and treaties into norms as it is the other way round.

3. Bentham supported gradual emancipation not out of concern over the rights of property but because he feared immediate emancipation would worsen material living standards for ex-slaves. This seems to me to be perfectly consistent with his overall moral philosophy. See Rosen 2005.

4. As Burke was a lifelong Whig there is some debate as to whether he is best understood as a conservative or as a classical liberal. He is best known for his critique of the French Revolution and defense of the ancien régime, but his "conservatism" certainly had a strain of laissez-faire and free market thinking, based on an acceptance of the stability-inducing character of private property, suspicion of government, and belief in the self-regulating nature of market activity. Thus he is perhaps best understood as a conservative in the American sense, and as embodying the fundamental contradiction of that category: defense of traditional values alongside belief in free market capitalism, which undermines those traditional values.

5. According to one of the movement's most important theorists, globalization has created a crisis for the human rights movement. During the Cold War, human rights ac-

tivists developed a clear set of moral principles and a variety of techniques to put those principles into practice. Especially after the Helsinki Accord (1973), these practices were remarkably successful. Today, both the moral position and practice of the human rights movement is in disarray (Ignatieff 2002). I argue later that globalization raises even deeper problems for human rights discourses.

6. For instance, in their best-selling textbook, Krugman and Obstfeld, after building the basic free trade argument under conditions that never apply (perfect competition, etc.) state and then simply dismiss moral philosophical questions, recognize the distributional consequences from trade but say this is not a reason for protection, demonstrate the logic of the factor price equalization theorem and then dismiss it as not relevant most of the time, and then acknowledge the existence of "intellectually respectable" market failure arguments for a tariff but say that in the "real world" it won't work (Krugman and Obstfeld 2005). Uncritically infecting young minds with this nonsense is a scandal.

7. "Free trade" evokes more positive references than the more accurate term "deregulated international commerce." See the excellent discussion in Daly 1993. The use of quotes around "free trade" may seem pedantic but I think it is necessary to problematize this powerful mantra.

8. These were the countries Ricardo used as examples in his original formulation of the theory of comparative advantage. Actually, the pattern of English-Portuguese trade was determined by a series of unequal treaties between the two countries. See Magdoff 1971.

9. And it is likely, as DeMartino (2000) argues, that the economic losers from freer trade started with less political capability to begin with. Otherwise they might have been able to prevent the policy that is so inimical to their interests. This weakness is likely the reason that losers from trade integration are rarely able to secure compensation. As DeMartino puts it, "The greater the level of inequality prior to a regime shift, the greater will be the capabilities failures that it induces, and the less adequate will be the level of compensation for the losers that is actually forthcoming" (207).

10. See also more generally Bhagwati 1998. But as Ignatieff (2001) notes, our most important human rights documents, such as the Universal Declaration, were, at the time of their signing, no better than aspirations and were in fact developed in response to the barbarism at the heart of the industrialized capitalist world in the 1930s and 1940s.

11. Srinivasan and other neoclassicals recognize that these results do not hold in the absence of perfectly competitive and complete markets. For instance, capital markets may not be sufficiently functional to allow investments that promote worker safety. Addressing market failures at their source—in this case the capital market—is preferable to using trade policy for them. They also recognize that the income distribution that emerges from freer trade may be unacceptable. Income transfers through taxation are again preferable to incorporating labor standards in trade agreements.

12. This is the same logic used by Wal-Mart spokesmen in their defense against crit-

ics who claim that Wal-Mart drives down wages and working conditions. In a remarkable two-page advertisement in the *New York Review of Books* Wal-Mart's CEO claimed that for the sake of 250,000 grocery store clerks and baggers, 35 million other Californians are being asked to pay billions of dollars more than they should for the necessities of life.

13. The countries that have been loudest in raising the labor standards issue—the United States in particular—stand accused of hypocrisy by the neoclassicals. They claim that the use of prison labor to produce items sold to the government and the inability of the Labor Department to effectively regulate sweatshops both indicate that the concern with trade stems from protectionism not altruism. The U.S. position on labor rights has generally been dominated by broad, foreign policy concerns and corporate interests. For detailed discussion of the U.S. position vis-à-vis core labor standards, see chapter 6.

14. Ignatieff 2001 is a clear and concise statement of human rights liberalism. There are, of course, disagreements among human rights theorists, but in my view, Ignatieff's is a particularly eloquent statement of a perspective that finds wide agreement. See the responses of Appiah, Hollinger, and Orentlicher in Ignatieff 2001.

15. See also Keck and Sikkink 1998, 39–78.

16. Ignatieff does not cite any major Marxist texts on this issue.

17. Furthermore, Ignatieff accepts the neoclassical approach to trade, so long as compensation is actually paid. "A human rights perspective on development for example, would be critical of any macroeconomic strategy that purchased aggregate economic growth at the price of the rights of significant groups of individuals. A dam project that boosts electro-generation capacity at the price of flooding the lands of poor people without compensation and redress is an injustice, even if the aggregate economic benefit of such a measure is clear" (2001, 167). For Ignatieff, then, compensation must occur for the Pareto principle to be invoked. I noted earlier that for the neoclassicals this is not strictly necessary and that there are problems with the principle even if compensation is paid.

18. More specifically the language and practice of labor rights grew in response to the industrial and communist revolutions.

19. "Rights are likely to be quite durable, stabilizing expectations in ways that would be thought desirable in almost any conceivable society, and yet also flexible, so that when conditions change radically a right rendered obsolete might pass painlessly out of existence" (Haskell 2000, 138).

20. In defining capitalism as a system of class relations or a system of market relations there are echoes of older debates over the transition from feudalism to capitalism and the conditions necessary for successful capitalist development, i.e., the Dobb-Sweezy and Brenner-Wallerstein debates (Hilton 1976; Ashton 1987).

21. See also Stanley 1993, especially chap. 2, 60–97.

22. More generally see Tomlins 1993, 223–93.

23. "Although many administrations have proclaimed full employment and adequate

housing as governmental goals, they are not constitutionally guaranteed rights as is, for example, a free press" (Meyer 1998, 11).

24. Gross 1999b, 68. On the orientation of the major human rights organizations and networks see Keck and Sikkink 1998 and Gordon, Swanson, and Buttigieg 2000.

25. See also Brody et al. 2001.

26. Gross (1999b, 67–68) discusses the religious underpinnings of labor rights.

27. For an argument against the right to protection from child labor from someone generally seen as a supporter of worker rights see Gould 2003.

28. "It is not only the state that has power to violate people's rights. Employers have explicit power over individuals' lives and there is the implicit power of the 'free market.' True liberty, therefore, is the ability to act successfully on one's choice, and not simply the freedom from interference by the state" (Gross 1999b, 69–70).

29. See especially Stone 1996. Some argue that the Wagner Act itself limited the self-organizing activity of workers. See S. Lynd 1997.

CHAPTER 5

1. As income inequality is not the focus here I do not take a side in the technology vs. trade debate. These do not seem to me to be separate processes but interlinked in important ways as causes of what Freeman (1996) calls the "de-institutionalization of wage norms" along with increased capital mobility, immigration, declining unionization, and the long-term decline in the minimum wage.

2. As discussed in chapter 4, the first two rights are most problematic for the contemporary human rights regime. See the section entitled "International Organization of Worker Rights," this chapter, for the ILO's reasoning for choosing these and not other rights.

3. Even economists sympathetic to collective bargaining are skeptical about including worker rights clauses in trade agreements. For instance, Richard Freeman argues that improvements in labor rights can be "paid for" through currency devaluation or tax increases (1994). To the extent that international solutions are necessary he favors product labeling that allows consumers to express their preferences for nonsweated labor rather than imposing trade-based labor standards. See also Freeman and Elliott, op cit.

4. The following chapter focuses specifically on U.S. policy.

5. For a detailed discussion see Ramstad 1990.

6. This section draws on the following histories of the ILO: Barnes 1926; Ghebali 1989; Alcock 1971; Shotwell 1934; Turmann 1922.

7. The conventions on freedom of association are the most widely ratified. The special Committee on Freedom of Association occupies a unique place within the ILO's subsidiary bodies and with its 3–3–3 makeup is the most truly tripartite and perhaps most effective of those bodies.

8. See especially ILO 2004.

9. The next several paragraphs are based on transcripts of interviews conducted at the ILO in Geneva in November 2002.

10. See the discussion in Ghebali 1989, chap. 4. These patterns were confirmed in interviews conducted with ILO staff in Geneva, Nov. 2002.

11. The most effective transnational rights networks have been those dealing with equality of opportunity and bodily harm. For details on this see Keck and Sikkink 1998, especially chap. 6. As I argued in chapter 4, international labor rights, as conceived by the ILO, fall partly within these categories but also include collective rights that sit uneasily within these essentially liberal categories.

12. According to staff members I interviewed, the dropoff in filings by American trade unions in the 1990s was to avoid embarrassing the Clinton administration.

13. The economists I interviewed at the ILO indicated without hesitation that their theoretical orientation was institutional, and many seemed to be reading key texts of the new institutionalism, such as Hall and Soskice 2001. ILO economists strike me as institutionalist in a specific way. They are eclectic, they draw from institutional work in political science and sociology as well as economics, and they see the institutional approach in labor economics as consistent with the core mission of the ILO. They also acknowledge that this causes problems when speaking to their brethren at the WTO or the Bretton Woods institutions because sometimes it literally feels like they are speaking different languages.

14. See, for instance, the ILO's approach to Poverty Reduction Strategy Program, *Decent Work and Poverty Reduction Strategies,* http://www.ilo.org/public/english/bureau/integration/download/tools/6_3_107_prsrefmanual.pdf

15. In trying to understand the differences in the kinds of knowledge produced by the ILO and the Bretton Woods institutions I have been influenced by the concept of "thought world" developed in Mary Douglas's (1986) *How Institutions Think.* One really has to spend time at the ILO, as its people and space are quite different from the bland bureaucracy one gets from its Web site, where one sometimes has to look harder than necessary to find the social justice mission that is at the heart of the ILO's work. A document that captures the very different thought world in the Washington institutions is the following webcast: *Joseph Stiglitz and Kenneth Rogoff Discuss Globalization and Its Discontents,* http://info.worldbank.org/etools/bspan/PresentationView.asp?EID=145& PID =325

16. One does tire of Stiglitz thinking he is always right, and it is likely that the discontent with globalization stems from psychology and culture as much as it does from economics (McIntyre 2004). Still, Stiglitz is no hack, and his dissent from official economic ideology has been both productive and admirable. His speech to the IRRA (Stiglitz 2000) is a fundamental text on democracy and collective worker rights.

CHAPTER 6

1. All statistics concerning the adoption and ratification of conventions come from the ILO's *ILOLEX Database of International Labor Standards,* which is found at http://www.ilo.org/ilolex/english/index.htm

2. One uses "designed" loosely here as Clinton's spokesmen spent most of the week beginning their statements with phrases like "What the President meant to say was . . ."

3. Compare the number of conventions ratified by the other Group of Eight large industrialized nations: Canada 28, France 103, Germany 74, Italy 93, Japan 41, Russia 53, and the UK 67.

4. They are Bahrain, Cambodia, Cape Verde, Eritrea, Gambia, Iran, Kiribati, Laos, Namibia, Nepal, Oman, Qatar, Somalia, St. Kitts, Turkmenistan, United Arab Emirates, and Uzbekistan.

5. Convention No. 144 reaffirms the ILO's tripartite structure by assuring that labor and employer associations, along with governments, may respond to ILO requests for information; Convention No. 160 pledges support for the ILO's statistics-gathering activities; and Convention No. 150 requires nations to support labor bureaus for the purpose of enforcing national labor standards.

6. The full texts of conventions are available online at http://www.ilo.org/ilolex/english/convdisp1.htm. The critical section of Convention No. 87 (Article 2) states: "Workers and employers, without distinction whatsoever, shall have the right to establish, and, subject only to the rules of the organization concerned, to join organizations of their own choosing without authorization." The critical section of Convention No. 98 (Article 4) states: "Measures appropriate to national conditions shall be taken, where necessary, to encourage and promote the full development and utilization of machinery for voluntary negotiation between employers or employers' organizations and workers' organizations, with a view to the regulation of terms and conditions of employment by means of collective agreements."

7. This was also the argument given to me by former Clinton administration officials working at the ILO in Geneva.

8. Principally, the National Labor Relations Act, Railway Labor Act, and Civil Service Reform Act.

9. See ILO Constitution, Annex, Article III at www.ilo.org/public/english/about/iloconst.htm#annex

10. Legal scholars challenged this interpretation based on a U.S. Supreme Court decision handed down soon after the ILO was established. In 1920, the Court overturned a lower court's ruling that a federal statute protecting migratory birds (which had been passed to fulfill obligations under the Migratory Bird Treaty Act) violated the Tenth Amendment (which addresses powers reserved to the states). In *Missouri v. Holland* (252 U.S. 416, 1920), the Supreme Court held that the federal government has the authority to pass all laws "necessary and proper" to carry out its treaty-making prerogatives. Therefore, some argued that, based on *Missouri v. Holland,* the federal government's ability to ratify ILO conventions is not "subject to limitations," the necessary trigger for the Federal State proviso to take effect (Chamberlain 1920; Tayler 1935).

11. Unfortunately, the business of the President's Committee is difficult to examine, since it typically meets behind closed doors in the interest of national security and to protect the confidentiality of U.S. treaty-negotiating positions.

12. See also the testimony of Abraham Katz of the USCIB who writes, "Almost all

countries understand that the United States does apply the body of international labor standards but does so through legislation that is different in detail" (106).

13. Convention 105 has since been ratified.

14. Potter argued that Convention No. 87 would subordinate employee rights to those of the union; would broaden the classes of workers covered by labor law; would revoke portions of the Landrum-Griffin Act, particularly those prohibiting persons with criminal records from holding union office; would repeal employer free speech provisions of the NLRA; would limit restrictions on the right to strike and secondary boycotts; would prohibit restrictions on union participation by members of subversive organizations; would repeal prohibitions on hot cargo agreements; would restrict the withdrawal of exclusive representation; would revoke limitations on the use of union monies for political purposes; and would remove limitations on the disaffiliation of local unions from national bodies and the dissolution of multiemployer units. According to Potter, Convention No. 98 would have many of the same effects, but also would limit discretion in instituting wage-price controls; would prohibit legislation restricting the scope of bargaining and distinctions between mandatory and permissive subjects; would provide union officials with special job protections; would modify the burden of proof and remedies under NLRA Section 10(c) (which concerns NLRB remedies); and would put the United States at the mercy of evolving ILO standards.

15. The USCIB is the official U.S. employer representative to the ILO. It took over this role from the U.S. Chamber of Commerce in 1980. According to officials I interviewed at the ILO in Geneva, it is essentially a shell organization.

16. This last statement is in Katz's written but not oral testimony.

17. Bhagwati 1998, 247–68.

18. "Message from the President of the United States Transmitting the Convention Concerning the Rights of Freedom of Association," *Congressional Record*, August 27, 1949.

19. The reference is not clear here. Some of the discussion concerned conventions No. 144 and No. 147. The former, on tripartite cooperation, was especially desirable as the Soviet countries would not be able to ratify, and this was a chance to embarrass them. See especially the discussion between Chairman Hatch and Secretary of Labor Brock (U.S. Senate 1985, 70). But Hatch clearly has a longer list in mind including core conventions No. 29, No. 105, No. 87, and No. 98.

20. See President George H. W. Bush's letter of transmittal at bushlibrary.tamu.edu/papers/1991/91021902.html

21. The Railway Labor Act was passed in 1926 and the National Labor Relations Act in 1935. Elements of both acts can be found in the Erdman Act, which was passed in 1898 but subsequently found unconstitutional by the U.S. Supreme Court (Millis and Montgomery 1945, 731–32).

22. The National Labor Relations Board ruled, in its Kentucky River decision, that millions of nurses were not eligible to organize. This is a striking but typical example of

the rulings of the Bush board, which had yet to take any oral arguments as of January 2008. The AFL-CIO filed a complaint with the ILO's Committee on Freedom of Association on this case in October 2007. No report has yet been issued on case #2608.

23. CFA case reports can be found online at http://www.ilo.org/ilolex/english/case frameE.htm.

24. The secretary was speaking on behalf of the Departments of Labor, State, Justice, Interior, and Navy, and the Federal Security Agency, all of which reviewed Convention No. 87.

25. The ILO Constitution is available online at http://www.ilo.org/public/english/about/iloconst.htm#a19p2

26. See, for instance, the discussion of the ratification of Convention 105 concerning the abolition of forced labor in the Senate at www.senate.gov/~rpc/rva/1021/102159.htm. It is not surprising that the extension of the market promotes some freedoms (in this case, freedom from forced labor) while limiting others, in this case the right to bargain collectively. See the discussion in chapter 4.

27. See the discussion in chapter 5.

28. See, for instance, Eric Helleiner (1994), *States and the Reemergence of Global Finance.*

CHAPTER 7

1. An interesting rupture in this debate was the French case in 1848 of applying labor rights to all, not just to women and children. Considerations of space prevent a full discussion of the various differences between the evolution of Anglo-American and French concepts of worker rights but for nineteenth-century France see Lynch 1988; Stone 1985; Weissbach 1989; as well as the discussion in Engerman 2003.

2. Note the absence of any movement toward labor standards in agriculture, due to the power of landowners and the ideology of the family farm, compounded perhaps by the difficulty of publicizing agricultural working conditions in the nineteenth century, as well as difficulties in enforcing worker rights on the farm.

3. As this book was going to press the Bush administration and the Democratic leadership in Congress agreed to include labor standards in bilateral trade agreements. Whether this marks a fundamental change in the U.S. position or a stopgap given the breakdown of multilateral trade talks is not possible to tell at the time of writing.

4. There were two new literary genres whose rise coincided with the British factory revolution, "the condition of the laboring population" book and the "book of factory abuses." The former tended to be based on direct and personal observation of working and living conditions and also tended to be reformist, Engels's *The Condition of the English Working Class* being an exception. The latter genre tended to draw on factory inspectors' reports and legislative hearings, showing the horrors of the system and the ne-

cessity for radical reform or revolution (Freedgood 2003). The middle chapters of *Capital* volume I are a classic of this type, although it was unusual for such books to have such a strong connection to political economy. Despite the brilliance of Marx's descriptions and analysis, with repetition this genre created the same "habit of horrified reaction" that often occurs in response to contemporary sweatshop conditions.

5. In his New Year's Day 1860 letter to Engels, Marx expressed dismay at Horner's abrupt resignation. That Horner was singular and not necessarily representative of a type is shown by the counterexample of the inspector William Cole Taylor (Freedgood 2003, 15).

6. See here also Stedman Jones 1983, 72.

7. The owners' opposition to limitations on the working day and on child labor was based on some arguments that are familiar from today's debates: freedom of contract, parental rights and family budgets, the imperatives of global competition (at that time from American producers), the infamous argument that all profits were obtained from the last hour's work, and that things were worse outside the mills. The idea that children are not free agents and form a special case is accepted by economic liberals today, though parents (and especially fathers) at the time disputed the state's rights vis-à-vis their own in the disposal of children's time.

8. Freedom of contract was as attractive to many workers as it was to owners. See Kirby and Musson, *The Voice of the People*, 367–68.

9. See Marx 1981, 592–99. But see also Bartrip and Fern (1983) who claim that safety inspection had little effect on accident rates.

10. This success and progress was always built through alliances with other classes and class factions. The landowners' defeat on the Corn Laws played no small role in their occasional support for the Factory Acts (Marx 1848). The history of American international economic policy in the twentieth century has been interpreted through the lens of class interest by Ferguson (1995) and Helleiner (1994).

11. We might also mention here activities like Jobs with Justice's Kentucky-Sonora Workers Exchange, which built solidarity between unemployed American workers and Mexican workers who had "taken" their jobs.

12. The only author who addresses these issues on a philosophical basis in this book is the industrial relations scholar Roy Adams who argues that workers do not have the right not to be represented, in the same way that they do not have the right to sell their physical being.

13. The growth of these collaborative networks of private actors can be understood as making up for both market and state failures. Some institutional authors have spun tales of how certain institutions foster "reflexive collaboration," and there seems a presumption in some of this literature that these reflexive collaborations will become evolutionarily stable strategies (Sabel, O'Rourke, and Fung 2000). This literature does not include workers' organizations or self-agency in any substantial way.

14. WRC does not do much public education. Officially, WRC sees alliances to build organizing capacity in the countries as good, but not the job of the WRC, "not our role." European unions do more in this area than Americans, especially the Dutch, Danes, and Norwegians. Among U.S. organizations the AFL-CIO's Solidarity Center does some worker education in the poor countries, with individual unions such as UNITE and increasingly SEIU also. Nonetheless, I argue that the WRC does empower workers and build solidarity because of the nature of its fact-finding and reporting process.

15. This cutting edge may be moving to China and Vietnam. Law and the psychology of the workers in these countries are very different than in Central and Latin America, and there is not much of an organizing infrastructure. Through the summer of 2007 in China it was acceptable to have an independent organization but not to call it a union. Whether the new Chinese labor law will change this situation is unclear, but so far none of the new factory inspector groups has been able to crack China. For my research some of the most useful organizations on Chinese labor issues are the Hong Kong Christian Industrial Committee, Labor Action China, and the National Labor Committee. The situation in India seems altogether different because factories are generally locally owned.

16. The Choishin plant in Guatemala was organized in response to pressure from Liz Claiborne and its independent monitor, who were themselves responding to an FLA investigation and the violent response to an earlier organizing attempt. But the campaign stagnated for two years before the state intervened on the side of the workers due to a desire to look good for the then upcoming debate over the adoption of CAFTA in the U.S. Congress (Rodríguez-Garavito 2005).

17. Reebok's Vice-President for Human Rights, Doug Kahn, left the company after the merger with Adidas.

18. *Brands* has become a commonly accepted term to define a particular kind of company, and distinguishes them from Taiwanese, Korean, or Chinese factory-owning capitalists. None of the interviewees for this book knew the origin of this term.

19. For instance, Brown 2006.

CHAPTER 8

1. Personal experience recounted to the author.

2. To the extent that a concern's activities are operationally separable, it may choose to organize the labor process either via the sweating system or the factory system or both. Hence, it is not implausible for a concern to organize its labor process through a combination of the two systems. And, equally, it is not implausible that new innovations, whether technological or organizational, might induce the firm to adjust the activities it allocates to each realm of labor market organization. In many minds, factory production is analogous to mass production. Some observers see the period since the 1970s as one of a retreat from mass production in favor of "flexible" production meth-

ods. This innovation is one that might arguably stimulate the aforementioned adjustment of the activities a firm allocates to each system of labor market organization. Thus, I would perceive that, like Wal-Mart, many firms are likely to structure their labor processes via some mixture of both systems.

3. There are of course important differences also. For instance, excessive work hours was one of the primary problems for the early factory working class, while irregularity of work hours is a bigger problem for Wal-Mart workers.

4. I use this dictionary definition of exploitation here to avoid a detailed exegesis of this term and its use by various schools of economic thought.

5. Marx's incisive review of the Factory Act inquiry suffices to undermine Smith's presumptions that an appropriate concern for others will cause the powerful to forbear from fully exercising their power in negotiations with those who are less powerful. See also chapter 3.

6. Walmart's People department claims that its central human resource strategies for its "associates" are an open door policy, open communications, managers as "servant leaders," and support for associates on and off the job. This mix of religious and family language, along with various team-building exercises and the lack of viable alternative employment in many of the small towns and suburbs where Wal-Mart locates its stores, combine to "manufacture consent" in many stores. The level of activism around labor issues and the alienation of the gentleman in our story indicate that this consent is now contested.

7. Effectively battling the morality of "grab it" and the strategy of creating social distance would take political leadership that could engage people as citizens and workers. Separating these identities seems characteristic of the most recently successful political strategies in both major parties in the United States. The Bush administration embraced Wal-Mart as an example of the kind of "economic success" that they hoped to bring to the United States as a whole. Speaking before 1,000 cheering Wal-Mart employees in May 2004, Dick Cheney pointed to Wal-Mart's success as a sign of the rightness of his administration's policies, particularly its tax cuts (*USA Today* 2004a). However bizarre the reasoning, Wal-Mart was not only ideologically in tune with that administration but was also a major financial supporter to Bush, Cheney, and their supporters in the Republican Party (*USA Today* 2004b; see also www.opensecrets.org). Hilary Clinton served on Wal-Mart's board of directors when she was a lawyer in Arkansas (Featherstone 2005). Other factions in the Democratic Party take a different line on these issues. See especially the report by the Democratic staff of the House Committee on Education and the Workforce, commissioned by Rep. George Miller of California, "Everyday Low Wages: The Hidden Price we all pay for Wal-Mart," at http://edworkforce.house.gov/democrats/WALMARTREPORT.pdf

8. See the discussion in chapter 7.

9. Freeman acknowledges that improving labor standards can have some impact,

though he argues that their effects on global poverty and living standards pale in comparison to the effects of macroeconomic instability, indebtedness, and the policies of the IMF and U.S. Treasury.

10. Note that from an anarchocommunist perspective this is exactly the wrong approach. Rather than getting a seat at the table it is more important to blow the table up. See Cockburn, St. Clair, and Sekula 2000.

11. Marcus Jiborn 2006, "The Power of Coordination" http://people.su.se/~guarr/Ideologi/Jiborn%20on%20Coordination%20power.pdf

REFERENCES

Adams, R. 1999a. Collective bargaining: The Rodney Dangerfield of human rights. *Labor Law Journal* 50 (3): 204–9.

Adams, R. 1999b. Labor rights are human rights. *WorkingUSA* (July–August): 72–77.

Adams, R. 2001. Choice or voice? Rethinking American labor policy in light of the international human rights consensus. *Employee Rights and Employment Policy Journal* 5:521–47.

Aidt, Toke, and Z. Tzannatos. 2002. *Unions and Collective Bargaining: Economic Effects in a Global Environment.* Washington, DC: World Bank.

Albert, A., and Y. Ramstad. 1997. The social psychological underpinnings of Commons's institutional economics: The significance of Dewey's *Human Nature and Conduct. Journal of Economic Issues* 31 (4): 881–916.

Albert, A., and Y. Ramstad. 1998. The social psychological underpinnings of Commons's institutional economics II: The concordance of George Herbert Mead's "Social Self" and John R. Commons's "Will." *Journal of Economic Issues* 32 (1): 1–46.

Alcock, Antony. 1997. *History of the International Labour Organization.* London: Macmillan.

Anner, M. 2001. The international trade union campaign for core labor standards in the WTO. *WorkingUSA* (Summer): 43–63.

Ashton, T. H., and C. H. E. Philpin. 1987. *The Brenner Debate: Agrarian Class Structure and Economic Development in Pre-Industrial Europe.* Cambridge: Cambridge University Press.

Balibar, E. 1993. What is a politics of the Rights of Man? In *Masses, Classes, and Ideas.* London: Routledge.

Bardhan, P. 2001. Distributional conflict, collective action, and institutional economics. In *Frontiers of Development Economics: The Future in Perspective,* ed. G. Meier and J. Stiglitz, 269–83. Washington, DC: World Bank.

Barnes, George N. 1926. *History of the International Labour Office.* London: Williams and Norgate.

Bartrip, P. W. J., and P. T. Fern. 1983. The evolution of regulatory style in the nineteenth century British factory inspectorate. *Journal of Law and Society* 10:201–11.

Beaumont, Gustave de, and Alexis de Tocqueville. 1964 (1833). *On the Penitentiary System in the United States and Its Application to France.* Carbondale: Southern Illinois Press.

Bellace, J. R. 1999. ILO fundamental rights at work and freedom of association. *Labor Law Journal* 50 (3): 191–95.

Bender, Thomas, ed. 1993. *The Anti-Slavery Debate.* Berkeley: University of California Press.

Benson, Susan Porter. 1988. *Counter Culture: Saleswomen, Managers, and Customers in American Department Stores, 1890–1940.* Urbana: University of Illinois Press.

Berlanstein, Lenard R., ed. 1993. *Rethinking Labor History: Essays on Discourse and Class Analysis.* Urbana: University of Illinois Press.

Bhagwati, Jagdish. 1998. *A Stream of Windows: Unsettling Reflections on Trade, Immigration, and Democracy.* Cambridge: MIT Press.

Bluestone, Barry, and Bennett Harrison. 1982. *The Deindustrialization of America.* New York: Basic Books.

Bodah, M. 1999. Congressional influence on labor policy: How Congress has influenced outcomes without changing the law. *Labor Law Journal* 50 (3): 223–29.

Bodah, M. 2001. Congress and the National Labor Relations Board: A review of the recent past. *Journal of Labor Research* 32 (4): 699–722.

Border, John. 1998. President terms certain rights "universal." *New York Times,* June 29, 1.

Borjas, G., R. Freeman, and L. Katz. 1997. How much do immigration and trade affect labor market outcomes? *Brookings Papers on Economic Activity,* 1–67.

Boydston, J. 1990. *Home and Work: Housework, Wages and the Ideology of Labor in the Early Republic.* New York: Oxford University Press.

Boyer, George R., and Robert S. Smith. 2001. The development of the neoclassical tradition in labor economics. *Industrial and Labor Relations Review* 54 (2): 199–223.

Bradley, Curtis. 1998. The treaty power and American federalism. *Michigan Law Review* 97:391–461.

Brody, R., Smita Narula, Arvind Ganesan, Joe Stork, Joseph Buttigieg, Jacinda Swanson, and Neve Gordon. 2001. Human rights and global capitalism: A roundtable discussion with Human Rights Watch. *Rethinking Marxism* 13 (2): 52–71.

Bronfenbrenner, Kate. 2001. *Uneasy Terrain: The Impact of Capital Mobility on Workers, Wages, and Union Organizing.* U.S. Trade Deficit Review Commission, http://www.ustdrc.gov/research/bronfenbrenner.pdf.

Brown, Sherrod. 2006. *Myths of Free Trade: Why American Trade Policy Has Failed.* New York: New Press.

Burawoy, Michael. 1985. *The Politics of Production: Factory Regimes under Capitalism and Socialism.* London: Verso.

Calzini, D., Jake Odden, Jean Tsai, Shawna Huffman, and Steve Tran. 1997. *Nike Inc.: Survey of Vietnamese and Indonesian Expenditure Levels.* Dartmouth: Amos Tuck School.

Chamberlain, J. P. 1920. Migratory bird treaty decision and its relation to labor treaties. *American Labor Legislation Review,* vol. 10.

Cockburn, Alexander, Jeffrey St. Clair, and Allan Sekula. 2000. *Five Days that Shook the World: Seattle and Beyond.* London: Verso.

Colby, J. UNICCO wages keep workers in poverty. *Cowl,* April 25, 2002.

Commons, J. R. 1924. *Legal Foundations of Capitalism*. New York: Macmillan.

Commons, J. R. 1931. Institutional economics. *American Economic Review* 21:648–57.

Commons, J. R. 1934a. *Institutional Economics: Its Place in Political Economy*. New York: Macmillan.

Commons, J. R. 1934b. *Myself*. New York: Macmillan.

Commons, J. R. 1964 (1909). American shoemakers: 1648 to 1895. In *Labor and Administration*, 219–66. Reprints of Economic Classics. New York: Augustus M. Kelley.

Commons, J. R. 1977 (1901). The sweating system. In *Out of the Sweatshop*, ed. L. Fink. New York: Quadrangle.

Compa, L. 2000. *Unfair Advantage: Workers' Freedom of Association in the United States under International Human Rights Standards*. New York: Human Rights Watch.

Compa, L. 2003. Workers freedom of association in the United States: The gap between ideals and practice. In *Workers' Rights as Human Rights*, ed. James Gross. Ithaca: Cornell University Press.

Compa, Lance, and Stephen F. Diamond, eds. 1996. *Human Rights, Labor Rights, and International Trade*. Philadelphia: University of Pennsylvania Press.

Cooke, William N., and Frederick H. Gautschi III. 1982. Political bias in NLRB unfair labor practice decisions. *Industrial and Labor Relations Review* 35 (4): 39–549.

Cooke, William N., Aneil K. Mishra, Gretchen M. Spreitzer, and Mary Tshirhart. 1995. The determinants of the NLRB decision-making revisited. *Industrial and Labor Relations Review* 48 (2): 237–57.

Cowie, Jefferson. 1999. *Capital Moves: RCA's Seventy Year Quest for Cheap Labor*. New York: New Press.

Daly, H. 1993. The perils of free trade. *Scientific American* (November): 50–57.

Dark, Taylor E. 1999. *The Unions and the Democrats*. Ithaca: Cornell University Press.

Dawley, Alan. 1976. *Class and Community: The Industrial Revolution in Lynn*. Cambridge: Harvard University Press.

DeBrizzi, J. A. 1983. *Ideology and the Rise of Labor Theory in America*. Westport: Greenwood Press.

DeMartino, G. 2000. *Global Economy, Global Justice: Theoretical Objections and Policy Alternative to Neoliberalism*. New York: Routledge.

Djang, T. K. 1942. *Factory Inspection in Great Britain*. London: George Allen and Unwin.

Dobbins, F., and J. Sutton. 1998. The strength of a weak state: The rights revolution and the rise of human resources management divisions. *American Journal of Sociology* 104:441–76.

Doeringer, P., and M. Piore. 1971. *Internal Labor Markets and Manpower Analysis*. Lexington: D. C. Health.

Douglas, Mary. 1986. *How Institutions Think*. Syracuse: Syracuse University Press.

Dulles, Foster Rhea, and Melvin Dubofsky. 1984. *Labor in America: A History*. 4th ed. Arlington Heights, IL: Harlan Davidson.

Dupuy, J. P. 1989. Common knowledge, common sense. *Theory and Decision* 27:37–62.

Engerman, S. 2003. The history and political economy of international labor standards. In *International Labor Standards,* ed. Kaushik Basu, Henrik Horn, Lisa Roman, and Judith Shapiro, 9–83. Malden, MA: Basil Blackwell.

Edwards, R. 1979. *Contested Terrain: The Transformation of the Workplace in the Twentieth Century.* New York: Basic Books.

Estreicher, Samuel. 1985. Policy oscillation at the Labor Board: A plea for rulemaking. *Administrative Law Review* 15:163–81.

Featherstone, Lisa. 2005. Down and out in discount America. *Nation,* Jan. 3, 11–15.

Ferguson, Thomas. 1984. From normalcy to New Deal: Industrial structure, party competition and American public policy in the Great Depression. *International Organization* 38:1.241–69.

Ferguson, Thomas. 1995. *The Golden Rule: The Investment Theory of Party Competition and the Logic of Money Driven Political Systems.* Chicago: University of Chicago Press.

Fields, G. 1990. Labor standards, economic development, and international trade: Conceptualizing labor standards and government's role in promoting them. In *Labor Standards and Development in the Global Economy.* Washington, DC: U.S. Department of Labor, Bureau of International Affairs.

Finnemore, M. 1993. International organizations as teachers of norms: The United Nations educational scientific and cultural organization and science policy. *International Organization* 47:565–97.

Fishman, Phil. 2002. AFL-CIO support for international worker rights. *Perspectives on Work* 6 (1): 34–36.

Fraad, Harriet, Stephen Resnick, and Richard Wolff. 1994. *Bringing It All Back Home.* London: Pluto.

Freedgood, Ellen, ed. 2003. *Factory Production in Nineteenth-Century Britain.* Oxford: Oxford University Press.

Freeman, Anthony. 1999a. Comment. *Labor Law Journal* 50 (3): 210–13.

Freeman, Anthony. 1999b. ILO labor standards and U.S. compliance. *Perspectives on Work* 3 (1): 28–31.

Freeman, R. 1994. A hard headed look at labor standards. In *International Labor Standards and Economic Interdependence,* ed. W. Sengenberger and D. Campbell. Geneva: Institute for International Labour Studies.

Freeman, R. 1996. Towards an apartheid economy. *Harvard Business Review* 74 (5) (Sept.–Oct.): 114–26.

Freeman, R. 1997–98. Program Report: Labor Studies. *NBER Reporter,* Winter. Cambridge: National Bureau of Economic Research.

Freeman, R. 1998. What Role for Labor Standards in the Global Economy. http://www .nber.org/~freeman/Papers%200n%20RBF%20website/un-stan.pdf 1998, 10.

Freeman, R. 2002. Program Report: Labor Studies. *NBER Reporter,* Fall. Cambridge: National Bureau of Economic Research.

French, H. 2005. Anger in China over threat to the environment. *New York Times,* July 19, A3.

French, J. 2002. From the suites to the streets of Seattle: The unexpected reemergence of the labor question, 1994–99. *Labor History* 43 (3): 285–314.

Friedman, Milton. 1962. *Capitalism and Freedom.* Chicago: University of Chicago Press.

Friedman, Milton, and Rose Friedman. 1979. *Free to Choose.* Orlando: Harvest Books.

Friedman, Sheldon, Richard W. Hurd, Rudolph A. Oswald, and Ronald L. Seeber, eds. 1994. *Restoring the Promise of American Labor Law.* Ithaca: ILR Press.

Galenson, Walter. 1980. *The International Labor Organization: An American View.* Madison: University of Wisconsin Press.

Garraty, John. 1979. *Unemployment in History: Economic Thought and Public Policy.* New York: Harper and Row.

Gernigon, B., A. Odero, and H. Guido. 2000. ILO principles concerning collective bargaining. *International Labour Review* 139 (1): 33–55.

Ghebali, V. Y. 1989. *The International Labour Organization: A Case Study of the Evolution of UN Specialized Agencies.* Dordrecht: Martinus Nijhoff.

Gibson-Graham, J. K. 1996. *The End of Capitalism (as we knew it).* London: Basil Blackwell.

Ginsburg, C. 1994. Killing a Chinese Mandarin: On the moral implications of difference. *Critical Inquiry* 21 (1) (Autumn): 10–36.

Glendon, Mary Ann. 2001. *A World Made New: Eleanor Roosevelt and the Universal Declaration of Human Rights.* New York: Random House.

Glickman, Lawrence. 1997. *A Living Wage: American Workers and the Making of Consumer Society.* Ithaca: Cornell University Press.

Gonzalez, Juan. 2001. *Harvest of Empire: A History of Latinos in America.* New York: Penguin.

Gordon, N., J. Swanson, and J. A. Buttigieg. 2000. Human rights: Emancipation. *Rethinking Marxism* 12 (3): 1–22.

Gould, W. 1993. *Agenda for Reform.* Cambridge: MIT Press.

Gould, W. 2003. Labor law for a global economy: The uneasy case for international labor standards. In *International Labor Standards: Globalisation, Trade, and Public Policy,* ed. R. J. Flangan and W. Gould, 81–128. Stanford: Stanford University Press.

Gramsci, Antonio. 1971. *Selections from the Prison Notebooks.* Edited and translated by Quintan Hoare and Geoffrey Nowell Smith. New York: International.

Greenhouse, Steven. 2004a. In-house audit says Walmart violated labor laws. *New York Times,* Jan. 13, A13.

Greenhouse, Steven. 2004b. Altering of workers' time cards spurs growing number of suits. *New York Times,* April 4.

Greenhouse, Steven. 2005. Labor Board's critics see a bias against workers. *New York Times,* Jan. 2.

Greenhouse, Steven, and Joseph Kahn. 1999. U.S. effort to add labor standards to agenda fails. *New York Times,* Dec. 3, A1.

Gross, James A. 1994. The demise of the national labor policy: A question of social justice. In *Restoring the Promise of American Labor Law,* ed. S. Friedman, Richard Hurd, Rudolph Oswald, and Ronald Seeber, 45–58. Ithaca: ILR Press.

Gross, James A. 1999a. A human rights perspective on U.S. labor relations law. *Labor Law Journal* 50 (3): 197–203.

Gross, James A. 1999b. A human rights perspective on United States labor relations law: A violation of the right to freedom of association. *Employee Rights and Employment Policy Journal* 3:65–96.

Gross, James. 2003a. *Broken Promise: The Subversion of U.S. Labor Relations Policy, 1947–1994.* Philadelphia: Temple University Press.

Gross, James, ed. 2003b. *Workers Rights as Human Rights.* Ithaca: Cornell University Press.

Hall, Peter, and David Soskice, eds. 2001. *Varieties of Capitalism: The Institutional Foundations of Comparative Advantage.* Oxford: Oxford University Press.

Harvey, David. 2003. *The New Imperialism.* Oxford: Oxford University Press.

Haskell, T. 1985. Capitalism and the origins of the humanitarian sensibility. *American Historical Review* 90 (2): 339–61.

Haskell, T. 2000. *Objectivity Is Not Neutrality.* Baltimore: Johns Hopkins University Press.

Head, Simon. 2004. Inside the Leviathan. *New York Review of Books,* Dec. 16, 80–89.

Heilbroner, Robert, ed. 1986. *The Essential Adam Smith.* New York: W. W. Norton.

Helleiner, E. 1994. *States and the Reemergence of Global Finance: From Bretton Woods to the 1990s.* Ithaca: Cornell University Press.

Hillard, M., and R. McIntyre. 1994. Is there a new institutional consensus in labor economics? *Journal of Economic Issues* 28 (2): 619–29.

Hilton, R. Editor. 1976. *The Transition from Feudalism to Capitalism.* London: New Left Books.

Hodges-Aeberhard, Jane. 1989. The right to organise in Article 2 of Convention No. 87. *International Labour Review* 128 (2): 177–94.

Howard, J. K. 1975. Doctor Thomas Percival and the beginnings of industrial legislation. *Occupational Medicine* 25:58–65.

Huggins, N. 1991. The deforming mirror of truth: Slavery and the master narrative of American history. *Radical History Review* 49 (Winter): 25–46.

Human Rights Watch. 2000. *Unfair Advantage: Workers' Freedom of Association in the United States under International Human Rights Standards.* New York: Human Rights Watch.

Hume, David. 1961 (1777). *Philosophical Essays Concerning Human Understanding.* Oxford: Clarendon.

Humphries, J. 2003. The parallels between the past and the present. In *International Labor Standards,* ed. Kaushik Basu, Henrik Horn, Lisa Roman, and Judith Shapiro, 84–91. Malden, MA: Basil Blackwell.

Hutchins, Betty L., and Amy Harrison. 1903. *A History of Factory Legislation.* London: P. S. King and Son.

Hymer, S., and S. Resnick. 1971. International trade and uneven development. In *Trade,*

Balance of Payments, and Growth, ed. Jagdish Bhagwati, Ronald Jones, Robert Mundell, and Jaroslav Vanek, 473–94. Amsterdam: North Holland.

Ignatieff, Michael. 2001. *Human Rights as Politics and Idolatry.* Princeton: Princeton University Press.

Ignatieff, Michael. 2002. The rights stuff. *New York Review of Books,* June 13.

ILO (International Labor Organization). 1919. *Constitution.* http://www.ilo.org/public/english/about/iloconst.htm.

ILO. 1944. *The Philadelphia Declaration.* http://www.ilo.org/public/english/about/iloconst.htm#annex.

ILO. 1997. *The ILO, Standard Setting, and Globalization.* Report of the Director-General. http://www.itcilo.it/english/actrav/telearn/global/ilo/law/ilodg.htm.

ILO. 1998. *ILO Declaration on Fundamental Principles and Rights at Work and Its Follow-Up.* Geneva: ILO Publications.

ILO. 2000. *Review of Annual Reports under the Follow-Up to the ILO Declaration on Fundamental Principles and Rights at Work, Part II.* Geneva: ILO Publications.

ILO. 2004. *A Fair Globalization: Creating Opportunities for All.* Report of the World Commission on the Social Dimensions of Globalization.

International Labour Review. 1949. The I.L.O. and the problem of freedom of association and industrial relations. *International Labour Review* 58 (5): 575–600.

Isaac, J. C. n.d. Thinking about the anti-sweatshop movement: A modest proposal. http://umass.edu.peri/pdfs.Isaac.pdf.

Jacoby, Wade. 2001. *Imitation and Politics: Redesigning Modern Germany.* Ithaca: Cornell University Press.

Jiborn, Marcus. 2006. The power of coordination. http://people.su.se/~guarr/Ideologi/Jiborn%20on%20Coordination%20power.pdf.

Kahn, Joseph, and David Sanger. 1999. Trade obstacles unmoved, Seattle talks end in failure. *New York Times,* Dec. 4, A1.

Kaufman, B. 1994. The evolution of thought on the competitive nature of labor markets. In *Labor Economics and Industrial Relations: Markets and Institutions,* ed. Clark Kerr and Paul Staudohar, 145–88. Cambridge: Harvard University Press.

Kaufman, B. 2004a. The institutional and neoclassical schools in labor economics. In *The Institutional Tradition in Labor Economics,* ed. Dell Champlin and Janet Knoedler, 13–38. Armonk: M. E. Sharpe.

Kaufman, B. 2004b. *The Global Evolution of Industrial Relations.* Geneva: International Labour Organization.

Kaufman, B, and J. Hotchkiss. 2005. *The Economics of Labor Markets.* 7th ed. Fort Worth: Thompson.

Keck, M., and K. Sikkink. 1998. *Activists Beyond Borders: Advocacy Networks in International Politics.* Ithaca: Cornell University Press.

Kirby, R. G., and A. E. Musson. 1975. *The Voice of the People: John Doherty, 1788–1854: Trade Unionist, Radical and Factory Reformer.* Manchester: Manchester University Press.

Klein, Naomi. 2000. *No Logo*. New York: Picador.

Kohr, M. 1997. The WTO and the battle over labor standards. www.globalpolicy.org/socecon/labor/wtolabor.htm.

Kristjanson-Gural. 2008. Postmodern contributions to Marxian economics: Theoretical innovations and implications for class politics. *Historical Materialism,* 16 (2).

Kruglak, Gregory T. 1980. *The Politics of United States Decision-Making in United Nations Specialized Agencies: The Case of the International Labor Organization.* Washington, DC: University Press of America.

Krugman, Paul. 1997. In praise of cheap labor. *Slate,* March 20, http://web.mit.edu/krugman/www.smokey.html.

Krugman, Paul, and M. Obstfeld. 2000. *International Economics.* 5th ed. Reading: Addison-Wesley.

Landes, David S. 1986. What do bosses really do? *Journal of Economic History* 46 (3) (September): 585–623.

Larimer, T. 1998. Sneaker gulag: Are Asian workers really exploited? *Time International,* May 11, 30–32.

Leary, Virginia. 1996. The paradox of workers rights as human rights. In *Human Rights, Labor Rights, and International Trade,* ed. Lance Compa and Stephen Diamond, 22–47. Philadelphia: University of Pennsylvania Press.

Lee, F. 2004. History and identity: The case of radical economics and radical economists, 1945–1970. *Review of Radical Political Economics* 36 (2): 177–95.

Lester, R. 1946. Shortcomings of marginal analysis for wage-employment problems. *American Economic Review* 36 (1) (March): 63–82.

Levinson, J. 2000. Dissenting statement. *Report of the International Financial Institutions Advisory Commission.* www.house.gov/jec/imf/ifiac.htm.

Levitz, J. 2002. Immigrants lament loss of fish processing jobs to Worker Rights Board. *Providence Journal,* Jan. 12, A-3.

Lichtenstein, Nelson. 1999. Workers rights are civil rights. *WorkingUSA* (March–April): 57–66.

Lichtenstein, Nelson. 2002. *State of the Unions.* Princeton: Princeton University Press.

Lin, J. 1998. Vietnam gives Nike a run for its money. *Philadelphia Inquirer,* March 23, 1.

Lorenz, Edward C. 2001. *Defining Global Justice: The History of the U.S. International Labor Standards Policy.* Notre Dame: University of Notre Dame Press.

Lynch, Katherine A. 1988. *Family, Class, and Ideology in Early Industrial France: Social Policy and the Working-Class Family, 1825–1848.* Madison: University of Wisconsin.

Lynd, Staughton. 1997. The Webbs, Lenin, and Rosa Luxemborg. In *Living Inside Our Hope,* 206–31. Ithaca: ILR Press.

Macgregor, David. 1996. *Hegel, Marx, and the English State.* Toronto: University of Toronto Press.

Madra, Y. 2004. The power of the New Institutionalism: Hegemony arising from heterogeneity. Mimeo.

Magdoff, H. 1971. Economic myths and imperialism. *Monthly Review* (May): 1–17.

Marglin, Stephen A. 1974. What do bosses do? *Review of Radical Political Economy* 6 (Summer): 33–60.

Marx, Karl. 1842. Debates on the law on thefts of wood. www.marxists.org/archive/marx/works/1842/10/25.htm#p1.

Marx, Karl. 1848. On the question of free trade. http://www.marxists.org/archive/marx/works/1848/free-trade/index.htm.

Marx, Karl. 1970 (1859). *A Contribution to the Critique of Political Economy.* New York: International Publishers.

Marx, Karl. 1981 (1867). *Capital: A Critique of Political Economy.* Vol. 1. London: Penguin.

Marx, Karl. 1993 (1894). *Capital: A Critique of Political Economy.* Vol. 3. London: Penguin.

McIntyre, N. 2002. Protests continue for UNICCO living wage. *Cowl,* April 11.

McIntyre, R. 2004. Globalization goes for therapy. *Rethinking Marxism* 16 (10): 101–8.

McIntyre, R., and M. Hillard. 2008. A radical critique and alternative to U.S. industrial relations theory and practice. In *Radical Economics and the Labor Movement,* ed. Frederic Lee and Jon Bekkan. London: Routledge.

Mehring, Franz. 1966. *Karl Marx: The Story of His Life.* London: Allen and Unwin.

Melish, J. 1998. *Disowning Slavery: Gradual Emancipation and "Race" in New England, 1789–1860.* Ithaca: Cornell University Press.

Meltzer, A. 2000. *Report of the International Financial Institutions Advisory Commission.* http://www.house.gov/jec/imf/meltzer.pdf.

Meyer, William H. 1998. *Human Rights and International Political Economy in Third World Nations: Multinational Corporations, Foreign Aid, and Repression.* Westport: Praeger.

Mihaly, E. The truth about third world workers. *Providence Journal,* June 3, 1998.

Milkovits, A. 2002a. Students protest in support of janitors. *Providence Journal,* April 5.

Milkovits, A. 2000b. PC tells students it won't intervene in janitors, subcontractor pay dispute. *Providence Journal,* April 6.

Miller, George. 2004. Everyday low wages: The hidden price we all pay for Wal-Mart. Report by the Democratic Staff of the House Committee on Education and the Workforce, commissioned by Rep. George Miller (C-CA) Senior Democrat. http://edworkforce.house.gov/democrats/WALMARTREPORT.pdf.

Miller, Michael. 1981. *The Bon Marché: Bourgeois Culture and the Department Store, 1869–1920.* Princeton: Princeton University Press.

Miller, Spencer, Jr. 1936. *What the International Labor Organization Means to America.* New York: Columbia University Press.

Millis, Harry A., and Royal E. Montgomery. 1945. *The Economics of Labor.* Vol. 3, *Organized Labor.* New York: McGraw-Hill.

Mishel, L., J. Bernstein, and J. Schmitt. 2001. *The State of Working America, 2000–01.* Ithaca: ILR Press.

Mishel, Lawrence, Jared Epstein, and Sylvia Allegretto. 2004. *The State of Working America.* Ithaca: ILR Press.

Monbiot, George. 2004. The fruits of poverty. *Guardian,* March 16.

Montgomery, David. 1993. *Citizen Worker.* Cambridge: Cambridge University Press.

Montgomery, David. 1996. Labor rights and human rights: An historical perspective. In *Human Rights, Labor Rights, and International Trade,* ed. Lance Compa and Stephen Diamond, 13, 16–17. Philadelphia: University of Pennsylvania Press.

Moore, M. 1998. *The Big One.* New York: Dog Eat Dog, Miramax.

Morse, David. 1969. *The Origins and Evolution of the ILO and Its Role in the World Community.* Ithaca: New York State School of Industrial and Labor Relations.

North, Douglass. 1990. *Institutions, Institutional Change, and Economic Performance.* Cambridge: Cambridge University Press.

Novak, J. 2002a. Fish plant fires workers who raised labor issues. *Narragansett Times,* Jan. 2.

Novak, J. 2002b. OSHA holds meetings for members of fish processing industry. *Narragansett Times,* Jan. 30.

Novak, J. 2002c. Workers Rights Board attempts to meet with Town Dock employees. *Narragansett Times,* Feb. 13.

Panitch, L. 2001. Reflections on strategy for labor. In *Working Classes, Global Realities: Socialist Register 2001,* ed. Leo Panitch and Colin Leys with Greg Albo and David Coates. New York: Monthly Review.

Peterson, Coleman. Transferring corporate culture through effective people practices. http://www.wspartners.com/RFL%20-%20WM%20Global%20Conference.pdf.

Piore, M. 1983. Labor market segmentation: To which paradigm does it belong? *American Economic Review* 73 (2): 249–53.

Piore, M. 2003. Stability and flexibility in the economy: Reason and interpretation in economic behavior. http://econ-www.mit.edu/files/1117.

Piore, M., and S. Safford. 2006. Changing regimes of workplace governance, shifting axes of social mobilization, and the challenge to industrial relations theory. *Industrial Relations* 45 (3): 299–325.

Polanyi, K. 1980 (1944). *The Great Transformation: The Political and Economic Origins of Our Time.* Boston: Beacon.

Polgreen, Lydia. 2006. War steals Congo's young by the millions. *New York Times,* July 30.

Potter, Edward E. 1984. *Freedom of Association, the Right to Organize and Collective Bargaining: The Impact of on U.S. Law of Ratification of ILO Conventions No. 87 & No. 98.* Washington, DC: Labor Policy Association.

Ramstad, Yngve. 1987. Free trade versus fair trade: Import barriers as a problem of reasonable value. *Journal of Economic Issues* 21 (1) (March): 5–32.

Ramstad, Yngve. 1990. The institutionalism of John R. Commons: Theoretical foundations of a volitional economics. In Warren J. Samuels, ed., *Research in the History of Economics Thought and Methodology,* vol. 8, 53–104. Greenwich, CT: JAI Press.

Ramstad, Yngve. 1998. Commons's institutional economics: A foundation for the industrial relations field? *Proceedings of the Fiftieth Annual Meeting of the IRRA* 1:308–19.

Ramstad, Yngve. 2001. John R. Commons reasonable value and the problem of just price. *Journal of Economic Issues* 35 (2): 253–77.

Ranciere, J. 1991. *The Nights of Labor: The Workers Dream in Nineteenth Century France.* Philadelphia: Temple University Press.

Ranciere, J. 2004. Who is the subject of the Rights of Man? *South Atlantic Quarterly* 103 (2–3): 297–310.

Rawls, John. 1971. *A Theory of Justice,* 131–42. Cambridge: Harvard Cambridge: Belknap Press of Harvard University Press.

Reid, P. A. 1974. The decline of Saint Monday, 1766–1876. In *Essays in Social History,* ed. P. Thane and A. Sutcliffe. Oxford: Clarendon.

Resnick, S. and R. Wolff. 2006. *New Departures in Marxian Theory.* London: Routledge.

Rockman, S. 2005. Class and the history of working people in the early Republic. *Journal of the Early Republic* 25 (Winter): 527–35.

Rockman, S. 2006. The unfree origins of American capitalism. In Cathy Matson, ed., *The Economy of Early America: Historical Perspectives and New Directions,* 335–61. University Park: Pennsylvania State University Press.

Rodríguez-Garavito, César A. 2005. Global governance and labor rights: Codes of conduct and anti-sweatshop struggles in global apparel factories in Mexico and Guatemala. *Politics and Society* 2:203–33.

Rodrik, D. 1997. *Has Globalization Gone Too Far?* Washington, DC: Institute for International Economics.

Rodrik, D. 2000. How far can international economic integration go? *Journal of Economic Perspectives* 14 (1): 177–86.

Roediger, David, and Philip Foner. 1989. *Our Own Time: A History of American Labor and the Working Day.* London: Verso.

Rosen, F. 2005. Jeremy Bentham on slavery and the slave trade. In Bart Schultz and Georgios Varouxakis, eds., *Utilitarianism and Empire.* Lanham: Lexington Books.

Ross, Robert. 2004. *Slaves to Fashion: Poverty and Abuse in the New Sweatshops.* Ann Arbor: University of Michigan Press.

Sabel, Charles, Dara O'Rourke, and Archon Fung. 2000. *Ratcheting Labor Standards: Regulation for Continuous Improvement in the Global Workplace.* Social Protection Discussion Paper No. 11. Washington, DC: World Bank.

Sanger, D. 1999. After Clinton's push, questions about motive. *New York Times,* Dec. 3.

Schlosser, E. 2001. *Fast Food Nation: The Dark Side of the All American Meal.* New York: HarperCollins.

Schneider, Greg, and Dina ElBoghdady. 2003. Stores follow Wal-Mart's lead in labor. *Washington Post,* Nov. 6, 1.

Scott, Joan. 1988. *Gender and the Politics of History.* New York: Columbia University Press.

Shotwell, James T. 1934. *The Origins of the International Labor Organization.* 2 vols. New York: Columbia University Press.

Silver, Beverly. 1994. Labor movements from a global perspective. www.jhu/~igscph/win94sil.htm.

Silver, Beverly. 2003. *Forces of Labor: Workers Movements and Globalization since 1870.* Cambridge: Cambridge University Press.

Simon, Herbert. 1979. Rational decision making in business organizations. *American Economic Review* 69 (4) (September): 493–513.

Smith, Adam. 1937 (1776). *An Inquiry into the Nature and Causes of the Wealth of Nations.* Modern Library Edition, ed. E. Cannan. New York: Random House.

Smith, Adam. 1976 (1759). *The Theory of Moral Sentiments.* Ed. D. D. Raphael and A. L. Macfie. New York: Oxford University Press.

Sonenscher, Michael. 1989. *Work and Wages: Natural Law, Politics, and the Eighteenth-Century French Trades.* Cambridge: Cambridge University Press.

Spar, D., and J. Burns. 2000. *Hitting the Wall: Nike and International Labor Practices.* Harvard Business School Case #9–700–047. Boston: Harvard Business School.

Srinivasan, T. N. 1998. Trade and human rights. In Alan Deardorff and Robert Stern, eds., *Constituent Interests and U.S. Trade Policies,* 226–53. Ann Arbor: University of Michigan Press.

Stabile, Don. 1997. Adam Smith and the natural wage: Sympathy, subsistence, and social distance. *Review of Social Economy* 55 (3) (Fall): 293–311.

Stanley, Amy Dru. 1993. *From Bondage to Contract: Wage Labor, Marriage, and the Market in the Age of Slave Emancipation.* Cambridge: Cambridge University Press.

Stedman Jones, Gareth. 1983. *Languages of Class: Studies in English Working Class History, 1832–1982.* Cambridge: Cambridge University Press.

Steinfeld, R. 1991. *The Invention of Free Labor: The Employment Relation in English and American Law and Culture, 1350–1870.* Chapel Hill: University of North Carolina Press.

Stiglitz, J. 2000. Democratic development as the fruits of labor. Keynote address, Industrial Relations Research Association, Boston, January.

Stiglitz, J. 2002. *Globalization and Its Discontents.* New York: Norton.

Stone, Judith M. 1985. *The Search for Social Peace: Reform Legislation in France, 1870–1914.* Albany: SUNY Press.

Stone, K. 1996. Mandatory arbitration of individual employment rights: The yellow dog contract of the 1990s. *Denver University Law Review* 73:1017.

Sugden, R. 1989. Spontaneous order. *Journal of Economic Perspectives* 3 (4): 85–87.

Tananbaum, Duane. 1988. *The Bricker Amendment Controversy.* Ithaca: Cornell University Press.

Tayler, William Lonsdale. 1935. *Federal States and Labor Treaties.* New York: Apollo Press.

Thurow, Lester. 1975. *Generating Inequality.* New York: Basic Books.

Tigar, M., and M. Levy. 1977. *Law and the Rise of Capitalism.* New York: Monthly Review Press.

Tomlins, Christopher. 1993. *Law, Labor, and Ideology in the Early American Republic.* Cambridge: Cambridge University Press.

Trubek, D., J. Mosher, and J. Rothstein. 2000. Transnationalism in the regulation of labor relations: International regimes and transnational advocacy networks. *Law and Social Inquiry* 25 (4): 1187–1211.

Turmann, M. 1922. The Christian social movement and international labour legislation. *International Labour Review* 6 (1): 1922.

USA Today. 2004a. Vice president Cheney visits Wal-Mart's home town. May 3.

USA Today. 2004b. Wal-Mart widens political reach, giving primarily to GOP. Feb. 2.

U.S. Department of Commerce, Economic, and Statistics Administration. 1999. *Other Footwear Manufacturing.* http://www.census.gov/prod/ec97/97m3162e.pdf.

U.S. Department of Labor. 1980. *Briefing Paper: ILO Convention 87 Concerning Freedom of Association.* Office of the Solicitor. Appended to *The United States and the International Labor Organization.* Hearings before the Committee on Labor and Human Resources, United States Senate, September 11, 1985.

U.S. Department of Labor. 1994. *Fact Finding Report.* Commission on the Future of Worker-Management Relations. Washington, DC: U.S. Department of Labor.

U.S. Department of Labor. 1997a. Report on freedom of association and the protection of the right to organize convention, 1948 (No. 87). Made pursuant to Article 19 of the ILO Constitution. Mimeo in author's possession.

U.S. Department of Labor. 1997b. Report on right to organize and collective bargaining convention, 1949 (No. 98). Made pursuant to Article 19 of the ILO Constitution. Mimeo in author's possession.

U.S. Department of State. 2001. *Labor Diplomacy: In the Service of Democracy and Security.* Advisory Committee on Labor Diplomacy. www.state.gov/g/drl/rls/10043.htm.

U.S. General Accounting Office. 1984. *Sustaining Improved U.S. Participation in the International Labor Organization Requires New Approaches.* Washington, DC: U.S. General Accounting Office.

U.S. General Accounting Office. 1994. *Data on the Tax Compliance of Sweatshops, 1994.* http://www.unclefed.com/GAOReports/ggd94–210fs.pdf.

U.S. House of Representatives. 1999. *American Worker Project: Securing the Future of American Families.* Subcommittee on Investigations, House Committee on Education and the Workforce. Washington, DC: GPO.

U.S. Senate. 1949. *Convention Concerning the Freedom of Association and Protection of the Right to Organize.* 81st Congress, 1st Session, Executive S.

U.S. Senate. 1985. The *United States and the International Labor Organization.* Hearings before the Committee on Labor and Human Resources, September 11. Washington, DC: GPO.

U.S. Senate. 1995. *Teamwork for Employees and Management Act of 1995.* 104th Congress, 2nd Session. Report 104–259. Washington, DC: GPO.

Wade, R. 2001. Showdown at the World Bank. *New Left Review* 7:124–36.

Waldron, Jeremy. 1987. *Nonsense Upon Stilts.* New York: Methuen.

Weissbach, Lee. 1989. *Child Labor Reform in Nineteenth Century France.* Baton Rouge: Louisiana State University Press.

Wheeler, H. 1999. Viewpoint: Collective bargaining is a fundamental human right. *Industrial Relations* 39:535–39.

Weil, D. 1994. *Turning the Tide: Strategic Planning for Labor Unions.* Lexington: Lexington Books.

Wilber, C., and R. Harrison. 1978. The methodological basis of institutional economics: Pattern model, storytelling, and holism. *Journal of Economic Issues* 12:61–89.

Williams, Eric. 1944. *Capitalism and Slavery.* Chapel Hill: University of North Carolina Press.

Williams, William A. 1964. *The Great Evasion.* Chicago: Quadrangle Books.

Williamson, Oliver E. 1980. The organization of work: A comparative institutional assessment. *Journal of Economic Behavior and Organization* 1 (1): 5–38.

Wood, A. 1995. How trade hurts unskilled workers. *Journal of Economic Perspectives* 9 (3): 57–80.

WRC (Workers Rights Consortium). 2005a. *Assessment re Easy Group, Easy Fashion Corporation, Allen Garments & Kasumi Apparel,* http://www.workersrights.org/Easy GroupReport9-20-05.pdf. Washington: Workers Rights Consortium.

WRC. 2005b. *Assessment re Far East Textile and First Apparel, Findings, Assessment and Status Report* http://www.workersrights.org/Far_East_and_First_Apparel_Report .pdf. Washington: Workers Rights Consortium.

Ziner, K., and P. Davis. 2001. Panel seeks probe of death. *Providence Journal,* Dec. 20.

Zizek, S., ed. 1994. *Mapping Ideology.* London: Verso.

Zweig, M. 1992. Teaching to student values in the early nineties. *Review of Radical Political Economics* 24 (2): 109–14.

Zwick, D., J. Denegri-Knott, and J. Schroeder. 2007. The social pedagogy of Wall Street: Stock trading as political activism. *Journal of Consumer Policy* 30 (3): 177–99.

INDEX

abolitionism. *See* antislavery movement
abstract universalism, 57
accountability, 135
Acheson, Dean, 118
Action Manufacturing Employment, 1
activists, 7, 52, 60, 75–76, 150, 172
    antislavery, 2
    antisweatshop, 6
    labor based, 49
    union, 123, 125
Adams, Roy, 191n12
Adidas, 159, 192n17
AFL-CIO, 76, 111, 115–16, 122, 192n14
Africa, 99
African American progress, 69
agricultural workers, 125, 190n2
Allen Garments, 155
American Institutional school, 3
American Revolution, 75
Americans with Disabilities Act, 166
Amnesty International, 162
anarchism, 151
antislavery movement, 67, 72–74, 76, 138, 162,
    173
    Bentham and, 183n2
    idealization of "free labor" in, 163
    worker rights and, 2, 178
    See also slavery
antisweatshop movement, viii, 5–6, 11, 56, 74,
    153, 177
    effects of, 12
    U.S. government initiatives for, 161
    See also new factory inspectors; sweating
    system; sweatshops; Worker Rights Con-
    sortium (WRC)
Apparel Industry Partnership, 36,
    149
Argentina, 61, 98, 172
Ashworth, John, 73–74
Austria, 18
Averato, Flori, 176

Balibar, Etienne, 55
Bardhan, Prahnab, 28–29
bargaining power, unequal, 85, 138
Barrera, Nasario, 38–39
Becker, Gary, 26
behavioral economics, 19
Bentham, Jeremy, 3, 54, 57–58, 78, 183n2
Bhagwati, Jagdish, 83–85, 95
The Big One (film, Moore), 137, 183n8
blocked exchange, 85
Bolshevik revolution, 2, 108
boomerang effect, 129, 133, 157
Boutros-Ghali, Youssef, 103
boycotts, 84
brand recognition, 172
Brazil, 150
Brenner, Robert, 29
Bretton Woods institutions, 99, 102
Bricker, John, 110–11
Bricker Amendment, 104, 111
Britain, 32
    See also England
Brock, William, 115
Bronfenbrenner, Kate, 82
Burawoy, Michael, 144–45
Burke, Edmund, 57, 58–59, 183n4
Bush, George W., 131–32, 193n7

Cambridge group, 25
Campaign for Labor Rights, 129
Canada, 125, 188n3
capabilities equality, 69
Capital (Marx), 20, 26–27, 134, 143–44
    as "literature of the factory," 190n4
capitalism, 21, 73–74, 169–71, 185n20
    antislavery movement and, 72, 162
    emergence of in America of, 22
    fascist forms of, 31
    human rights tradition of, 69
    Marxist view of, 31–32, 70
capitalist development, 70